LÉON
Bakst

Alexander Schouvaloff

LÉON

The theatre art

Sotheby's Publications

'Every subject, every model, every part of the human body, that is designed without passion, without the joy of life, is a work utterly barren and false. Colour should afford a joy for the eye.'

LÉON BAKST

First published in 1991 for Sotheby's Publications by
Philip Wilson Publishers Ltd
26 Litchfield Street
London WC2H 9NJ

ISBN 0 85667 391 9

Designed by Andrew Shoolbred
Typeset in Photina by Tradespools Ltd, Frome, Somerset
Printed and bound by Khai Wah Litho Pte Ltd, Singapore

Frontispiece Set design for *Thamar*, 1912, 740 × 860
MUSÉE DES ARTS DÉCORATIFS, PARIS

Endpapers Textile design, 1923
LADY ST JUST COLLECTION

The pen and ink decorations throughout are by Bakst and were used by him when he designed *The Contemporary Ballet* by Valerian Svetlov, St Petersburg, 1911

Contents

List of Illustrations

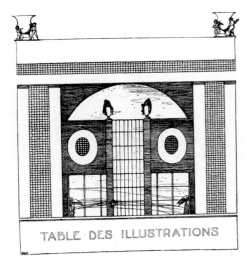

Acknowledgements

This book would not have been possible without the enormously generous help I received from a great many people:

First, I should like to express my thanks to Asya Chorley of Sotheby's and her colleagues Kate Garmeson, Stephane Cosman Connery, Charlotte Hill and Eliot Woolf who gave me so much help with the illustrations.

I am especially grateful to Sallie Blumenthal, Marina Henderson, Alice Hodgson, Lady St Just, Nina and Nikita Lobanov-Rostovsky, John Cavanagh, Kyril FitzLyon, Vladimir Gvozdev and Richard Nathanson who have all been particularly helpful in different ways.

Much of my research was done in museums, galleries and libraries. Curators everywhere were most co-operative and quick to answer questions or make their material available. I thank them all most warmly: Susan Tripp and F. Lloyd of the Evergreen House Foundation, Baltimore; Judy Weinland and Edith Schmidt of the Museum of Fine Arts, Boston; Jeanne Newlin of the Harvard Theatre Collection; Georgeanna Bishop, Anita Jones and Melanie Harwood of the Baltimore Museum of Art, Claire Hudson, Rhiannon Finamore, Andrew Kirk, Susie Mapp, Leila Meinertas, Sarah C. Woodcock and Graham Brandon of the Theatre Museum, London; Francesca Franchi of the Archive Office, Royal Opera House, London; Valerie Mendes of the Victoria and Albert Museum, London; Henrietta Susser and Calvin Brown of the Metropolitan Museum of Art, New York; Ann Percy of the Philadelphia Museum of Art; Lynn Doherty and Kathryn Mets of the Museum of the City of New York; Robert Evren of the Museum of Modern Art, New York; Madeleine Nichols of the Dance Collection, New York Public Library, New York; Craig Hartley of the Fitzwilliam Museum, Cambridge; Lesley Hoskins, Archivist at Arthur Sanderson & Sons Ltd, London; Peggy Tolbert of the Minneapolis Institute of Arts; Shannon Halwes of The Museum of Fine Arts, Houston; William K. Clark of the Cincinnati Art Museum; Dr M. Josephus Jitta of the Gemeentemuseum, The Hague; Cécile Giteau, P. Tourniac and André Veinstein of the Département des Arts du Spectacle, Bibliothèque Nationale, Paris; Nicole Wild of the Musée de l'Opéra, Bibliothèque Nationale, Paris; Marie-Jeanne Geyer of the Musée des Beaux Arts, Strasbourg; Marvin Conerly of the *Baltimore Sun*; Peyton Skipwith of The Fine Art Society; Irina Naumovna Duskina of the Bakhrushin State Theatrical Museum, Moscow; Natalia Ivanovna Alexandrova of the Pushkin Museum, Moscow; Marina Igorovna Tsanovetskaya of the Theatre Library, Leningrad; Tatiana Vladimirovna Sventorzhetskaya of the Russian Museum, Leningrad; Irina Evstigneeva and Natalia Metelitza of the Museum of Theatrical and Musical Arts, Leningrad; William H. Crain of the University of Texas at Austin.

I owe an enormous debt of gratitude to Sally Prideaux, my editor. I greatly value her sympathetic enthusiasm, observant eye and monumental patience. I also thank Andrew Shoolbred who designed the book with such sensitivity.

Throughout this project my wife, Daria, has been the greatest support and has shared all the excitements of discovery and the occasional disappointments. All her constant encouragement, comment and thoughtful criticism have been of inestimable helpfulness. This book would have been impossible without her.

Note

Russian dates are given in the old style followed by the new date in brackets. The difference increased by one day every century; in the nineteenth century the difference was twelve days, in the twentieth century it is thirteen days.

Productions are called by their most common name. Most of them were first performed in France with a French title. When they were performed in England or America some titles were translated into English, some not.

There has been inconsistency about spelling 'Ballets Russes'. I have spelt it with an 's' as it almost always was in the Souvenir Programmes, and consider that Ballet Russe, without the 's', more usually refers to Colonel de Basil's Company which was formed after Diaghilev's death.

Russian names are spelt in their most usually accepted form: thus 'Diaghilev' rather than 'Diaghilew' or 'Diaghileff', except in direct quotations when the original spelling has been retained.

Except where otherwise stated, I have made all the translations from Russian and French. Bakst's French, though fluent, was often strange, idiosyncratic and sometimes difficult to follow. The translations try to give the meaning without altogether losing his style.

Quotations in the text can mostly be traced in the bibliography by the date, or, in the case of newspaper reviews, from the date of the first production. Manuscripts are in the Bibliothèque Nationale and Archives Nationales, Paris; the Russian Museum and the Theatre Library, Leningrad; the State Tretyakov Gallery, Moscow and the Victoria and Albert Museum, London.

The designs by Bakst are all in pencil and watercolour or gouache unless otherwise stated. In the captions to the illustrations, measurements are in millimetres, height before width. The date after the title is that of the first production; if the date of the design is different it follows in brackets.

Preface

The first time I saw Léon Bakst's work in art galleries and Sotheby's sale rooms I was astonished by the power of his sensual images. Bakst is rightly best known through his costume designs. He was unique. He has had his followers, his imitators and even his denegrators but there has never been another theatrical designer to match him for the vigour, colour and expressiveness of his drawing.

Bakst's theatre had vanished and there was a lot of uncertainty about his work. I went in search of his theatre. I visited Russia, France and the United States where I found hitherto unrecorded productions designed by him. In Russia I spoke to the distinguished art historian, Irina Pruzhan, whose pioneering book on Bakst is, by her own admission, scant after he left Russia, but whose expertise was exceedingly helpful. In France I saw one of Bakst's surviving neices who told me touchingly about her uncle and revealed his character. My knowledge of both Russian and French has allowed me to incorporate a lot of new material and previously unpublished manuscripts and letters. I have also been able to correct a number of previous mistakes and disentangle some of the misapprehensions and controversies surrounding his work. Others doubtless remain. The most thrilling discoveries for me, apart from Bakst's letters and the new productions, were all the designs for *Orpheus* now in the Pushkin Museum in Moscow, more than a hundred perfectly preserved, unfaded costumes for *The Sleeping Beauty* in a warehouse of the Museum of the City of New York, the recently meticulously restored theatre in Evergreen House, Baltimore, and, above all, to see so many of his drawings.

There is something special about Bakst. While I was looking at his portrait by Modigliani in Washington two teenage American blondes in pale blue sweatshirts, pink silky trousers and white trainers came up and one said to the other 'I like this guy.'

Léon Bakst by Rip
Ink and watercolour, 260 × 205
SOTHEBY'S/PRIVATE COLLECTION

Rip was the pseudonym of Georges Thenon who wrote and produced *Aladin ou la Lampe Merveilleuse* which Bakst designed in 1919

Léon Bakst was thirty-five years old when he designed his first work for the theatre in 1901. He had found his true vocation. During the twenty-three years until his death in 1924 at the age of fifty-eight he revolutionized theatre design and became, according to his own ambition, the 'most famous painter in the world.'

This book is about his work for theatre. It is not a biography of Bakst, although it begins with a sketch of some key moments of his life quoting in full, for the first time, a revealing autobiographical statement. Nor is this another history of the Ballets Russes for whom he designed his most important productions. Diaghilev and his ballet company have been written about extensively, but usually more from the point of view of Diaghilev himself, the company, and the choreography rather than the designers. Lynn Garafola in her recent and constantly riveting book also delves deeply into audiences and business matters. Of course, Bakst's name occurs frequently in any discussion of the Ballets Russes, and his drawings are always used to illustrate the various ballets he designed. He is generally credited with the flamboyant success of the company and from the beginning critics praised his work but lacked an adequate vocabulary of superlatives: they reacted as if stunned by repeating the word 'sumptuous' again and again. It is as if his treatment of all his ballets were identical when in fact each one was separately considered and individually conceived. This book is about Bakst's work on the productions he designed for the stage: ballets, plays, operas, and revues for Diaghilev, Anna Pavlova, Ida Rubinstein and other managements. The productions are described in chronological order (not every one is described, but every known work for the theatre whether it reached the stage or not is listed on pages 240–48.)

You would have to be in your seventies to have seen a production designed and staged by Bakst, and much older to have seen any of the productions he personally staged for the Ballets Russes. Last year I talked to an aristocratic old lady in her nineties who remembered seeing *The Sleeping Princess* in 1921 and going to it several times to see different dancers dancing the part of Aurora. 'What was it like?' I asked. 'Oh, it was lovely.' 'Yes, but how was it lovely?' 'It was wonderful, so beautiful.' She could remember it only in a haze of happy memory rather than clear recollection. The theatre is a perishable art.

It is impossible to recapture exactly what those productions were like. There is no contemporary film, there are only, black and white photographs. Memories are very short, even those of the participants. There is a film of Bronislava Nijinska trying with Léonide Massine to piece together the choreography for *L'Après-midi d'un Faune*, a ballet which she had helped to create and in which she danced, but she cannot remember what happened. She looks at Baron de Meyer's photographs and still cannot remember. Even so, photographs are better than nothing, and the ones in this book have been chosen primarily to show the results and effects of Bakst's work rather than particular dancers or choreographic moments. Better yet are photographs with verbal descriptions. When discussing and describing Bakst's productions I have quoted from contemporary critics because they were present and what they wrote at the time gives us the best idea of what they were like. I often quote Cyril Beaumont because more than other critics he wrote simply, without striving for effect, and described exactly what he saw. His direct, unfussy descriptions have veracity.

Best of all are the designs, but even they give a disproportionate and distorted view. Bakst is celebrated, collected and prized largely for his costume designs, but one costume design, or even a group of designs for the same production, while being exquisite works of art, do not represent what happened on stage. A play or a ballet may have had several sets and several hundred costumes. The theatre is a three-dimensional art, akin to architecture or sculpture. The designer has to be an architect who knows how to build, but impressions of buildings rather than real ones, and a sculptor who understands the human frame. He also has to be a dressmaker, making fantastical costumes rather than fashionable frocks. The individual designs do not give the total effect but they show the line and indicate the colour. Bakst was famous for his vivid colour and his erotic line. He was also the first great designer for whom every aspect of the production – sets, props, lighting, costumes, wigs, make-up – was of equal importance and who saw the whole stage as a single work of art. His greatest contribution to the art of the theatre and his most permanent influence has been to establish the importance of the role of the designer. His set designs, costume designs, costumes and even pieces of scenery are now in museums, but the theatre is not a museum art. His was the necessary presence to animate his theatre and no revival has succeeded in recapturing the perfection of his work. A re-production in the theatre is actually impossible. Although his own theatre vanished with his death and now appears dated, the way our theatre is today owes a lot to him.

Bakst was reticent about his work, preferring others to write about it, but I quote a number of his hitherto unpublished letters as well as statements and interviews in which he discusses his method and his ideas. As so often happens with artists after their death, Bakst suffered a period of neglect. Perhaps he was thought to be merely an artist of his time, even though in his time he was supreme. Sheldon Cheney in *The Theatre* wrote: 'It was Léon Bakst who created the most sumptuous of the Ballets Russes backgrounds. No modernist simplification of the setting for him! He took the old muddy painted scenery, sifted the mud out, poured in buckets of raw color, and created stage pictures of more prodigious proportions, vaster spaces, and more overwhelming colorfulness than any ever invented before.' The art of theatre certainly changed, even during his lifetime, as he observed in an article written towards the end of his life (see Appendix 2, p. 238). At the time this was like a hopeless testament but now the theory of theatre art has come full circle, and painting and colour dominate again.

Serge Diaghilev and Léon Bakst, caricature by Jean Cocteau

Rosenberg to Bakst

Lev Samoilovitch Rosenberg was born on 27 April (9 May) 1866 in Grodno, in White Russia near the Polish border, to a middle-class Jewish family which had originally come from Germany. Lev's father and mother moved from Grodno to St Petersburg soon after he was born. He had an elder brother, Isaiah, and two sisters, Sophie and Rosa. Bakst, at one time 'Baksht' or 'Baxter', was his mother's maiden name. Later he always pretended snobbishly that he had been born in the capital and also, perhaps out of vanity, that he was two years younger than he was. Reference books and catalogues still often give 1868 as the year of his birth. Perhaps his pretence was in order to be closer in age to his particular friends and colleagues Alexandre Benois, born in 1870, and Serge Diaghilev, born in 1872.

Few facts are known about his early life, but he later told his biographer André Levinson (1923), in evidently happy recollection, that as a small boy he regularly used to visit his 'noble and vaguely mysterious' grandfather in his 'home of dreams.' There his 'greatest delight was the large gilded parlor, with panels of yellow tapestry, with furniture of rock and shell-work in the style of 1860, with its white marble, its yellow flower stand, filled at all times with rare plants, and its four gilded cages in which canary birds were chirping.' The boy was obviously deeply affected by the opulence of his grandfather's house. He was the idol of the child and more than anyone else was instrumental in establishing Lev's taste and sensibility.

Bakst gave the best insight into his development as an artist and showed how the theatre affected him at an early age in a revealing interview about his childhood given to the *New York Times* (27 January) during his first visit to America in 1923. He explained that the reason for the brilliant decorative effects of his paintings came from his love for Adelina Patti and that his infatuation dated back to the time when he was a little boy in Russia; he had taught himself to read and write and was very anxious to go to the opera. When his elder brother went he would waken him early in the morning to have the whole story told to him, and finally, it was decided that he should be taken. 'Mr Bakst told of being dressed in his little velvet suit, of seeing the Emperor and the members of the royal family at the opera, the brilliant lights, a great crystal chandelier and all the people in beautiful clothes and diamonds . . .' Then he said:

> . . . there was great applause, and there appeared upon the stage a beautiful creature with great dark eyes. It was Adelina Patti. It was love at first sight, and I told my father so quite seriously when I reached home and that I intended to marry her. I was taken to the opera again the next week, but something terrible happened. It was *La Sonambula*, I think, and Patti, robed all in white, drank a glass of water, clasped her throat and fell to the ground. Then there arose the most furious shrieks of a small boy. I grasped the lace of my mother's gown and I begged the theatre doctor, who was in our box, to go and cure the beautiful lady who was ill. He took me into the corridor, but I would not be comforted. Then, to my surprise, I found myself, a little, crying boy, in a room with a beautiful lady with dark eyes. The doctor had taken me to Patti.

Léon Bakst by Amadeo Modigliani
(1884–1920), 1917
Oil on canvas, 553 × 330

Léon Bakst
Photo by Choumoff, Paris

Taken in his studio 112 Boulevard
Malesherbes, Paris. Bakst is holding a
Chinese porcelain figure; other objects
include oriental bowls, a Chinese
dragon, Indian elephants and a Buddha.
The photograph has usually been
printed the wrong way round

To sooth me, she gaily put rouge on each of my cheeks and made me very black, long eyebrows. That way I went back to the box, and there was great trouble to wash it off. But it was my early experience at the opera and the influence of the dark eyes of Adelina Patti which gave me the trend to my style of painting.

Bakst first thought seriously of becoming a painter when he was twelve years old after he had won a prize at the 6th Gymnasium in St Petersburg with a portrait of the poet Zhukovsky. His father disapproved of his ambition but the boy continued to draw and paint in secret. Eventually his father relented. Bakst chose a conventional academic start to his profession as a painter for, after one unsuccessful attempt, he enrolled as a student at the Academy of Fine Arts in 1883. In 1886 Bakst entered a controversial painting for the Academy's Grand Silver Medal. The trauma that he experienced as a result of his entry remained with him for the rest of his life and is described very movingly in this unpublished autobiographical note which he wrote to Jean de Pierrefeu in about 1913:

Léon Bakst
Photo by Choumoff, Paris

Like all painters who are just beginning I used to hide in a little corner and watch eagerly to see what impression my painting was making. Invariably the same thing happened which then made me very miserable. The teachers would approach, scrutinize, step back, step forward, bend their proud heads first to the left, then to the right, wave their brushes about in great gestures, and next morning when I would ask them in a voice trembling with emotion what they thought of my work I would invariably be given one of these replies: 'My dear chap, I don't think I saw your canvases,' or 'I was in such a hurry I hardly saw them,' or 'Yes, quite interesting, but badly lit.' Little by little I saw a wall of hostile silence go up around me fortified by an intense supervision of everything I did and said; a supervision, need I say, from which every so often arrows and sparks full of subtle poison and burning stings burst forth. But the real thunderbolt struck when the theme set for the examination was 'The Blessed Virgin Weeping over the Body of Christ' from the New Testament. I brought to the St Petersburg Academy of Fine Arts a large canvas, realistically painted, on which I had depicted a gloomy, damp vault where an old mother, distraught from grief, her eyes reddened by bitter tears, with white disshevelled hair, her clothes torn, in a crisis of despair, an old mother holds in her feeble hands the mutilated and dreadfully tortured body of her son.

The jury met the following day, and, as I watched some of the privileged few, who still held the secret of our success or failure, coming out of locked doors, I met strange looks sometimes staring at me with curiosity, sometimes turning away in scorn. I came to the conclusion that I should not expect good news, but what I saw when I entered the room has made a lasting impression on me. While my fellow students were busy looking for the 'medal' on a piece of paper stuck to the bottom of their canvases to send them beneficently on their way, a crowd was gathering in front of my picture. It was lacerated with two diagonals of thick chalk marks on the fresh paint, and scratched on the paint in large letters were the words 'The Council of the Academy of Fine Arts strictly disapproves of this kind of painting.' I then left the examination room and never returned.

A very hard life was waiting for me: everywhere I went, I never got any serious work, people turned away from me, and I reached rock bottom when I was obliged to paint shop signs and colour by hand printed alphabets for children's bookshops. However, I sometimes managed to go on exhibiting my work and I would sell my pictures for 20–25 francs, including the frame, happy to be able to exhibit at all and not be obliged to give up the hope of becoming a 'good painter' one day.

You cannot begin to realize what a frightening predicament it is for a young painter, with conviction and faith in himself and who knows 'he can do it', to see the easy success of his fellow artists who know only too well how to please the public. One fine day, I was with a friend as poor as me going round an exhibition where a young fashionable portrait painter painting in light, sweet colours of a nauseous prettiness was obviously going to have an unbounded success, and I said to him, smiling: 'Look, we are poor and despised, we will never succeed like this. Shall I do the same, and then once I have made my fortune, I promise I will discard such a vile palette and such slack drawing and begin to do 'true' art?'

My friend had an incredulous smile: 'You would never be able to leave this kind of work behind – the richer you are the more you want and then . . . take care, remember Gogol's novel *The Portrait* [in which a portrait comes to life]; all these fashionable painters poison themselves for the rest of their lives.'

But this was a decisive conversation for me. I abruptly changed my style; I became urbane, a liar, characterless and smart; a flatterer and a toady, and success came quickly. In three or four years I had an enormous number of commissions. I painted the whole of the 'Faubourg St Germain' of St Petersburg; I became a painter at the court of a Grand Duke and fortune largely compensated for the banal and flat style of my painting of this period. It was a nightmare.

But there was another compensation. I took a fiendish pleasure in changing my style just as abruptly, and going back to my first ideals. It is impossible not to smile, thinking about this time, just one year, one year, when little by little all 'fashionable society' turned against me, and began to whisper that they did not know what had happened to Bakst, that he has suddenly lost all his 'good taste', all his feeling for restraint in colour and in drawing, and that some demon of 'frivolity' has overcome him. I then began designing for the theatre in St Petersburg and collaborating in an avant-garde artistic journal *The World of Art*. Now began my stubborn campaign for

Alexandre Benois by Léon Bakst, 1898
Watercolour and pastel, 645 × 1003
THE RUSSIAN MUSEUM, LENINGRAD

This marvellous and sympathetic
portrait catches exactly the cosy but
studious intellectual art historian who
was his friend

the arts which I worship. I decided to dedicate my life to art, to do battle for it whatever
the cost, to uphold its supremacy and independence over all other interests. I had the
means; no matter the cost to myself or the wounding insults I and my work attracted,
I had established my name in my own country. At each attack I responded with new
works which doubled the fury. I faced my attackers and now, at the peak of my happiness, I am expelled from the city of my birth, from St Petersburg, and not one painter
from the Academy of Fine Arts has whispered a word to say that it is a disgrace; a disgrace for the city of my birth, a disgrace for the country which I tried my best to glorify
throughout the world.

Bakst has telescoped time. The sense of rejection and failure was to some extent to remain
with him all his life but his years of real struggle as an artist continued until 1892 when he
was commissioned by Count Dimitri Benckendorff to paint an official picture on the yawn-
ingly boring subject of Admiral Avelan's arrival in Paris marking the Franco-Russian
alliance. This commission had its compensations. It kept him going until 1900 and gave him
the excuse to visit Paris often where he also studied in Rodolphe Julian's studio and attended
classes given by the Finnish painter, Albert Edelfeldt.

A turning point came in March 1890 when Bakst met Albert Benois who introduced him to his younger brother Alexandre who had the year before gathered round him a group of enthusiastic young artists and writers. They called themselves the 'Nevsky Pickwickians'. The first members included the painters Evgeny Lanceray (Benois' nephew), Constantin Somov, Walter Nouvel, described by Benois as being 'a passionate musician, a magnificent reader of music' and Dimitri Philosophoff, described as 'a great lover of literature'. They met regularly at the Benois' house to discuss artistic ideals, philosophical notions and aesthetic principles. Alexandre introduced Bakst to the group in the autumn of 1890. At the same time they were joined by the painter Nicholas Roerich and Serge Diaghilev who, arriving like 'a country bumpkin' from the distant provincial town of Perm, was introduced by his cousin Philosophoff. 'It would be a mistake,' wrote Benois later, 'to consider our circle . . . as a sort of society which pursued definite moral aims . . . Questions of morality and philosophy interested us deeply . . . but, on the whole, our circle had a purely artistic and aesthetic character, which did not blend easily with any kind of rigorous morality. One of its characteristics was our love of a joke and appreciation of the comic side of life.'

Diaghilev was the only member of the group who was not a creative artist in the conventional sense of the word, although he had the vision to exploit the talents of others. Being an impressario is creative in its own right. He shaped the group and formed it into an artistic team with defined objectives. In the autumn of 1897 Diaghilev met Savva Ivanovitch Mamontov who owned banks and factories, was chairman of several railway boards, and who was one of the most influential patrons of art in Russia at the end of the nineteenth century.

Illustration for *The World of Art* magazine, 1902

Eagle colophon for *The World of Art*
magazine, 1898

When he met Diaghilev for the first time he is supposed to have exclaimed: 'From what soil springs this mushroom?' But Mamontov quickly recognized his talent and agreed to subsidize, with Princess Tenisheva, the first issues of a magazine planned by the group, with Diaghilev as editor, to be called *The World of Art*. This influential magazine was published from 1898–1904. Bakst was largely responsible for the graphic design and drew the eagle colophon for the magazine. The group itself also took on the name 'The World of Art' and under its auspices, administered by Diaghilev, began to organize exhibitions and then concerts. Eventually The World of Art developed into Diaghilev's Ballets Russes. Diaghilev and Bakst became particular friends. Of all his collaborators during the formation and successful establishment of the Ballets Russes, Bakst was Diaghilev's staunchest ally and his most original and talented artist. They saw eye to eye. But they were both highly strung, excessively volatile and excitable. Inspite of the fact that they trusted each other's taste and opinion they regularly had the most thundering rows, yelling at each other, which sometimes ended in blows. Their friends were appalled by their fury which they thought was vulgar and ill-bred, but Diaghilev and Bakst always made up their quarrels and strengthened their friendship. One thing, however, rankled. Bakst did not share Diaghilev's negligent attitude towards money, and although he continued to complain about not being paid he began to make money out of selling his designs. Money was the cause of their final break, but he worked for Diaghilev on more productions for the Ballets Russes than anyone else, did his best work for him and, to some extent, lost his sense of direction when their collaboration ended. Alexandre Benois expressed the policy, or ideal, of the company in his *Reminiscences of the Russian Ballet* (1941): 'It was no accident that what was afterwards known as the *Ballets Russes* was originally conceived not by professionals of the dance, but by a circle of artists, linked together by the idea of Art as an entity. Everything followed from the common desire of several painters and musicians to see the fulfilment of the theatrical dreams which haunted them; but I emphasize again that there was nothing *specific* or *professional* in their dreams. On the contrary, there was a burning craving for Art in general.'

In 1902 Bakst met Liubov Gritzenko and they fell in love. She was the widow of a painter and one of three daughters of Pavel Tretyakoff, a rich business man and founder of the gallery that bears his name. Of the other daughters, one married Dr Serge Botkin, a court physician, and the other the pianist and conductor Alexander Ziloti. Bakst and Gritzenko wanted to get married but Russian law did not allow marriage between a Jew and an Orthodox. Bakst therefore had to become a Christian and discovered that the easiest way was to be converted to Lutheranism in Finland. The couple were married on 12 November 1903. Changing his religion had a catastrophic effect on Bakst. It is possible that he was not previously aware of how strongly he felt Jewish, but becoming a Christian was the catalyst in provoking a profound depression. All his life he was to fall victim to these periodic depressions and although his marriage lasted seven years, and he had a son, it seems fairly certain that his depression was the cause of the break-up. The couple were divorced in October 1910 with the Emperor himself signing the papers. Bakst returned to Judaism. Husband and wife, however, continued to be very fond of each other and corresponded frequently. From about this time Bakst lived permanently in Paris at 112 Boulevard Malesherbes while his wife stayed in Russia with their son, André, who was born in 1907. He paid a heavy price for returning to Judaism for in October 1912 he was exiled as a Jew at twenty-four hours' notice, delayed for two weeks on the intervention of S. D. Sozanov, Minister of Foreign Affairs. Some part of the establishment had been cruelly vindictive. In 1914, on the nomination of three members, including his patron Count Benckendorff, he was elected a member of the St Petersburg Academy which gave him the right to return to Russia, but he was prevented from doing so by the First World War. He never returned.

What was Léon Bakst really like? There is almost nobody left alive who knew him. His niece remembers a delightfully charming, solicitous, attentive and elegant uncle who combed down his thin, long hair carefully over his head to hide his baldness. She first saw him during his profound depression in 1914 and remembers the shock of seeing him in his studio, unshaven, with long fingernails, unaware of anyone. He suffered two other long periods of depression, in 1920, and finally in 1924. The cause of his death is uncertain. There is the unfounded rumour that he died of syphilis. This is as preposterous as the various tales about his sexuality; they vary from his having been a homosexual – look at his relationship with Diaghilev, all those quarrels were based on sexual jealousy – to his having been a sex maniac sleeping with every girl in sight – look at all those erotic, almost pornographic drawings. Bakst's depravity was malicious gossip. He wrote to his friend André Saglio: 'I was amazed to learn "that I amuse myself by painting the naked legs of dancers"!!! If this were not so absurd I would have protested.' Prince Peter Lieven probably sustained the rumour when in *The Birth of the Ballets Russes* (1936) he referred to Bakst's 'depraved' life. Bakst fell in love all the time but there is no evidence that he had a string of mistresses or even one mistress although there is a description of him being infatuated with a French actress, following her to Paris, only to be jilted by her. He *was* very fond of women, and, apart from his wife, had a very close relationship with three others: Anna Pavlova, Ida Rubinstein and Maria Kousnezoff. He may have had a 'fling' with Maria Kousnezoff but his relationships with the other two were chaste and business-like. There has been a lot of speculation about whether Bakst and Rubinstein were lovers but from what they said about each other in interviews and letters it seems perfectly clear that they were not. Bakst was sexually maladroit and timid and besides he loved his wife and remained faithful to her. He was able to satisfy his sexual appetite by expressing his erotic fantasies in his drawings, and it is precisely because he was starved that his drawings are so sexually powerful.

His character is elusive. He kept his private and professional life separate. He had few true friends but many acquaintances and professional colleagues. Some of his contemporaries

The Yellow Sultana, 1916
465 × 680
SOTHEBY'S/PRIVATE COLLECTION

Bakst painted several flagrantly erotic Sultanas or odalisques based on his studies of nudes. As well as this one (before sex) there is a Pink one (after sex) painted in 1914 and a less obviously erotic Blue one painted in 1910. They take their titles from the colour of the turbans, although the Blue one is sometimes called 'Red' from the colour of her trousers. There is also a smaller Black one in a different style. Because of their 'oriental' character they have been associated quite wrongly with *Schéhérazade* and even called costume designs

recorded their impressions of him. These brief comments, like snapshots, were recorded mostly in hindsight and are therefore blurred; they are not necessarily deceitful nor are they entirely truthful. But they create an image:

Alexandre Benois (1941): 'Everyone who saw Bakst will agree with me that he was a man of great charm, but the Bakst of *those* days [1890s] was quite exceptionally delightful. Later, when he was at the height of his fame, it was difficult to imagine how modest and shy he had been as a young fellow. His near-sighted eyes and very fair lashes, his sibilant voice and slight lisp, imparted something half-comical and touching to his personality.'

Walter Nouvel: 'Bakst was a charming and talented man, with a rich imagination, and highly amusing and witty. But he had his defects. He was extraordinarily vain, adored publicity and fame, thought too much about his own career, and, in order to achieve his goal, sometimes used means which we found unattractive. Besides, he was unbalanced, suspicious, hot-tempered, inconsistent, and one could not always trust him as he was not always sincere, and he whined. These defects annoyed Diaghilev, and Bakst, in turn, used to get agitated by his dictatorial attitude in exploiting the talent of others; and this was the reason for their constant quarrels.'

Tamara Karsavina (1954): 'I met him for the first time at a dress rehearsal (*The Fairy Doll*), a dandified young man in appearance, pernickety in his ways. Bakst won through at once.'

Bronislava Nijinska (1982): 'I remembered seeing him in the spring sunshine of Monte Carlo, not extravagently dressed like Stravinsky, but always neatly turned out, wearing a white shirt with pink stripes, a dark pink bow tie and, of course, always the flower in his buttonhole. His prominent blue-grey eyes looking out over the pince-nez, which he rarely removed, his red hair carefully combed over his small, round, balding head, with that pompous moustache beneath his large, arched nose. One could not call him handsome, but beneath his attractive individuality one sensed the artist.'

Serge Grigoriev (1953): 'On my right sat a man with curly red hair, very carefully brushed, with lively, slightly laughing eyes and clean-shaven cheeks. He was elegantly dressed and smelt of scent . . . He spoke with a curious accent, giving his 'r's a guttural pronunciation. As I noticed later, he greatly amused Diaghilev, especially by his accent.'

Jean Cocteau letter to Misia Sert (Gold, A., 1980): 'Bakst, a huge society parakeet with a ''violon d'Ingres'' on his head, a monster of Jewish duplicity, jealous of anybody loving anybody else, and capable of anything to stop their being happy. Boasts a lot and never sleeps with anyone. He is not liked among the female dancers, which was a surprise to me, as I thought he would be popular in that field. His moustache is the object of great hilarity among them.'

André Levinson (1923): 'I fondly recall the dandy, with his liking for little conceits of elegance, collecting the compliments, with a quizzing smile, from a whole aviary of dancers in their tutus.'

Paul Morand: 'A rumpled, tubby man with spectacles, sparse red hair, a ridiculously dapper military moustache, and a comical lisp.'

Prince Peter Lieven (1936): 'With him one always felt happy and amused and at perfect ease, knowing that if Bakst was there everything would be pleasant and merry. This combination of good nature with his involuntary drollness was the secret of Bakst's particular charm.'

Maurice Martin Du Gard (1925): 'The last time I saw Léon Bakst was one afternoon at the Opéra, during a technical rehearsal of the revival of *Le Martyre de Saint Sébastien*. He was going up and down the centre aisle of the stalls, with the seats covered in dust-sheets, holding a portable telephone, with gold pince-nez on his nose, and a large rosette of the Legion of Honour in his buttonhole. He was adjusting the complicated lighting cues. He was putting in the final touches.'

Valerian Svetlov (a quaint translation, Réau, L., 1927): 'Léon Bakst was deeply imbued with the European "correctness" which found its expression in his way of dressing, always unimpeachable, as well as in the accuracy with which he carried out the orders, and in his methods of working . . . I often called at his studio on the Boulevard Malesherbes and I could not conceal my enthusiasm at the sight of the strict order that reigned in Bakst's studio. It resembled rather a rich flat of a man of taste than a painter's studio; and when I gave utterance to my admiration, he used to say: "There is nothing to be astonished at; the disorder is an obstacle to regular work. When everything is in order, the thoughts are in order as well, and work is smoothly running on. You know yourself what a supreme importance is accuracy and speed in the scenographer's work."

In the vast and elegant sitting-room which served as studio, there stood elegant furniture, a few large tables, an American writing desk on which several richly leather-bound books with gilt edges were destined for recording all orders received, all invitations accepted; other albums of great size contained excerpts from papers and reviews with criticisms of his works. I wonder where those albums, so important for everybody undertaking a work on Bakst, are now? [Yes, indeed!] There were also two easels and a small moveable estrade for the model, when Bakst had to paint a full-size portrait.

To the right of the sitting-room, there was a bedroom, a cosy little chamber with a broad bed. I was always impressed at the sight of so many drugs in the small sideboard and on the night-table. Bakst's health was far from being strong and he had to follow different courses of treatment. On the left from the sitting-room, a few steps lower, there was a large room which Bakst called his "picture gallery". In that gallery there were many cubistic pictures and

Opposite, above left
Costume design for an elder at Theseus'
court in *Hippolytus*, 1902
280 × 210
SOTHEBY'S/PRIVATE COLLECTION

Right
Costume design for 2 slaves in *Phaedre*,
1923
295 × 225
SOTHEBY'S/PRIVATE COLLECTION

Below, left
Costume design for 4 soldiers in *Oedipus
at Colonus*, 1904
280 × 215
SOTHEBY'S/PRIVATE COLLECTION

Right
Costume design for Pollux in *Hélène de
Sparte*, 1912
280 × 208
ASHMOLEAN MUSEUM, OXFORD

These four drawings show two
examples from many which illustrate
how Bakst, early in his theatrical career,
designed certain costumes and then
adapted the same drawing for later
productions by making only minor
changes to the figure and decorative
details. He usually applied this 'short
cut' only to minor characters. Costume
design is more concerned with the
appearance of the final costume on
stage, than with the appearance of a
design on a piece of paper. Costume
designs are working drawings which is
why they also often include annotations
and written instructions to the
costumier. Simultaneously, however,
Bakst also developed his unique style of
making 'one-off' costume designs
which, because they were appreciated
as drawings, he then copied and
sometimes enlarged

among them those of the founder of the cubism and Bakst's personal friend, Pablo Picasso . . .

Bakst was not fond of anybody being present while he was at work. He used to shut himself up and nobody could penetrate into his house . . . To work with Bakst was a real delight; he was a delicate, well-bred man; even when he did not agree with somebody, he used to defend his own opinions but hesitatingly and was liable to yield the ground as soon as he met with a weighty argument. Alien both to self-esteem and to blind obstinacy, he was a very sincere and simple man.

Bakst loved Russia ardently. I remember with what a profound sadness he spoke of Bolshevism which was beginning to destroy Russia's moral, spiritual and artistic value . . . He was not fond of political discussions and tried to avoid them. He did not care to communicate to everybody his convictions and intimate opinions; at the close of his life, he was leading a life of nearly a recluse.

One of the reasons for shunning the world was the bad state of his health. I knew that when amidst his tactful and soft speech there appeared signs of irritation, when he uttered his opinions with a note of intolerance, all this was a symptom that a crisis of a deep neurasthenia was at hand. He had to undergo such crisis several times, when staying in Paris. When he became the prey of this grave disease, the door of his flat was hermetically closed and nobody was admitted except the nurse whose permanent presence became altogether necessary. He lay in bed motionless, presenting the lamentable aspect of a man exhausted physically and morally. Such fits could not last long. Then they passed and we saw him again in good humour and energetically beginning new work.

But the heavy sickness was watching this painter, poet and thinker, until it threw him definitely down in the prime of his brilliant talent, of his all-embracing activity.'

Bakst used to refer to the theatre as his 'evil genius'. He chose to practise his art and produced his greatest artistic effects in the most ephemeral form. When he was asked, once, if he regretted that so much of his work had already disappeared, he shrugged his shoulders and replied, 'It is all comparative: only the creative force in the artist's soul survives.'

Fortunately, many of his designs have survived and we know his art through them, but they give a false and distorted view because they are seen as objects in isolation and not as finished costumes and sets in an integrated ensemble. Bakst's genius, however, was to be able to transmit in his costume designs, the spirit, or the soul of the character, and in his set designs, the atmosphere of the place as well as the technical details and visual instructions about how they should all be made. He also, inimitably, expressed the movement of the dancers or the pose of the actors. Bakst wrote to Robert de Montesquiou: 'I have just come up against a really cock-eyed estimation of "decorative art"! What are graphic drawings if they are not "decorative art"? And anyway is there a single painting which does not enter the realm of "decorative art" even though it has its own special purpose?' Although his style of drawing was individual he evolved, especially for minor characters, several basic formulas for making costume designs. They became frequently repeated patterns on which he simply changed the decorative details. The repetition of these drawings has meant that they have sometimes been attributed to the wrong productions. Apart from his economic use of 'templates', the unique character of Bakst's drawing is that he varied his style according to the nature of the production and designed each costume to fit the particular role as he saw it; his designs are like portraits. Gerald Siordet was one of the first to remark on this characteristic: 'Bakst is a real student, a genuine scholar in costume. His designs are no mere archaeological resurrections of the wardrobes of the past; neither are they the summary, impressionistic stock-in-trade of the quick change artist. He is, indeed, a kind of bright, particular chameleon. He will settle into the strange, distorted glamour of the East, or the simple graces of archaic Greece, or the fierce, gay medley of the Middle Ages, and presently will bring you forth not dresses merely but *personages* who move with ease and certainty each in his own time, and yet retain the stamp of their creator.' No other theatre designer has done this in the same way. Most designers change their style over the years, but *none* changes styles for different kinds of productions. This makes Bakst's work on paper an interpretation of the staging as well as an accurate visual record.

Furthermore, while his *sense* of colour was always vividly the same, the way he used it changed from one production to another. He thought that colour had symbolic meaning and that therefore certain colours created particular moods. Sometimes he used colour in blocks moving up and down stage or from side to side, sometimes the set would be vividly strong and the costumes muted, sometimes vice versa, sometimes both would contrast or even clash with each other. The whole stage was his 'canvas'; sky borders, back cloths, floor cloths, furniture, props and costumed figures were all part of his three-dimensional moving picture. The illustrations in this book clearly demonstrate his different styles and colour ranges but they cannot show the effect of the ensemble.

Bakst is best remembered for the 'sumptuousness' of his sets and costumes and for bringing vivid, pure colour to the stage. Jean le Seyeux in *Comoedia* in 1922 described the effect of his work: 'No costume designer knows how to juggle with colours as well as he does . . . Léon Bakst, uses all the brightest as well as the most neutral colours. He knocks them about, puts them together, controls them, contrasts them so that the colours, whether bright or dull, always retain an intense luminosity. I have seen costumes by Bakst, howling with colours, which off stage look like colourless and shapeless tawdriness.

'He takes a period and then his genius transposes it and resets it into ours maintaining its principal outlines. That is the true art of costume. There are no costumes more genuine, more whimsical, more powerful, more sumptuous, more mannered, more delicate, more savage than the costumes of Léon Bakst.'

Bakst himself best described what he meant by colour and its effect in the theatre in an interview with Georges Gombaut in 1919:

> I have a taste for intense colour; and I have tried to achieve a harmonious effect by using colours which contrast with each other rather than a collection of colours which go together. The eye used to be saturated with undisturbed visions, and I have tried to use a more resonant scale. Art is only contrasts. Besides, I have invented nothing: look at a bunch of flowers, not cunningly arranged by a gardener, but picked by the innocent hand of a child, and you will see harmony in the pure colours of nature; it is up to the painter to rediscover his palette. This trend is most perfectly expressed in the theatre: the curtain goes up, the public's imagination is seized by the harsh plainness of the colours, it is roused, it is like the effect of a shot from a gun.'

An aspect of his drawing which has caused endless confusion is the copying. It is a minefield. When Bakst realized that there was a market for his designs he began to make them with greater care, first either copying them himself or having them copied by assistants. These copies were for the workshops and on them Bakst would often have written and signed extensive notes and instructions to scene painters and costumiers; this has led people wrongly to suppose that the whole drawing was by him. The presence of notes, however, does not mean that Bakst definitely did not do the drawing. Sometimes the drawings and the notes were signed by Bakst as 'Copie d'après Bakst' (Copy after Bakst) and unscrupulous dealers have been known to paint out, or cut out the words 'Copy after'. Beware. Bakst copied many favourite designs himself, often enlarging the original, but he was not deceitful and generally signed his copies with the right date. Bakst signed and dated nearly all his work. After his death, Rasamatt, the husband of one of his nieces, removed much of the work remaining in his studio, had a stamp made of an approximate signature and another with his own name, *G. Rasamatt, Dépositaire exclusif des oeuvres de Léon Bakst*, and tried to sell everything off whether it was by Bakst or not. There are several ways of detecting a fake, you can look at the paper, the watermark, the signature, the date, but the best way is to look at enough real Baksts – then the fakes are unmistakable.

Bakst had a long and successful association with The Fine Art Society in London which began in June 1912 with his first one-man show in London. The managing director, enthused by seeing a performance of the Russian Ballet, decided at once to mount an exhibition of Bakst's designs. Huntly Carter, critic and theatre historian, described in his introduction to the first catalogue Bakst's artistic aim '. . . to express rhythmic movement, supple, precise, and harmonious. He is one of the advanced decorators of to-day who are occupied with drawing action, that is something seen and put down in a flash. It has been aptly said that he clothes a movement, not a mannekin. He uses the supple movements of the dancer's body and the fluid lines of her drapery symbolically. The flow of both indeed form a lyrical

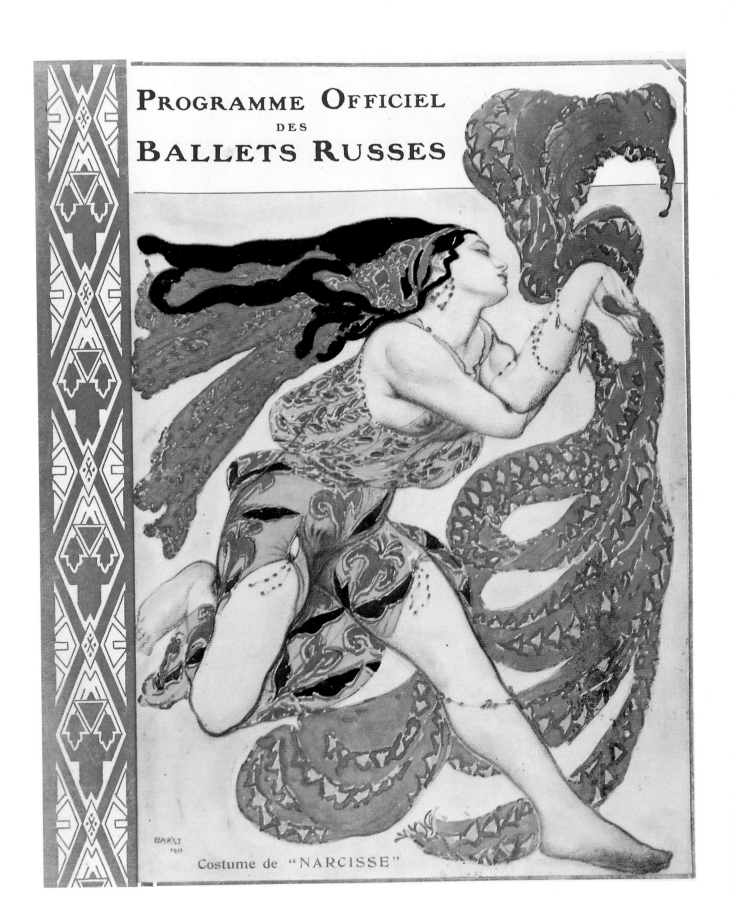

PROGRAMME OFFICIEL
DES
BALLETS RUSSES

BAKST
1911

Costume de "NARCISSE"

Left
Costume design for a Bacchante in
Narcisse, 1911
285×220
SOTHEBY'S/PRIVATE COLLECTION

Right
Costume design for a Bacchante in
Narcisse, c.1923
675×480
MUSÉE NATIONAL D'ART MODERNE, CENTRE
GEORGES POMPIDOU, PARIS

These three designs show Bakst copying
himself. In the initial drawing (left), the
figure has been worked out, the basic
shape defined. In the finished design
(opposite), the figure is more sensual,
the shading more erotic, an
extraordinary combination of
movement and languor, with all the
details finished for reproduction. The
third drawing (right), with a signature
stamped after his death, is Bakst's own
unfinished enlargement for exhibition
purposes. Was it unfinished because
Bakst just left it, or did he see that it was
not as good as the previous one, that the
life had gone from it?

Opposite
Costume design for a Bacchante in
Narcisse, 1911

Reproduced on the cover of the
Souvenir Programme of the Ballets
Russes, 1911
Reproduction 310×200

accompaniment to her inner passions. They roll with a luscious rhythm in harmony with the rhythm of her soul.' Very early Bakst's drawing inspired extravagent admiration.

Other one-man shows in London followed in 1913 when The Fine Art Society published the English edition of the luxurious *The Decorative Art of Léon Bakst*, and in 1917 when several designs were shown from Pavlova's production of *The Sleeping Beauty* in New York in 1916. Prices then ranged between £35 and £140 with an average of about £40. In 1927, just over two years after his death, there was a Memorial Exhibition when the average price for a costume design had dropped to about £25. Recent prices at auction for a costume design can be up to £55,000.

One of the directors of The Fine Art Society in 1913 was W. A. Propert, who wrote the first contemporary assessment of the Russian Ballet, published in 1921, with a chapter on Léon Bakst. He thought he was: 'A figure-draughtsman of first-rate ability, a landscape-painter very sensitive to the lines of hills and the building of trees, a colourist without fear and a remarkable manipulator of water-colour, his predilections have been for the exuberant and the sumptuous, and the proof of his excellence can be measured by the failure of his numerous copyists ... He has founded a school, but he is likely to be its only master ... there can be no doubt that his is the most outstanding figure among the painters who worked with Diaghilev during the first five years of his enterprise ... within the walls of the theatre, the terrain which he had deliberately chosen for his work, he remains in many ways unrivalled.'

A theatre design is primarily a statement of intent. It may or may not also be a work of art in its own right. Bakst produced many works of art on paper but the true manifestation of his art was on stage. And yet he knew, better than anyone, that theatre is also the art of compromise; the designer has to rely on others to fulfil his intentions.

31

Towards the end of the nineteenth century, theatre design in Russia and everywhere else in Europe had reached a level of stultified mediocrity. It was Savva Mamontov who did more than anyone to reinvigorate the theatre in Russia by inviting easel painters to design the sets for his private opera productions. This innovation, influenced by The World of Art group, was then taken up by the Imperial Theatres where Bakst found his vocation. Once he learnt his craft, however, he was much more than just a painter designing sets and costumes as an additional attraction to the look of a play. He was equally concerned with every aspect of the production, the sets, the props, the costumes, the make-up, the lighting, the whole staging as well as influencing the choreography. As he acquired more experience so his role as designer assumed greater importance and his reputation became pre-eminent. He always insisted on getting the best out of people, and, by all accounts, succeeded.

He wrote some of his thoughts on the role of theatre designer to Huntly Carter in about 1913:

> I think the time when the director ruled the roost in theatrical production has gone for ever. The cerebral 'mind' which dominated the theatre for so many years is giving way to the scenic 'mind', and the 'tone' of the whole effect will henceforth (and for a long time in the future it seems to me) be determined by the painter. The evolution of theatre is leaning towards a scenic ideal, and sometimes beautifully inventive theatre appears to be weak and unimpressive when the 'vision' has not first been realized in an artistic way; in the same way as a painting which is too literary is not to the taste of a true connoisseur of art.
>
> So, pride of place to the painter in the theatre! Now it is the painter (just as earlier it was the scholarly director) who has to create everything, know everything, foresee everything and organize everything. It is the painter who must know all about archaeology as well as the latest trends, who has to understand the subtlety of the 'circumstances'; and who has to decide on the style of the play; the thousands of details which go to make up the whole thrilling and imposing effect of a fine theatrical production will henceforth depend on his scenic good taste.
>
> Gone is the time when the humble scene painter, that ignorant, younger brother of kings of the palette, gave in to the bad taste absurdities of learned directors. The leaders of this theatre, which is evolving all the time and which is taking on this new form, will now be recruited from the ranks of artist painters of the highest intelligence. The era of realism in the theatre is finished – everyone feels it more and more every day.
>
> For me the play and its framework is a continual transformation of a large painting unified by a style which is expressed in the smallest pictorial, scenic or even 'phonetic' details. This absolute unity must be guided by a mind which first and foremost

sees things scenically because it is now clearer than ever that the interpretation of a play is more a three-dimensional art than a literary one. Otherwise, what is the point of a stage, acting, scenery, costumes, props all of which add to the impression of a play which can be read just as easily at home without a theatre.

Just as in a painting, the 'decor' cannot have elements of form and colour in it other than those specially chosen by a single scenic mind which unites everything in perfect harmony. It is goodbye to scenery designed by a painter blindly subjected to only one part of the work, to costumes made by any old dressmaker who strikes a false and foreign note in the production; it is goodbye to the kind of acting, movements, false notes and that terrible, purely literary wealth of detail which make modern theatrical production a collection of tiny impressions without that unique simplicity which emanates from a true work of art.

The theatre is the most transitory of the arts and it vanishes into inaccurate memory without the controlling presence of the original artist passionately insisting on getting everything right. When, for example, *Schéhérazade* was revived after his death in the 1930s it was a very diluted affair. G. E. Goodman noticed in *The Dancing Times* that: ' . . . the total effect gives one the impression that "making do" has been rather too much the order of the day. There are surely enough photographs and sketches of the original *décor* in existence to make it a fairly easy matter to reconstruct this scene in all its first lushness and extravagence, even if the actual scenes and designs are no longer available. If a certain modernization has been attempted, the public should be informed in the programme and thus be given someone to blame for tampering with history. Bakst cannot be modernized, even if he does not wear very well.' The critic missed the point; photographs and sketches are not enough. With the original designer no longer available to oversee the production the effect cannot be the same. Theatre design cannot be a second-hand art.

The theatre art

Before Greece:
1901–1907

Frontispiece for *The Contemporary Ballet*
by Valerian Svetlov, St Petersburg, 1911,
originally designed for the programme
cover for *The Heart of the Marchioness*,
1902

The first venture into theatre by The World of Art group ended in a production which did not take place.

Prince Sergei Mikhailovitch Volkonsky (1860–1937) was appointed director of the Imperial Theatres on 22 July 1899. He wanted to liven up their image which had become rather stuffy, and one of the first things he did was to appoint Diaghilev to produce a revitalized *Year Book*. The new edition, published in 1900, which included a reproduction of a programme cover design of Pierrot and Columbine by Bakst for the Hermitage Theatre, was a magnificent example of book production and was complimented by everyone including the Tzar. But it had gone way over budget. Volkonsky loyally supported Diaghilev against the criticism of extravagence and in January 1901 commissioned him to produce Léo Delibes' *Sylvia*. A production of this ballet had been in the minds of The World of Art group for some time. Delibes was a favourite composer but as *Coppelia* was already in the repertoire and as there was no-one, in the group's opinion, who could dance the name part in *Lakmé*, they pestered Volkonsky with the idea of *Sylvia* until he acquiesced. Something of a mish-mash was planned for it was agreed that Alexandre Benois, Constantin Korovine, Evgeny Lanceray and Léon Bakst would all have a hand in the design. The production began to arouse a lot of unpleasant envious gossip from other departments in the theatre and, at the last minute, Volkonsky lost his nerve and told Diaghilev that he could not have sole responsibility for the production but that it had to be under the final control of the directorate of the Imperial Theatres. Diaghilev was offended and refused these conditions. The artists supported Diaghilev who told Volkonsky that if he could not be responsible for the production he would refuse to go on editing the *Year Book*. Volkonsky, adamant, asked him to resign and gave him five days to think about it. Diaghilev refused, whereupon Volkonsky dismissed Diaghilev under Paragraph Three of Article 838 of the 'Rules of State Service'. This meant 'dismissal without pardon' and 'dismissal without reason given and without appeal' and was used in conjunction with Article 788 which stated that it was entirely a matter for the authorities to determine whether an employee was capable of carrying out his functions as a civil servant or not. (Similar rulings apply today in certain English museums.) A person dismissed according to Paragraph Three could never be employed by any state department again. (This rule caused so much hardship that it was repealed in 1905.) Diaghilev appealed to his friend the Grand Duke Sergei Mikhailovitch who apparently said that if he were in Diaghilev's shoes he would not resign either. Diaghilev therefore wrote to Volkonsky saying that he would not resign, but on the same day, 15 March 1901, the dismissal was officially announced in *Pravitelstvennom Vestnike* (*The Government Herald*) and could not be rescinded. Diaghilev was in disgrace. And the production of *Sylvia* was cancelled. It was just as well; Volkonsky was right, it would have been a scrambled mess. The single surviving drawing by Bakst (opposite) is a charming figure study

Costume design for the Viscount
Holding a Stick in *The Heart of the
Marchioness*, 1902
280 × 178
THE FINE ARTS MUSEUMS, SAN FRANCISCO

He is already concerned with character
as well as costume. The stick is a
frequent prop in Bakst's designs and
balances the pose

КОСТЮМЪ „ВИКОНТА"
(ПАНТОМИМА „LE COEUR DE LA MARQUISE")

in pale colours but not yet an effective costume design. (He was, however, totally confident
and convincing by 1910 when he designed a similar costume for Anna Pavlova as Diana.)
Soon afterwards, in July, Volkonsky himself had to resign after the scandal which followed
when he had the audacity to fine the prima ballerina Kshessinska, once the mistress of the
Tzar. Volkonsky was succeeded by Vladimir Arkadievitch Teliakovsky (1861–1924). Since
Diaghilev could no longer work for the state he turned to the West a few years later, and so it
is likely that had the production of *Sylvia* taken place as planned, there may well have been
no Ballets Russes.

Although Diaghilev was now without an official position the Imperial Theatres continued to employ the artists and other members of The World of Art group. Bakst was asked to
design a production of the French one-act pantomime-ballet *Le Coeur de la Marquise* (*The
Heart of the Marchioness*) for the Hermitage Theatre, the Tzar's private theatre where the performances were only attended by the imperial family and members of the court. Bakst

Preliminary drawing for costume design for Nijinska as one of the 12 Dolls in *The Fairy Doll*, 1903
295 × 260
THEATRE MUSEUM, LONDON

Bronislava Nijinska in her *Early Memoirs* (1982) remembered: 'I was a pink doll, and I remember what a delight it was for me as a child as I put on each detail: the pink open-work socks over white tights, ruffled pantalettes showing beneath the short, full, ruffled, white muslin skirt of the dress. I had a wide pink ribbon over one shoulder tied in a bow below the waist, and tiny pink bows tied on each wrist just above short white gloves. Over my curly locks I wore a light, lacy bonnet tied with a ribbon under my chin'

designed a classical, semi-circular setting and historically accurate costumes in the Directoire style of the 1790s. The costume designs are delicate, romantic drawings again more appropriate to book illustrations than to the theatre but they already show in their different poses Bakst's distinctive feel for individual character (p. 36). *Le Coeur de la Marquise* was only

given two performances, the first on 22 February (7 March) 1902, and was judged to be a success. Bakst, however, complained in a letter to Benois that the scene painter Oreste Allegri had coarsened all his colours and 'improved' all his decorative details without consulting him: 'Not one of the colours is as on my drawing, not a single pattern has been left alone. There was nothing I could do about it, but it's a pity. All whites and greens! Everything is drowned in candy colours in the very best of taste'. Benois himself later remembered in his *Reminiscences* (1941) 'Against the white background of the exquisite little *empire salon* the costumes stood out in a most distinctive harmony of shades.' The taste of the day had not yet come round to Bakst's stronger colours.

Almost a year later Bakst designed another production for the Hermitage Theatre. This was the one-act ballet *Puppenfee* (*The Fairy Doll*) by Bayer performed only once on 7 (20) February 1903. *Novoe Vremia*, under the headline 'Performance and Ball at the Hermitage', reported that their Highnesses appeared at 9 o'clock and that the Empress, dressed in black, was attired in diamonds and emeralds, that His Majesty the Emperor, in naval uniform, sat in the middle of the front row with Her Majesty the Empress beside him, and that to her right was His Majesty the Heir to the Throne, and then it listed other members of the Imperial family and the court who were present. The performance was well received and, according to *Novoe Vremia*, dinner was served at midnight, and dancing, in which the Emperor and Empress took part, went on until half-past two. The reporter mentioned that Bakst had designed the set, costumes and props but did not consider it necessary to express any opinion about the production.

This ballet, however, created such a good impression that it was revived on 16 February (1 March) at the Mariinsky Theatre for the closed winter season. It seems a strange decision when the critic of *Novosti i Birzhevaya Gazeta* (*The News and Stock Exchange Gazette*) made this comment: 'There is nothing original in this music, but it is not lacking in melody and is good for dancing,' but 'where after all we already have ballets like *The Nutcracker* with wonderful music by Tchaikovsky, the production of *The Fairy Doll* seems to be rather superfluous.' He does not mention Bakst who was praised in the *Journal de St Pétersbourg* (the French language newspaper): 'The sets and costumes from designs by M. Bakst are exquisite in their rightness and charm. The change of scale which he effects between the first and second scenes is of particular interest, and makes us want to see this young painter's work more often in the theatre because he seems to have a real talent for it.'

Called by its French title, *La Fée des Poupées*, this ballet was in two scenes set in a toy shop transposed from a small town in Germany to St Petersburg. The set for the first scene was an accurate representation of the interior of a large toy shop in the Gostinny Dvor, in St Petersburg in the middle of the nineteenth century. The sides of the shop were lined with showcases of dolls and shelves of other toys; there was a large clock on the wall above red plush chairs; a rocking horse centre stage and at the back of the set, like an extra diversion, two large windows in an arcade overlooked the street where passers-by could be seen coming and going by the audience. Bakst's effective theatrical trick was in the change he made between the realism of the first scene which was in human scale and the fantasy of the second with the architecture and furniture enlarged to be in scale with the dolls.

Dolls were an obsessive theme running through Bakst's career and in these costume designs he set himself a pattern for other ballets of the same genre which are reflected in designs for *Le Carnaval*, 1910 (pp. 79 and 85); *Les Papillons*, 1912 (pp. 126 and 127); *La Boutique Fantasque*, 1917, intended as a new version (p. 230), and *La Nuit Ensorcelée*, 1923 (pp. 230 and 231). In the drawings Bakst makes a careful distinction between the humans who look real and the delicate wide-eyed dolls stuck on stands which look as if they are made of china (pp. 37 and 38). As models both for the humans and the dolls Bakst used figures from the Russian porcelain factories of Gardner and Popov. Many of the designs for this ballet are still in museums in Russia, and evidence of their success is that Bakst had the unusual distinction of having a set of twelve of them reproduced as postcards to be sold for the benefit of the Red Cross.

The *corps de ballet* for this production was made up of children from the Imperial Ballet School and two of the pupils were Vaslav Nijinsky and his sister Bronislava then thirteen and twelve years old respectively. Bronislava in her *Early Memoirs* (1982) remembers: 'Even now I can relive the enchanted memory of the costumes. It was our first contact with the painter, Lev Samoilovitch Bakst, watching him create his designs. Before this I had worn only stock costumes from the wardrobe, but for *The Fairy Doll* each costume was individually designed and we were all specially measured ... Vaslav was a wooden soldier and wore a blue jacket and black trousers, designed so that the soldiers really looked as though they had been carved out of wood. Their trousers and boots made one triangle and their blue jackets made another.' Nijinska also remembered that Bakst was meticulous about their make-up and applied it himself in order to be sure to create the complete look that he wanted in each of his characters. 'I had two bright red round spots on my cheeks and long eyelashes that Bakst had drawn on my face.'

Before *The Fairy Doll* Bakst had already produced the first of his Greek designs for a production of *Hippolytus* by Euripides at the Alexandrinsky Theatre (one of the Imperial Theatres) in St Petersburg on 14 (27) October 1902. Artistic standards had been slipping there for some time with a weak repertoire of boring contemporary plays and third-rate productions. Teliakovsky, determined not to let standards slip further, appointed P. P. Gneditch as artistic director. He introduced a repertoire of classic Russian and western European plays, enlisted the co-operation of members of The World of Art, and commissioned artists to design the productions.

Hippolytus, translated by Dimitri Merezhkovsky, had already been performed successfully in a private theatre in 1900. Now Bakst was chosen to design the new production because he was already a well-known painter and could be relied upon to do the necessary research in order to achieve the desired authentic and historically accurate effect. The Greek theme recurs often in Bakst's theatre. His ideas developed and his eyes were opened to a new palette of colours after his visit to the country in 1907 but he did all the necessary basic research at the Hermitage Museum while working on this production, which then served him as a solid foundation for the future. Merezhkovsky's translation emphasized the symbolic aspect of the play and Bakst realized that his ideas were not compatible. He warned Teliakovsky in a letter dated 11 (24) April 1902: 'I'm afraid there is going to be a mutual misunderstanding between the translator and the painter because the one is going to ask the other to do things which will be contrary to the style and arrangement of the set.' Bakst, as a theatre designer, already had very specific ideas. In *The Story of the Artist's Life* (1923), André Levinson described (quoting Bakst and in a slightly curious translation) what Bakst tried to do: '... the problem was that of adapting the essential dualism of the Greek tragedy ... to the arrangement of the modern theatre, with its odd-shaped stage, like a box opened towards the side of the spectators. Bakst made the attempt ... By raising the background of the stage he made the foreground available for the proscenium, with the altar of the god of the tragedy in the middle ... At the end the leader of the chorus would ascend the steps which connected the proscenium with the platform in order to pronounce Fate's supreme sentence upon the protagonist who had been prostrated by the gods. Thus, for the first time, an attempt was made at a logical dissociation of the rhythmic and dramatic elements of the ancient theatre.' This was all very well in theory but apparently it did not succeed in practice. The critic of the *Journal de St Pétersbourg* was unaware of the theory and was brutal in his review: '*Hippolytus* has been a long time in preparation, and the director, counting on creating quite an event, spared no expense. M. L. Backst [*sic*], a painter of merit, has designed a novel set and has made all the drawings for the costumes. The properties, except for the cardboard altar, were well matched ... Furthermore, there was incidental music composed by M. E. Overbeck, and a certain number of students were engaged for the season at 25 roubles a month and introduced into the chorus in order to raise their spirits. One would have thought, therefore, that given all this, and notably with the gracious personal participation of M. Merezhkovsky the scenic effect of the production could only be magnificent. It was nothing of the kind. The setting, the statues, the costumes, the wigs, indeed even the altar, which was not even cardboard, and the music, which tried to be authentically Greek (a few very ancient hymns had been found), none of this could produce the unbelievable illusion and transport us into a seemingly fantastical environment. Classical simplicity, grandeur, majesty, dignity, all the principal elements which form the basis of this kind of performance were entirely lacking at the Alexandrinsky Theatre. As for the acting, that was even worse.' This illustrates the dilemma of all theatre design: how far should a designer go to be authentic, that is, historically accurate, and what is considered to be authentic anyway? In this case the critic was clearly not convinced. Successful theatre design depends upon conviction rather than authenticity. The critic of *Novoe Vremia*, Yuri Beliaeff, obviously had inside information for he was much more sympathetic to Bakst's ideas. Although he was no more complimentary about the acting he was more impressed by the aims of the production: 'A lot of artistic endeavour and special preparation was called for from the talented M. Bakst for the design of the set and costumes. I met him in the half-lit cellars of the Hermitage Museum where he poured over fragments of antiquities, and

Act 5 of *Hippolytus* at the Alexandrinsky Theatre, St Petersburg, 1902
MUSEUM OF THEATRICAL AND
MUSICAL ARTS, LENINGRAD

The actual set was a cumbersome and very artificial interpretation of the design. The scene looks very dated now

Set design for *Hippolytus*, 1902
287 × 408
THE RUSSIAN MUSEUM, LENINGRAD

The design, drawn as if from the side of
the dress circle, is like an impressionistic
sketch in an impossible scale for the
stage

Above
Costume design for a Herald in
Hippolytus, 1902
290 × 210
MUSEUM OF THEATRICAL AND MUSICAL ARTS,
LENINGRAD

The first costume design with the *élan* of
movement. Bakst, obviously pleased
with the result, later copied this design
which is in a private collection

Right
Costume design for Lady in Waiting to
Phaedra's court in *Hippolytus*, 1902
290 × 210
PRIVATE COLLECTION

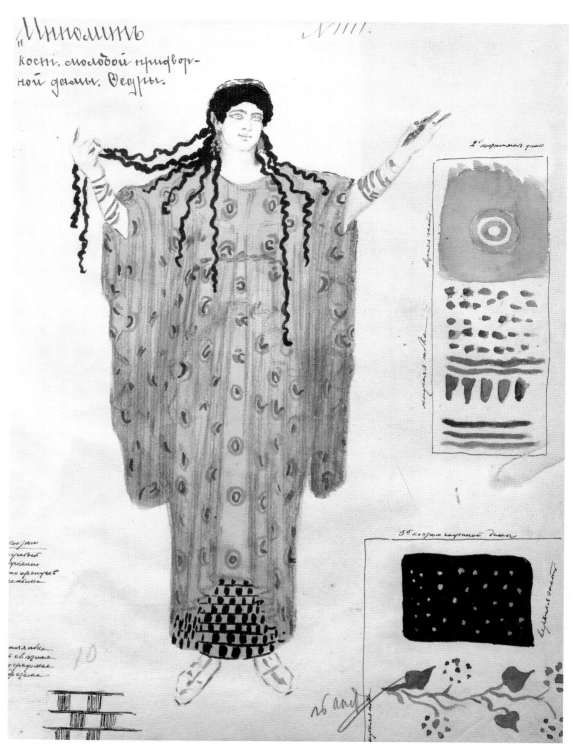

he made sketches of essential reference material from all kinds of sources: tombs, vases, and special books. It was a considerable achievement to create a novel setting while maintaining a sense of plausible classical Greek life. On the stage there were no usual Greeks in the Empire style, or worse, Greeks from operettas, but there were Greeks from Etruscan vases, bas-reliefs from sepulchres and the latest excavations. The costumes were handsome and novel, the make-up for the most part was terracotta … As far as the set is concerned it has been well thought out which is something that cannot be said of how it has been built and painted. The columns of the palace of Theseus are flat and have no thickness and therefore leave the setting without any sense of perspective. The statues of Artemis and Aphrodite need to be real statues and not paper cut-outs. I also agree with the general opinion that the clouds should be done lightly as if in movement, or otherwise not to paint them at all to achieve the effect of airiness.' Beliaeff pinpointed another problem that every designer has with every production, namely the difficulty of interpretation when having to rely upon other craftsmen. We have already seen in his comments about the scenery for *The Heart of the Marchioness* that Bakst was very sensitive to this. He was again thwarted by *Hippolytus* because of an argument about the painting of the clouds among the members of The World of Art. There were those who supported Bakst, like Philosophoff, and those who did not, especially the director of the theatre. Bakst was not yet sufficiently confident either to paint the set himself or to see that it was painted according to his requirements. He knew that there was something wrong with the clouds and, with his knowledge, the directorate of the Imperial Theatres asked Constantin Korovine (1861–1939) to amend the decor. As soon as Korovine had finished his work there were all kinds of arguments for and against among members of The World of Art. Philosophoff in *The World of Art* (No. 9–10, 1902) wrote: 'By repainting the clouds (the decor) on the one hand was made simpler and less pretentious, but on the other hand, by getting rid of the feeling of decadence, it was emasculated. A passive, empty sky diminished the significance of the architectural part of the scenery and all the action on the earth beneath it.' Too much was read into the symbolism of the set. The photographs of the production confirm the opinion of the critic of the *Journal de St Pétersbourg*. It all looks very ham-handed (p. 41).

Argument and intrigue were like yeast to the group, but the letter which Bakst wrote on 18 February 1903 to Liubov Gritzenko reads like a true description of The World of Art at the time:

> … our circle is tight; indeed, after fifteen years' experience (put to the test) it has strengthened and there can be no surprises! We have got so used to each other, we have grown fond of our defects, we have forgiven each other everything long ago, and if we quarrel until we are exhausted then in moments of common danger we stand by each other as if we are being shot at by soldiers on all sides! A. Benois, V. Nouvel, Seriozha Diaghilev, Kostia Somov, Dima Philosophoff, Zhenia Lanceray, A. Ostrou-

mova, A. Nurok, Pavka Koribut, Serov and your humble servant – that's the core of our society: friends who would never betray each other.

After *Hippolytus* the Alexandrinsky Theatre decided to mount Sophocles' tragedy *Oedipus at Colonus* and the same production team was brought together again. The first performance was on 2 (22) January 1904 but the preparations began nearly a year earlier. On 2 March 1903 Bakst wrote to Gritzenko: 'There was a final decisive meeting about *Oedipus* today ... Of course it would be wonderful to go to Greece and do lots of painting there, other studies of mountains, other horizons and shady damp places with luxuriant greens. It would bring freshness and truth to the atmosphere of my landscape scenery, not to mention local colour ...', and on 12 March he wrote to her: 'What is Greece? I dream about it hopefully. I so love the classical world. I expect some kind of revelation there. Oh, the Acropolis! I need it because it has become too imaginary for me and not real at all ... I am taking the costumes for *Oedipus* with me [to Menton], I have to do thirty designs.' Bakst was with Gritzenko in Menton and made a number of landscape studies for the set. He planned to return to Russia via Rome and Greece but in Rome he caught a cold, ran out of money and therefore had to abandon his visit to Greece. His work on the scenery was not going well. On 8 June he wrote to Gritzenko: ' ... I have made an awful pile of rocks! It is as if everything is in a "petrified" state. The mountains are pure Menton and the olive trees are like Greek olive oil. I want to make everything darker, more despairing, more frightening. I am still not satisfied with what I have done. I have worked a lot today, changed a lot, and still have not achieved what I want.' The sets were never completed to his satisfaction but the costumes were much more successful. For the first

Oedipus at Colonus at the Alexandrinsky Theatre, St Petersburg, 1904
MUSEUM OF THEATRICAL AND MUSICAL ARTS, LENINGRAD

This scene also looks very artificial and dated now

Costume design for the Women of the
Chorus at Colonus in *Oedipus at Colonus*,
1904
280 × 215
BAKHRUSHIN MUSEUM, MOSCOW

time in this production Bakst combined the discipline of the authentic with that freedom from slavish authenticity which is required for theatrical effect. The critics were again divided in their opinions. 'Solus' in *Novosti i Berzhevaya Gazeta* was quite ruthless in his attack: 'First of all we simply do not understand archaeological productions. The tragedy should be in a setting which is contemporary with the author, i.e. the fifth century and not in some different one of fairytale princes and ancient myths. The chorus and the other characters must be Greeks of the period in which we are used to imagining them to be, i.e. the period of Sophocles and not as if they are balding fishermen from some Flemish village. Beauty is beauty and it is not without importance in Greek art. Beards made out of rows of pipes are just absurd. They can be shown like that through the convention of Greek drawing or sculpture but not in real life. Indeed the "Alexandrinsky" Greeks were beneath criticism. There was not a single beautiful face, not a single graceful body. Where has all that Greek beauty gone? Furthermore, there were no men on the stage. Oedipus, like an old man, does not even rate. M. Yuref, with his naked legs and a disastrous make-up which made his face like a fat old hag, looked completely effeminate. M. Korvin-Krukovsky in spite of a fierce expression also reminded one of a woman in "a certain condition" thanks to an extremely ill-fitting and tasteless costume. The sets were very unsatisfactory. Athens was shown from a height as if from the top of Mount Ararat. One set represented a wild place, "silent and motionless", painted in parched monotony as if it had been squeezed out in front of the audience. While in actual fact Athens is visible from Colonus set in a deep blue sea where the Aegean disappears beyond the shore of Argolida... Bakst has bare rocks and no horizon. It is scandalously negligent and could have been avoided by just a modicum of attention to the matter in hand.' But Beliaeff in *Novoe Vremia* was again more sympathetic: 'A few words of praise must be said about the external appearance of the production. Although there is a certain pretentiousness about it ... there is in general a lot of good taste, application and talent. The costumes are irreproachable, and if the colours had been a little paler the impression they create would have been even more winning. M. Bakst's settings were extremely effective but the whitish background bordered too sharply with the dark foreground. And perhaps there is just too much of everything: trees, columns, statues, stones. There is in all this no classical simplicity.'

Beliaeff was a friend of the theatre who supported its work. Theatres need critics like that. He also understood what Bakst was trying to achieve and generously praised his contribution to the production, but the existing photographs again give the overwhelming impression of something old-fashioned and second-rate conforming more to the opinion of other critics (p. 45).

About this time an exotic and eccentric girl came into Bakst's life. She was very tall, angular, bony with enormous black eyes. There was something androgynous about her which later appealed to both homosexual men and women, and at the same time, judging from portraits

46

and photographs, she was also very feminine and sexy. She was very rich, she was Jewish, she was Ida Rubinstein. Both her parents had died when she was a child and she was brought up in St Petersburg very strictly by her aunt and uncle. They encouraged her interest in the arts and even allowed her to take private lessons in acting and dancing. She longed for a life in the theatre, but no young girl from a good family could be allowed seriously to contemplate becoming a professional actress. However, she was a very determined girl and longed to test her talents in front of an audience. She decided to mount a production of *Antigone*. In an interview, 'Mes Roles et mes Chasses', which she gave for *Lectures pour Tous* in Paris in 1913, Ida Rubinstein extravagently remembered how she first met Bakst, ' . . . and what a good idea I had at that moment of approaching Léon Bakst to design the costumes and sets. This great artist, with his fierce and uncompromising originality, rejected those conventions which usually overload and distort revivals of classical plays. He evoked that primitive, slightly barbaric and naked age when Oedipus screamed and Antigone wept. He gave the human frame and silhouette that sense of tragedy which is the resounding impression one gets from reading the text. Since then Léon Bakst has never deserted me. I concluded a kind of artistic alliance with him which is extremely important to me. His collaboration in all my efforts has been very precious.' Rubinstein always 'hyped' everything but she was right about Bakst. Without him she would not have survived.

The collaboration continued throughout Bakst's career and he, in turn, recalled the first encounter in an interview with Louis Thomas in 1924:

> She did what she wanted. At the age of fifteen or sixteen, she felt a leaning towards the stage . . . And she made her debut at a private performance, attended by the whole of Petrograd society, by playing – in Russian, of course – one act of Sophocles' *Antigone*.
>
> 'And what did the audience say?'
>
> . . . there were quite a few sceptics who wished for nothing more than to be able to make a lot of witty remarks if she came a cropper. But . . . her success was immediate and decisive. A goddess was born.
>
> 'Had you foreseen this triumph?'
>
> Yes, so much so that I dragged Diaghilev along to the play . . . He was tossing around in his head at the time his plan to tour Europe, and he instantly had the idea of making Mademoiselle Rubinstein into a Cleopatra.

Bakst's memory is not quite accurate. Ida Rubinstein was born on 5 (17) October 1885 so in April 1904 she was nearly nineteen, but for some reason Bakst always rather liked her to be younger than she was, just as he concealed his own age. Although Diaghilev may well have been taken to the performance he was not at that time thinking of casting *Cleopatra*. *Antigone* was given privately only once as a charity performance. Bakst had persuaded her to restrict the evening to one act of the play and, because of her 'position in society' and the attitude towards actresses, Ida Rubinstein, using her patronymic, appeared under the pseudonym of Lvovska.

The anonymous notice in *Novoe Vremia* on 18 April (1 May) 1904 read: 'On Friday 16 April in the New Theatre Sophocles' *Antigone* was presented with Mme Lvovska in the name part . . . The acting was very inexperienced and very uneven. The outward appearance of the play was very beautiful and could not have been more appropriate to the classical role but it could not conceal many missed cues and disproportionate expressions of feeling. It was clear that for the time being she is just a talented student . . . She should work on her voice and diction and then perhaps a talent, which at present we can only surmise, will be revealed.'

André Levinson, however, remembered the production differently: 'I clearly remember this unique production. And I see again the proud maiden as she is wrapped in the numerous and complicated folds of her black mourning robe. In working out this conception Bakst had drawn his inspiration from a tombstone or else had deciphered the clever pattern from the sides of a Greek vase.' This piece of business invented by Bakst forestalls Cleopatra's controversial entrance in the Ballets Russes's *Cléopâtre* in 1909, which caused so much trouble with Benois (pp. 72 and 93). Levinson then continues with an extravagent eulogy of Rubinstein: 'Later this young woman with her disconcerting and mysterious beauty, this mystical virgin, voluptuous yet frigidly cold, with a will of iron beneath a fragile frame, and possessed of a haughty and cold intelligence, who dresses in eccentric clothes, became one of the Muses of our artist [Bakst]. Hers was the gift of driving his imagination to exasperation. Even after many years had elapsed she still held for him the all powerful attraction of the strange, of the unreal, of the supernatural. His Muse – perhaps that is not the right term: rather, his Friendly Demon.'

On 20 April 1904 Bakst wrote to his wife that he had started his portrait of Diaghilev. A little later he wrote to say that Diaghilev was not good at posing and complained, telling Bakst to make him more handsome and less fat, 'I nearly threw the brushes at him.' On 4 June Bakst wrote: 'It is difficult to work with Seriozha [Diaghilev]. I have to call up my reserves of calm and patience a hundred times a session and put up with a stream of stupid remarks. Then I started to talk to him about his miserable attachment. His face lit up, fire in his eyes . . . The pose is sure, daring, considered. Well, we shall see.' It was two years before this revealing and truthful portrait of Diaghilev, with his old nanny in the background tenderly keeping watch over him, was finished.

In 1905 Diaghilev arranged a sensational exhibition of nearly 2,300 Historical Russian Portraits at the Tauride Palace in St Petersburg. This was the first time that so many portraits had been assembled together, and the last because many of them vanished after the revolution, looted or destroyed. Bakst designed the settings for the paintings in which colour played an important part in creating the right atmosphere. The first room, the rotonda,

Serge Diaghilev (1872–1929) and his
Nanny by Léon Bakst, 1904–1906
Oil on canvas, 1610 × 1160
THE RUSSIAN MUSEUM, LENINGRAD

There are very few portrait paintings of
Diaghilev, but many caricatures. This is
the most revealing painting. The old
woman in the background not only
gives the painting depth but puts
Diaghilev firmly in his place

arranged like a monument to Peter the Great, was in dark green, the end of the eighteenth century in deep red, the beginning of the nineteenth century in blue, the 1860s and 1870s in pale coffee-colour, and the last room in grey. This gradual fading of colour symbolized the fact that Russian art had finally reached an end. Encouraged by the success of this exhibition, and with the formal patronage of the Grand Duke Vladimir, Diaghilev began his Russian seasons in Paris in 1906 with an exhibition of Russian Art which opened at the Grand Palais on 6 October. There were 750 exhibits by Russian artists, divided into three sections: Novgorod, Moscow and Stroganov icons; painters and sculptors of the eighteenth and beginning of the nineteenth centuries, and The World of Art painters. Bakst was again responsible for the settings. On 26 October 1906, *Novoe Vremia* reported that 'Bakst was clever enough to present them as if on a plot of Russian earth in a distant, foreign land. Shrubs were brought from Russia ... The copse in which the sculpture was concentrated was like a reconstruction of a shady corner of Peterhof.' Bakst began the art of exhibition design.

A charity performance in aid of the Society for the Prevention of Cruelty to Children at the Mariinsky Theatre, St Petersburg on 10 (23) February 1907 marked the beginning of a long and successful professional collaboration between Michel Fokine, choreographer, and Léon Bakst, designer. Fokine was an innovative genius. Born on 13 (25) April 1880, he joined the Imperial Ballet School at the age of nine, passed the final examinations with distinction in 1898, and in the same year made his debut at the Mariinsky Theatre. He was a dancer of great ability but he felt that ballet had become too bogged down by tradition. He was determined to free it from the conventions which he thought were destroying it as an art form and therefore turned his mind to choreography. He had already formulated some of his ideas by 1904 when he suggested a production of *Daphnis and Chloë* to Teliakovksy. With the scenario he attached some explanatory notes of which the following is an extract quoted by Cyril Beaumont in *Michel Fokine and his Ballets* (1935): 'In ballet the whole meaning of the story can be expressed by the dance. Above all, dancing should be interpretative. It should not degenerate into mere gymnastics... The dance should explain the spirit of the actors in the spectacle. More than that, it should express the whole epoch to which the subject of the ballet belongs.

For such interpretative dancing the music must be equally inspired. In place of the old-time waltzes, polkas, pizzicati and galops, it is necessary to create a form of music which expresses the same emotion as that which inspires the movements of the dancer. The harmony which these dances must have with the theme, the period, and the style, demands a new view-point in the matter of decoration and costume. One no longer demands the eternal short skirts, pink tights, and satin ballet shoes. One can give way to the freedom of artistic fantasy...

The ballet must have complete unity of expression, a unity which is made up of a harmonious blending of the three elements – music, painting, and plastic art.'

Costume design for Mr Goldfalden as
Leporello in *Don Juan Rejected*, 1907
205×90
SOTHEBY'S/PRIVATE COLLECTION

Although Fokine and Bakst worked together almost continuously until 1914 and then again in 1920–21 there is no insight in Fokine's *Memoirs* (1961) into Bakst's character or revelation about their working relationship except that he obviously admired Bakst as a designer and said so: 'A fabulous painter, able to reproduce lines of the human body on paper or canvas in the most complicated perspectives – able to project, through the medium of his brush, a great plastic originality,' but this is almost the only comment. They were successful professional colleagues but not great friends.

Fokine did not follow his own precepts for their first collaboration which was the first version of *Chopiniana*. (There had been a *pas de deux* earlier, *The Flight of the Butterflies*, on 9 April 1906 with the students Elena Smirnova and Vaslav Nijinsky.) *Chopiniana* to Chopin's music was a suite of dances in five scenes with no real connection between them. For no apparent reason, one of the scenes developed into a Waltz with Anna Pavlova and Michael Obukov dancing the parts of Taglioni and Pierrot in costumes designed by Bakst. The sets were from stock and so were some of the other costumes, but *Novoe Vremia* noticed that those by Bakst were 'very stylish and elegant'. Pavlova's was based on contemporary lithographs of Taglioni. It was revised for the second version of *Chopiniana* in 1908, and it was Valentin Serov's sketch of Pavlova in the revised costume which Diaghilev used for the first poster for the Ballets Russes in Paris in 1909. But *Chopiniana* in Paris became *Les Sylphides* designed by Alexandre Benois.

Billed as coming before *Chopiniana* but actually second, was *Eunice*, another new ballet by Fokine. Based on an episode in the novel *Quo Vadis*, one of the dances, an Egyptian dance, was developed the following year into *Egyptian Nights* which in turn led to *Cléopâtre* in 1909. It is not unusual for works for the stage to go through a long process of development. Sometimes it is just tinkering and leads nowhere, but sometimes, as with *Eunice* the changes lead to improvements and ultimate satisfaction. Most of the costumes were again from wardrobe stock, from a production of *Aïda*. Bakst was responsible for seeing to the alterations and for designing the costumes for Kshessinska as Eunice, the dancers of the Torch Dance and some of the others.

However, a more important production for Bakst at the beginning of 1907 was *Don Juan Rejected* because he designed the three sets and all the costumes. It was first performed in St Petersburg on 12 (25) March. This verse play turned the familiar story of Don Juan on its head and showed, in three acts, Don Juan rejected by three women – a wife, a nun and a seductress. Bakst's designs are rare examples of his straightforward historical interpretation of the late medieval period without fantasy. His drawings, too, are straightforward, not very detailed but full of character. He still took time not to make short cuts with the pose and paid attention to hands and feet. Later, hands would often disappear into a few suggestive lines but the designs for *Don Juan* show how well he could draw them. His work was praised in *Rech*: 'An excellent supplement to the text were the settings by Bakst – especially the

Michel Fokine (1880–1942) by Valentin
Serov (1865–1911), 1910
Sanguine
THE RUSSIAN MUSEUM, LENINGRAD

Fokine was Diaghilev's first
choreographer. Above all, he created
the short dramatic ballet and, with
Bakst as designer, established the
reputation of the Ballets Russes. They
continued to be colleagues after they
both left Diaghilev. Serov, a member of
The World of Art group and a close
friend of Bakst, was the greatest portrait
painter of his day. This drawing was
made in 1910 at the time of the second
great season of the Ballets Russes in
Paris

courtyard of the Carmelite monastery (Act 2)', and in *Novoe Vremia*: 'The moorish costumes
and sets of old Seville assembled from drawings by Bakst were most effective,' but the same
critic wrote, 'Only M. Gaydeburov was any good as Don Juan. Mme Skarskaya was not bad as
the nun Teresa but all the other actors were terrible. In the last scene one of the seductresses
dressed in a turban made the whole theatre laugh with her affected and vulgar style of acting. What was she doing with all those contortions and jumps! There were not many people
in the audience.' *Don Juan Rejected* was a failure but although it was rejected by the public it
did no harm to Bakst's career.

Greece and the beginning of the Ballets Russes:
1907–1909

In May 1907 Bakst at last fulfilled a dream. He travelled to Greece with his friend the painter Valentin Serov (1865–1911). This journey had the profoundest effect upon Bakst and radically affected his palette. He had derived his knowledge of Greece from museums and to some extent believed the scholarly myth that the classical world was refined and pale. He had suspected a world of brilliant colour, now he saw it; the journey was both a revelation and a confirmation. On 5 May they sailed from Odessa to Constantinople (Istanbul) where they spent two days before arriving in Athens on 9 May to be met by an explosion of colour and light. Bakst and Serov wrote to their wives almost every day and so their itinerary has been established accurately for the first time from their letters. Bakst wrote on 10 May from the Hôtel Grande Bretagne: 'I was absolutely delighted by Constantinople – colourful, dirty, picturesque, oriental... We have been round the museum of antiquities, a lot of excellent and new things for me... The Acropolis is pure delight. Serov says "It makes me want to cry and pray." ... but in its severity of colour and form it is just like *Oedipus at Colonus*!!! Only not so colossal. Everything is more colossal in tragedy than in nature.' Serov on 13 May, still in Athens: 'We are working in the museum – there are wonderful archaic female coloured figures ... Bakst is a pleasant companion, but a dreadful molly-coddle, and is constantly afraid of catching some kind of chill. He hardly walks, is afraid of getting over tired – but eats a lot.' They were in Crete from 16 to 20 May when, before returning to Athens, Bakst wrote: 'The museum at Candia is staggering with the unexpected revelations of the secret past of Greece discovered during the recent digs.' Sir Arthur Evans was then in the process of uncovering the ruins of the Palace of Minos at Knossos which were such a surprise to everyone at the time. From Athens Bakst and Serov went to Corinth, Delphi, Patras, Olympia and Corfu where they arrived on 6 June. On the 7th Serov wrote: 'It is jolly hot. I wash and change my clothes all the time. Bakst only comes to life here in the evening and even then hardly moves which does not prevent him from sweating all the time and being afraid of catching a chill. I decided to sweat, there's nothing else to be done.' From Corfu Bakst went to Paris via Brindisi on 12 June and Serov returned to Russia.

Bakst and Serov spent a lot of time sketching in the countryside and in museums. One of Bakst's sketchbooks, which is probably typical of them all, is in the New York Public Library at Lincoln Center. It includes general views of the places they visited, figures in landscapes, people in boats, and also several pages of sketches (some coloured) of houses in Knossos, and bare-breasted Cretan women with details of jewellery, ornaments and decorative patterns which Bakst later incorporated in his costume designs. Indeed the visit is henceforth reflected, sometimes with accuracy, sometimes with variation, sometimes with distortion, in all his work. Bakst's great talent lay in using and adapting designs for a total, unified effect on a grand scale.

In 1922 Bakst finally wrote down his impressions of this journey and the short book, *Serov and I in Greece: Travel Notes*, was published in Russian in Berlin in 1923 but has never been translated. It is like a sketchbook in which he described in words the colour, the shimmer, the blaze, the smell and the sound of Greece.

> Greece is so surprising. The line of sandy, rust-coloured rocks is cut through with the horizontal, dark yellow lines of a fortress where, seen from afar looking like toys, tiny soldiers march in columns. And higher up there are scattered clumps of dust-grey olive groves, and higher still there are more naked rocks, wild, classical, mottled like a leopard skin, with irregular, dark brown spots. A bright, blinding light pours from the silver morning sky and caresses the white, sensual cupolas of the turkish buildings so much that it hurts, baking my neck, my shoes, my hands. I put them in my pocket and discover with dismay the erotic photographs which were thrust upon me on deck yesterday by a dirty old Greek just as we were setting sail from Piraeus. I throw the snaps, pathetic nocturnal aphrodisiacs, into the water: they are absurd in this bracing, wide-awake landscape. A breeze carries an attractive fresh smell of the island from the shore. What is the smell? Vegetation warmed by the sun, orange blossom, gentle smoke.'

The book is a chronicle of such word pictures, but the two artists were also in search of classical Greece:

> We wanted everything as classical as possible . . . to get close to Homer . . . Everything seemed pretty to us, and going on here just the same now as it had been three thousand years ago. An eighty year old shepherd in a goat-skin waistcoat and short leather trousers with a brown, sun-burnt, scarred face sat down on a bench close to us. He spread out some pieces of charred meat on his knees and slowly chewed them with his toothless gums. Under thick grey eyebrows his faded eyes looked vacantly ahead in reverie. Directly opposite him a large, dirty sheep-dog had been sitting for an hour on his hind legs nodding his clever head first to the right and then to the left. He gazed passionately at the mouth of his master while convulsively swallowing his saliva and whining respectfully. 'Valentin, Valentin,' I said with excitement 'Look, Ancient Greece, Homer.' I almost cried from emotion, 'Shouldn't we go and get our sketchbooks?'

Back in Russia Bakst designed two costumes for a charity performance at the Mariinsky Theatre on 22 December 1907 (5 January 1908). One was for Tamara Karsavina in an Egyptian Torch Dance choreographed by Fokine to music by Arensky; this was really the first version of *Cléopâtre*. The scene was described in *Novoe Vremia*: 'The costume, designed by Bakst, is Assyrian rather than Egyptian. The stage is dark. The torch bursts into flame in the dancer's hand. Then what appears to be a whole series of snapshots from a motley of Assyrian pottery is flashed before our eyes. The illusion is total, the fascination is complete. And finally the dancer freezes holding the smoking torch high above her head. The vision disappears.'

Costume design for Tamara
Karsavina (1885–1978) in
Torch Dance, 1907
308×233
THE RUSSIAN MUSEUM, LENINGRAD

The other costume became the most famous ballet costume in the world but many people are astonished to discover that it was originally designed by Bakst. This was Pavlova's Swan costume (p. 56). *Novoe Vremia* was moved by the performance: 'If a ballerina can imitate the movements of the most noble bird on stage then it was achieved by this swan.'

On 8 March 1908 there was a charity performance at the Mariinsky Theatre which included two ballets by Fokine in which he developed some previous ideas. *Egyptian Nights* (for some reason in French titled in the singular, *Une Nuit d'Egypte*) took the Torch Dance of two months earlier closer to *Cléopâtre*. The story was taken from Pushkin and so was not as trite as usual. The ballet with music by Arensky and choreography by Petipa was originally planned seven years earlier and the costumes, designed by E. Ponomarev, had all been made.

Anna Pavlova (1881–1931) as the Swan
in *The Swan*, 1928
Photograph by Nicholas Yarovoff
THEATRE MUSEUM, LONDON

The solo *Le Cygne*, first choreographed
by Fokine in 1905, became completely
identified with Pavlova and she
performed it everywhere she went. It
was so important to her that in 1931
when she was dying she asked her maid
to get her Swan tutu ready. Made of
swan's feathers over spangled white net
the costume was obviously remade
many times and therefore probably
changed considerably over the years
without Bakst having any control over
the changes; but no-one noticed the
differences

Fokine liked the male costumes but according to Cyril Beaumont 'he disliked those intended
for the female characters, which consisted of *maillot*, ballet-shoes, and the short and full bal-
let-skirt adorned with an Egyptian decorative motif . . . He took close-fitting blouses, belted
them with scarves, and in this simple manner achieved a reform in ballet costume.' It was not
quite as simple as that because Fokine asked Bakst to advise on the costumes as well as on the
lighting and to design a new costume for Pavlova and Karsavina who danced the solo in the
Jewish Dance which had the most successful costumes of all. The set, 'On the Shores of the
Nile' was a backcloth from the opera *Aïda*.

The second ballet of the evening was the revised version of *Chopiniana* to a new selection
of music. Fokine now transformed it into a purely classical ballet which he called *Reverie*

Romantique, on which he said 'I tried to return to the ballet the conditions of its period of highest development.' Bakst's costumes were all based on Pavlova's costume of the year before, and Fokine remarked: 'I was surrounded by twenty-three Taglionis.'

After the season Fokine went to Switzerland for his summer holiday but he was followed there by Ida Rubinstein who insisted on continuing her dancing lessons which she had begun with him in St Petersburg. She was intending to mount a production of Oscar Wilde's *Salomé* with herself in the title role and Fokine was teaching her the Dance of the Seven Veils. As Fokine says in his memoirs: 'It was not a complete rest,' but he adds charitably, 'The work on the Salomé dance was unique in my life. I had to teach Rubinstein simultaneously the art of the dance and to create for her the Dance of Salomé.'

Rubinstein had engaged Bakst to design the costumes and set for the production which was performed at a charity performance on 3 (16) November at the Mikhailovsky Theatre. The Dance of the Seven Veils by itself was repeated on 20 December (2 January) 1909 and some commentators say that the performance at the Mikhailovsky Theatre never took place. But there is no reason to suspect Bakst's memory or to suppose that his recollections are mere invention. In an interview in 1924 with Louis Thomas, Bakst described the difficulties they encountered with the production: 'Mme Rubinstein gathered round her the best actors from the Imperial Theatres in Petrograd ... She rented a theatre; there was an unparalleled extravagence about the decor and costumes.' It was the first production of *Salomé* in Russia but the Holy Synod banned it as it was a sacrilege to show the head of John the Baptist on stage. However, after many remonstrations they agreed that the production could take place provided that none of Wilde's words was spoken. Bakst then immediately called a meeting of all the actors at Rubinstein's house. 'Since the words were forbidden I proposed that both gestures and words should be mimed exactly as if the actors were speaking but without the sound. My dodge was adopted and *Salomé* became a kind fantastic ballet. The whole of Petrograd went mad with joy.' But there was another snag. Two hours before the performance was due to take place Bakst arrived at the theatre to find the Chief of Police already there demanding the head of John the Baptist and announcing that he had orders forbidding it to be shown on stage. Bakst tried to explain that it was only made of papier mâché, but the Chief of Police insisted on removing it. The production took place without the head on the dish. 'One of the unique details of the evening,' recalled Bakst, 'and one which gave a lot pleasure to the audience, was the empty dish brought to Salomé on which we could see in our mind's eye the head of John the Baptist ... it was total theatrical illusion.' Unfortunately only one costume design, for Salomé herself, survives from this production (p. 59). The erotic, heavily beaded costume, accurately made from the design, must have been quite noisy to wear, and quite shocking for the audience of the time. But Ida Rubinstein was always prepared to shock. 'She always wanted to be a dramatic actress,' said Bakst, 'and so because *Salomé* became a ballet thanks to the Holy Synod and she was successful in a silent role, it was

BAKST.

58

Costume design for Ida Rubinstein
(1885–1960) in *Salomé*, 1908
455 × 295
TRETYAKOV GALLERY, MOSCOW

Opposite
Costume design for Anna Pavlova in
Swan Lake, 1908
670 × 440
ROBERT L. B. TOBIN COLLECTION, MARION
KOOGLER MCNAY ART MUSEUM, SAN ANTONIO

Ida Rubinstein as Salomé, 1908
Photograph by Boassonn

actually chance that led her to accept a dramatic mime part in the company being formed by Diaghilev. She left with the Ballets Russes and made her enormously successful debut in *Cléopâtre* in 1906.' Bakst got the date wrong but that does not nullify the rest.

On 24 July 1908 Bakst had written to his wife: 'Yesterday evening Arguton [Argutinsky-Dolgorukov] and Valechka [Nouvel] called to see me and told me about Seriozha's [Diaghilev's] new plans. He wants to give a Russian ballet in the spring in Paris: *Armide*, *Giselle*, and a new one written by one of our composers, probably Akimenko, and to give the sets and costumes to Shura [Benois] and to me – so it's all wrapped up.' This is a crucial letter because it establishes first the fact that Diaghilev himself laid the basic plan for the following season in Paris and secondly that the plan included a new ballet, specifically on a Russian theme. During May and June 1908 Diaghilev had ambitiously and successfully presented as his third season in Paris six performances of the opera *Boris Godunov*, introducing Fedor Chaliapin to the West. Diaghilev wanted to expand his next Paris season but for practical reasons Diaghilev decided to present only one complete opera, *Ivan the Terrible* (again with Chaliapin); one act of *Russlan*, and the last act of *Judith* by Alexander Serov for which Bakst designed the finale, 'The Beseiged Town', while Valentin Serov, the composer's son, designed the first scene, 'Holopherne's Tent'. Robert Brussel in *Le Théâtre* wrote: 'The second [scene] which is by

III. PARIS — Place du Châtelet — Théâtre du Châtelet

Théâtre du Châtelet, Paris
Contemporary postcard

The first season of the Ballets Russes in 1909 (officially the Fourth Russian Season) took place at this theatre, as did the seasons of 1911, 1912 and 1917. When Gabriel Astruc, the French impressario, arranged the first season the theatre was in a very dilapidated condition. Diaghilev immediately had the whole place re-decorated, and a new stage had to be laid

Mr Léon Bakst is in a delightful range of colours and suggests the harmonious beauty of a heavily fortified town which has finally found peace and which is bathed by a pale blue, calm and peaceful oriental night.' As a novelty, Diaghilev included several new ballets in his programme.

Thus it was the fourth season that became the first of the Ballets Russes. It began at the Théâtre du Châtelet in Paris on 18 May 1909 with the public dress rehearsal (in France as glittering as a gala) of *Le Pavillon d'Armide*, the *Dances from Prince Igor* and *Le Festin*. The Russian ballet historian and friend of Bakst, Valerian Svetlov, described the usual organized chaos during rehearsals in *The Contemporary Ballet* (1911): 'In the vast basement great trunks of props, costumes, lights, and scenery were being unpacked. Forty thousand kilos. On stage behind the backcloth the sheep which appear in the third act of *Armide* were roaming around. Tcherepnine, the composer, conducted the orchestral rehearsals of *Armide*. Cooper, the conductor from Moscow, conducted *Igor* and *Festin*. Fokine was tireless and the dancers were tireless. Everyone worked with only brief interruptions from morning till midnight. Everyone was exhausted and became excitable as before a decisive battle but the work progressed in an atmosphere of amicable harmony. Sometimes there were little upsets, the conductor would not give way to the choreographer and vice versa. But everything was usually quickly settled in a friendly way. Everyone recognized how important it was to work together and without argument for the sake of their art . . .

A buffet was improvised on upturned cases at the back of the stage as it was out of the question to leave the theatre for meals and the dancers went there to eat during their breaks. Then the French and Russian carpenters finished the food and clinked their glasses.'

While Diaghilev made himself responsible for transforming the theatre, Gabriel Astruc (the French impressario) made sure that the season got off to a good start by inviting an audience for the *répétition générale* consisting of the most glamorous members of society as well as eminent artists, critics and writers, and in the front row of the grand circle he cunningly arranged a line of beautiful young ladies alternately blonde and brunette.

The 'Russian ballet' referred to by Bakst must have been based on the Russian fairy story of the Firebird but it had not been composed. Therefore Diaghilev, finding himself short of a ballet, arranged for a suite of dances from operas and ballets already familiar to the dancers to be presented under the general title, *Le Festin*. One of the dances in *Le Festin* was called *L'Oiseau de Feu* (*The Firebird*) with Karsavina and Nijinsky for whom Bakst designed the costumes. These were the first costumes by him to be seen in the West but there has been endless confusion about the title of this *pas de deux* and about the Firebird's costume. Stated as simply as possible, the *pas de deux* is actually the Blue Bird *pas de deux* from the last act of Tchaikovsky's *The Sleeping Beauty*. In the original version by Petipa (1890) the man is the Blue Bird. In Fokine's version Karsavina's role was called 'Oiseau de Feu' (Firebird), but Nijinsky's role, although transformed into a Prince, was called 'Oiseau d'Or' (Golden Bird).

Vaslav Nijinsky as L'Oiseau d'Or (or the Hindu Prince) in *The Firebird*, one of the suite of dances in *Le Festin*, 1909
BIBLIOTHÈQUE NATIONALE, MUSÉE DE L'OPÉRA, PARIS

Costume design for Vaslav Nijinsky (1889–1950) as L'Oiseau d'Or (or the Hindu Prince) in *The Firebird*, one of the suite of dances in *Le Festin*, 1909
335 × 215
PRIVATE COLLECTION

BAKST

Detail of Vaslav Nijinsky's costume in *Le Festin*, 1909

The inventory (in the Astruc Papers in the Dance Collection in the New York Public Library at Lincoln Center) for Nijinsky's costume stated:
'L'Oiseau d'Or (Nijinski)
1 faded green coloured jerkin embroidered with gold silk and precious stones. Belt and dalmatic (both sewn on to the costume), white faille embroidered with gold silk, pearls and precious stones, sleeves in knitted silk
1 purplish satin loin-cloth with gold fringes and metal motifs
1 green silk trunk-hose
1 faded green coloured silk body-stocking trimmed with metal motifs
1 white skin head-dress embroidered in gold with motifs in precious stones
2 pairs white shoes trimmed with gold stones

Left
Tamara Karsavina as the Firebird in
Stravinsky's *The Firebird*, 1910
BIBLIOTHÈQUE NATIONALE, MUSÉE DE L'OPÉRA,
PARIS

Right
Costume design for Tamara Karsavina
as the Firebird in Stravinsky's *The
Firebird*, 1910
343×215
SOTHEBY'S/PRIVATE COLLECTION

Bakst made many designs for the costume of the Firebird. This character fascinated him
for she frequently reappears in his work. The first design appeared on the cover of *Comoedia
Illustré* on 15 May 1909 (p. 66). This magazine, published by Maurice de Brunoff, made an important contribution to the success of the Ballets Russes and the fame of Bakst by devoting
many articles to the company and having high quality reproductions of the designs. He also
published the splendidly illustrated Souvenir Programmes for the Ballets Russes and Ida
Rubinstein's galas. This cover design and a not totally dissimilar one (also p. 66) were both
untitled and undated on the drawings. They were reproduced in Jean-Louis Vaudoyer's article in *Art et Décoration* (1911) under the title 'Costume pour *L'Oiseau d'Or*', but both, stated as
belonging to the Comtesse de Béarn, were exhibited at the Musée des Arts Décoratifs in July
1911 under the title of 'Costume pour *L'Oiseau de Feu* (Mme Karsavina)'. Both drawings were
used as a basis for this first Firebird's costume except that they have trousers when the costume itself did not as can be seen from the detailed inventory (Astruc papers in the Dance Collection of the New York Public Library at Lincoln Center):

L'Oiseau de Feu (Karsavina)
1 crêpe de Chine and tarlatan dress with satin ribbons, embroidered with gold, pearls,

precious stones and feathers behind
1 white satin head-dress, ostrich feathers, spangles, pearls, precious stones, etc
1 necklace in gilt metal with precious stones
2 pairs bracelets in gilt with precious stones
1 yellow silk body-stocking

Unfortunately the colour of the dress is not specified and the whole costume, particularly the head-dress, was simplified from the designs for practical reasons. In both variations Bakst lets his fantasy play. The heavily decorated body was topped and tailed with feathers billowing to create the illusion of a delicate fluttering bird poised for flight. When the design came to be made, Bakst's expert costumier Madame Marie Muelle, who from now on made most of his costumes, obviously had to interpret it into a dress for dancing that would work and be comfortable for the dancer on stage while maintaining the illusion required by the designer. There was a disagreeable coda connected with this costume when Madame Muelle was accused of unlawfully copying Karsavina's costume for Pavlova's American tour. She wrote to Bakst on 10 December 1910: 'I have just discovered that M. de Gunzbourg [who was subsidizing Diaghilev at the time] thinks that I have made the same *L'Oiseau de Feu* costume for Mlle Pavlova as I did for Mlle Karsavina. This, if nothing else, is a huge mistake.

On instructions from M. Clustine I made a costume for London which was taken to America and which was made up like a breast-plate of precious stones stitched on, and a skirt of ostrich feathers.

It was not to my taste but as it was ordered I made it without turning a hair for fear of putting them on the trail of Karsavina's marvellous costume. M. de Gunzbourg goes so far as to suspect that I took the costume to copy it the night it was missing from the Opéra. That is absurd because when I make a costume I remember it.

I am sorry to trouble you but I should be very upset if you thought that I could possibly do such a thing.

I have made a ballet for America from such bad designs that I kept remembering all the wonderful ideas of shape and colour which you taught me, and I had to restrain myself from copying any of your marvels.' They had a mutual respect and admiration for each other's work.

Bakst also designed the Firebird's costume for Stravinsky's ballet *The Firebird* in 1910 (p. 64). The drawing is of an elongated bird levitating rather than flying but the photograph of Karsavina wearing the costume shows that Madame Muelle in this case followed the drawing very closely, again only having to simplify the head-dress. Beaumont described seeing *The Firebird* for the first time: 'The whirring of wings grew louder and a figure radiating

Variation of costume design for Tamara Karsavina as L'Oiseau de Feu in *The Firebird*, one of the suite of dances in *Le Festin*, 1909. Reproduced in *Art et Décoration*, 1911

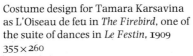

Costume design for Tamara Karsavina as L'Oiseau de feu in *The Firebird*, one of the suite of dances in *Le Festin*, 1909
355 × 260
SOTHEBY'S/PRIVATE COLLECTION

Reproduced on the cover of the Souvenir Programme for the Ballet Russes, 1909 and in *Art et Décoration*, 1911

Costume design for Vera Fokina as the
Tsarevna in *The Firebird*, 1910
355 × 221
MUSEUM OF THEATRICAL AND MUSICAL ARTS,
LENINGRAD

Ida Rubinstein would not travel with
the Ballets Russes on their tour to the
USA, and it was at Bakst's suggestion
that Flora Revalles, an opera singer, was
cast as Cleopatra and Zobeïda in
Schéhérazade. Bakst had seen her
perform in Geneva and persuaded
Diaghilev to engage her. (See also p. 96)

orange light flashed across the dark background. A moment later, Karsavina, glowing with
orange radiance, darted upon the stage, flitted about the tree, and vanished among the
shadows.

The costume which Bakst had designed for her was a charming conception, a woman's
head and shoulders emerging from a bird-like body. She wore a greenish bodice, the top edge
trimmed with feathers, the lower ending in a mass of swansdown fitting close to the hip. Over
her pink tights she wore trousers of fine orange gauze which, as they caught the light, made
her legs seem to emanate an orange glow. Her hair was dressed in two long plaits which fell
over her breast, while her head was covered with a cap decorated with curved feathers.'

Bakst also designed the costumes for the Tzarevna and the Tzarevitch, while Alexander Golovine designed the sets and all the other costumes. He designed new versions of all three costumes for Stravinsky's *The Firebird* in 1913, 1915 and again in 1917.

Tchaikovsky's *pas de deux* was still called *The Firebird* when Pavlova danced it on her
American tours in February and October 1910. It was then retitled *L'Oiseau d'Or* (*The Golden
Bird*) when she and Nijinsky danced it in London in November 1911. *L'Oiseau d'Or* then
became known as *L'Oiseau et le Prince* which is how Cyril Beaumont saw it in 1913 and then

finally in 1915 this *pas de deux* from *The Sleeping Beauty* was again retitled to *La Princesse Enchantée* (*The Enchanted Princess*). A consistent element in all the designs is the inverted heart-shaped design motif on the midriff. The Firebird herself became more and more crude and by the final version she was quite grotesque.

Cléopâtre has appeared as a refrain to Bakst's career so far. When the curtain went up after the first interval at the Théâtre du Châtelet in Paris on 2 June 1909 Bakst's reputation as a theatre designer triumphed. For the first time a designer became as much the talk of a town as the stars. After he had seen the ballet in London in 1911, Cyril Beaumont wrote: 'Bakst's setting evoked the dramatic mood essential to the ballet. It represented a temple in the Egyptian desert. On either side were gigantic, sombre, basalt figures which dominated the scene and made the dancers seem insignificant in proportion. In the distance were the pink columns of a temple, while the horizon was bounded by the blue waters of the Nile.' Jean-Louis Vaudoyer's article (1911) was more precise: 'The scene represented a huge hall surrounded by bulbous columns on which were hieroglyphic designs; between each of these columns there was a colossal statue of a helmeted god. All this part of the scenery was bright orange. It seemed as if an eternal sun had been incorporated into the stone and shone out of it. In the background, between the columns, was the blue Nile with its blurred banks; the floor of the hall was covered with paving of lapis-lazuli. A lighter blue awning was attached to the sky borders. Nothing could be simpler. No furniture, no wings. Besides, flats do not actually exist in Russian theatre scenery; they have been replaced by cut cloths which hang from the flies to the floor like back-cloths.' The interesting observation here is the reference to the floor and the ceiling showing the importance that Bakst attached to filling the whole stage for the total picture and not merely confining his set to the back and sides. *Cléopâtre* was different from *Egyptian Nights*. The main difference was that Bakst and Fokine had persuaded Diaghilev to give the part of Cleopatra to Ida Rubinstein. They had great confidence in her ability, but most of all they were sure of her star quality. 'It is irritating,' Bakst later remembered in his interview with Louis Thomas, 'to listen to a minor actor who wants to change something or add some silly bit of business to a work of talent or genius, but it is the artistic duty of a director or manager of a company who finds himself in the presence of a bird with enormous wings to extend the support, enlarge the cage, so that it may fly more easily.'

Jean Cocteau described Ida Rubinstein's sensational first appearance (Alexandre, A., 1913): '... balanced on the shoulders of six stalwarts, a kind of chest of gold and ebony was born aloft ...

The chest was placed in the centre of the temple, its doors were opened, and from it was lifted a kind of glorified mummy, swathed in veils, which was placed upright on ivory pattens. Then four slaves subjected it to a marvellous manipulation. They unwound the first veil, which was red wrought with lotuses and silver crocodiles, the second, which was green with all the history of the dynasties in golden filagree upon it, the third, which was orange

Costume design for the Bacchanale in
Cléopâtre, 1909 (1910)
280 × 205
SOTHEBY'S/PRIVATE COLLECTION

shot with a hundred prismatic hues, and so on until they reached the twelfth, which was of indigo, and under which the outline of a woman could be discerned. Each of the veils unwound itself in a fashion of its own: one demanded a host of subtle touches, another the deliberation required in peeling a walnut, a third the airy detachment of the petal from the rose, and the eleventh, most difficult of all, came away all in one piece like the bark of a eucalyptus tree.

The twelfth veil of deep blue released Madame Rubinstein, who let it fall herself with a sweeping circular gesture.' Bakst invented the unforgettable business of the entrance and the stripping of the veils, although, later, Benois claimed to have done so (see p. 93); this was the first production in which Bakst mastered his use of a particular and personal gamut of colours. All the costumes fitted in to the colour scheme of the set to become an intrinsic and inseparable part of the total stage picture. Vaudoyer added that Bakst : 'Found an arrangement of colours and a cut of the clothes for the costumes of *Cléopâtre* which fixed in a most felicitous way the impression we get from Egyptian paintings and granite sculptures. Nothing vague or hazy; all the outlines were firm and precise; the colours were powdery and matt. We were truly in the land of stone, sand and sun ... We usually see sets which are made ''after something better'' and almost always they dash the ideas we have imprudently formed in our minds before seeing them. So we should acknowledge M. Bakst who has gone beyond what we could imagine by using for his job as designer talents which an artist of his worth usually prefers to use for less perishable works of art.' Vaudoyer again put his finger on the main point. Bakst, still reeling from his visit to Greece and having absorbed all his research into Greek and Egyptian antiquity, collected his impressions and transformed them into a series of pseudo-archaeological costume designs while being quite clear in his mind about the composite effect he wanted to achieve on stage. A better tag would be 'baksto-archaeological' because the colour is unmistakably his and also because many of the individual drawings for *Cléopâtre* became templates for later productions such as *Le Martyre de St Sébastien* (pp. 118–25), *Le Dieu Bleu* (pp. 134–42), *Judith* (p. 121) and *Phaedre* (pp. 225–28). The costumes were seen before the designs but Huntly Carter in his prefatory note to an exhibition at The Fine Art Society in 1914 wrote: '*Cléopâtre* illustrated his mastery of chromatic combinations, and the use of the five primary colours in endless harmonies, as well as his right understanding of the note of style to be found in coherence and uniformity. The whole was held together by a tremendous design or framework into which he poured characteristic Egyptian motives which were caught up and repeated in the movements, costumes, and even in the ornaments worn by the dancers. This dominant mood flowed uninterruptedly from beginning to end and thus his contribution to the Ballet was seen to be the essential line and colour of one great rhythmic movement. He provided, indeed, the connecting links of a whole series of rhythms.' With his drawings for *Cléopâtre* Bakst devised choreography on paper.

Although Diaghilev's Ballets Russes never performed in Russia, reports about their performances throughout Europe appeared regularly in Russian newspapers and magazines and the theatre-going public in Russia was well informed about the company's activities and successes in the West. Alexandre Benois was a frequent contributor to the daily newspaper *Rech* (*Speech*) and wrote long and serious articles about art and about the various productions in Paris. Of Bakst's contribution to *Cléopâtre* he wrote on 25 June (8 July) 1909: 'It was fascinating, and I mean *fascinating*, starting with Bakst's scenery which was beautiful and well thought out but hurriedly and rather roughly painted in granite-pink and sombre violet. Against this strange, truly southern, fervid and suffocating background the rich purple of the costumes glowed like fire, the gold gleamed, and the black plaited wigs were menacing as, like a coffin or sarcophagus, the locked casket of Cleopatra marked all over with hieroglyphs entered the stage.'

Cléopâtre was a huge success. The stamina and enthusiasm of the audiences was such that it was even given some extra performances at the end of a long evening after the opera *Ivan the Terrible*. Bakst could write to his wife on 17 June 1909: 'In a word, the greatest success of the season was *Cléopâtre* if only because the house was full at the end and we gave it with extraordinary results (34 thousand [francs] take a day) and even at the end Chaliapin did not fill the house. It is flattering for the ego, but not much good for the pocket.' He obviously felt,

Costume design for a dancer in
Cléopâtre, 1909
280 × 210
MR AND MRS N. D. LOBANOV-ROSTOVSKY
COLLECTION

This undated design was reproduced
several times in contemporary
magazines but was not properly
identified. In *Apollon*, September 1910 it
was reproduced twice with one caption
being 'Oriental Dance' and the other
'Costume from *Cleopatra*', in *T.P's
Magazine*, 1911, it was called simply 'A
ballet dancer', in *Art et Décoration*, 1911,
it was surprisingly called 'Costume
oriental pour *Thais*'. It could be an early
version of Cleopatra's costume. The final
costume worn by Ida Rubinstein (see
p. 68) is different but is based on
similar ideas. There are also
similarities between this costume and
those designed for the Jewish Dancers
which is how it is described by
Zilberstein

Opposite
Costume design for a Jewish Dancer in
Cléopâtre, 1909 (1910)
315 × 230
SOTHEBY'S/PRIVATE COLLECTION

as usual that Diaghilev was not paying him enough.

Cléopâtre quickly became one of the most popular ballets and stayed in the repertoire for many years. In 1917, during the South American tour of the Ballets Russes, the railway truck containing all the scenery and costumes caught fire from a spark in a tunnel between Rio de Janeiro and Sao Paulo and although the costumes were safe the scenery for *Cléopâtre* and *Le Spectre de la Rose* was destroyed. Serge Grigoriev, the *régisseur* or company manager, improvised at the time by using the scenery of *La Péri* also designed by Bakst, for *Cléopâtre*, but then Diaghilev commissioned new scenery from Robert Delaunay and some new costumes from Sonia Delaunay. Cyril Beaumont saw the new production in 1918 in London: 'I went to see *Cléopâtre*, now deprived of its original setting by Bakst, which always filled you with a sense of impending tragedy the moment you saw it. In its place was a new setting by Robert Delaunay, conceived in the violently contrasted colours and cubist shapes then regarded as the most advanced artistic expression . . . The majority of the Bakst costumes were not those of the original production, but a medley of dresses adapted from *Le Dieu Bleu* and other ballets, which, naturally, did not harmonize with the new setting.' This production seems to have been slapdash and ill-conceived. It is always a problem to maintain a popular production and impossible to recreate it without the original designer, or even partially redesign it and hope for the same effect. It was a serious lapse in Diaghilev's judgement.

Alexandre Benois in *Rech* 19 June (2 July) 1909 summed up the general effect of the first ballet season: 'Neither Borodin, nor Rimsky, nor Chaliapin, nor Golovin, nor Roerich, nor Diaghilev was triumphant in Paris, but the whole of Russian culture, the whole peculiarity of Russian art, its conviction, freshness and spontaneity, its savage strength.' Benois, already jealous, left out Bakst from his list. But before the season was over Diaghilev was planning the next. Bakst wrote to his wife on 17 (30) June, 'Because of Diaghilev I can be sure of not sitting on a sand dune. For next season he has commissioned the ballet *Daphnis and Chloë* with music (also commissioned) from Ravel, and with Fokine and Ravel we have put together an interesting libretto. It will be put on at the Grand Opéra in April.' From now on Bakst's work was almost exclusively for the theatre. The next season was indeed at the Opéra in Paris but it was in June not in April and it did not include *Daphnis and Chloë*.

'The most famous painter in the world': 1910

Bakst was naturally very pleased by his personal success but he did not boast about it except to his wife and a few close friends. He was always outwardly modest about his work but decisive, and never manifested his inner doubts or dissatisfactions. He was always reticent with the press, and gave only very few interviews mostly towards the end of his career. He also wrote very little himself about his work, generally leaving it to others to discuss his art and cultivate his fame. As can be seen from the bibliography, many people began very quickly to write articles and appraisals; for the most part they are merely wordy eulogies with occasional insights. Bakst always got an amazingly good press.

In 1909 a new art magazine called *Apollon* was started in Russia which was widely read and became almost as influential as the earlier *The World of Art* although it was never so lavish. It was published regularly until 1919 and contained, as well as essays, reports and reviews of artistic events including detailed accounts of the Ballets Russes seasons in Paris. Bakst designed the first cover for the magazine, based on the columns of the Palace at Knossos, and he contributed a long and thoughtful article, 'The paths of classicism in art', which was published in the second and third numbers. (The article also appeared in French in June 1910 to coincide with the Ballets Russes season.) In this article Bakst did not specifically discuss theatre except for an allusion to Isadora Duncan and the 'new' choreography but, by stating very plainly and unequivocally his own views about art, he explains why he found fulfilment in working in the theatre. After a general exposition about the past and a critical statement about the present Bakst continued:

> Thus, the art of the future seeks a simpler form . . . Three qualities distinguish the composition of practically every child however little talent he has: sincerity, movement and bright, pure colour. These are exactly the qualities which modern painting has finished up by destroying . . . sincerity, movement and bright, pure colour is attractive in a child's drawing because it also belongs to all classical periods of great schools of art. Children's love of bright, pure colour is the natural taste; it is that of nature itself, which so magnificently colours animals, birds, butterflies and flowers with a surprising and startling boldness . . . The drawing of children, its movement, synthesis and colour, has become the enigma which many artists today try to resolve. They are also attracted by peasant and folk art; and the most cultured study the classicism of the great schools.'

For Bakst the most glittering examples of the artist of the future were Gauguin, Matisse and Maurice Denis. One of the pertinent reasons why he cited these artists, and, by implication, he included himself among them is because:

> For twenty-five years landscape has prevailed almost completely over man . . . man has been nothing more than an occurrence on the landscape . . . the art of the future will adopt the cult of man and his nakedness.

Cover design for *Apollon* magazine, 1909, pencil, pen and black ink, on cardboard 257 × 213

Bakst got carried away and concluded his statement in baroque style:

> Painting in the future means that the artist must renounce his old mania for shocking the public and his vulgar desire to be all the rage.
>
> The artist must be bold, simple and original.
>
> Painting of the future requires a concise style because fiddle-faddle has become intolerable; there has been enough of it.
>
> The components of painting recently have been air, sun and foliage; those of the future are man and stone.
>
> Painting of the future will be forced into chasms of primitiveness, into unexplored regions of a stony style in order to separate it from the over-cultivated painting of today opposed to any experiment.
>
> Painting of the future will begin by hating the old in order to produce a new generation of artists who will follow, perhaps reluctantly, the new and as yet unknown path which opens today.
>
> And after having distractedly glided over the polished forms of Hermes and Praxiteles our divining eye will stop in spite of itself at children's drawings; conscious that light will come among the childish murmurs of a newly hatched classical art.

The Théâtre National de l'Opéra, Paris
Contemporary postcard

The familiar and famous landmark designed by the architect Charles Garnier. The second season of the Ballets Russes (officially the fifth Russian season) in 1910 took place here as did the seasons in December 1911, 1914, the only performance in 1915, 1919–20, 1920, 1922. After that the Ballets Russes performed in smaller theatres in Paris except for two performances in 1927 and four in 1928–29. All of Bakst's work for Ida Rubinstein was first performed at the Opéra

Paris - PLACE DE L'OPÉRA

Costume design for Ludmilla Schollar
(1888–1959) as Estrella in *Le Carnaval*,
1910
315 × 245
MUSEUM OF THEATRICAL AND MUSICAL ARTS,
LENINGRAD

Russian dancers in *Le Carnaval*, from the special supplement to *Comoedia Illustré*, 15 June 1910

The dancers are in the costumes for the *Valse Noble*, the spots and the stripes in the inverted triangles were reddy-brown

Bakst chose the art of the theatre, a very public and risky art, in which to apply these bold principles. Nothing could be simpler than *Le Carnaval*. Fokine was asked to produce a new ballet for a charity masquerade ball sponsored by the magazine *Satyricon*. The ball, organized by the magazine's publisher, Michael Kornfeld and a young poet, Paul Petemkin, took place at the Pavlova Hall (no connection with the dancer) in St Petersburg on 20 February 1910.

Fokine had wanted for some time to arrange a ballet adapted from the story and characters in *Scènes Mignonnes*, a suite of piano pieces by Schumann. He invented a succession of romantic interludes and fleeting meetings danced by appropriately masked guests at a masquerade ball. Fokine, in his memoirs, wrote: 'From the titles indicated on the music, such as "Harlequin", "Columbine", "Pantaloon", "Pierrot", and "Papillon", I was able immediately to visualize and construct the picture of the ballet: the series of separate characters, linked one to the other. Fokine always worked fast; *Le Carnaval* had three days rehearsal. Artists of the Imperial Theatres were forbidden at that time from appearing in any other theatres so all the dancers had to appear in masks to avoid being disciplined. There is therefore some confusion about who danced which part (see p. 242).

Bakst, asked to design the set and costumes, was given a very small budget and almost no time. He used some costumes from other ballets. Those for Harlequin, Columbine, Pierrot and Pantaloon had been designed in 1908 when Fokine had arranged a harlequinade for a *Bal Poudré* for the Russian Mercantile Society. Some of the girls' crinolines came from *The Fairy Doll*. Among the new costumes was one for Bronislava Nijinska as Papillon (p. 85). According to Fokine's memoirs: 'The female performers were all chastely dressed in large hoop skirts with lace-fringed, long white pantaloons showing slightly above the ankles. Their very appearance seemed to say: "Don't touch me".' Bakst had learnt the successful effect made by seeing groups of similar, rather than identical, costumes. The original set was just draped curtains and Bronislava Nijinska described how Meyerhold as Pierrot '. . . made full use of the innovative decor by Léon Bakst, the many folds of the pleated curtains, with concealed slits, draped around the semi-circular stage . . . Each of his appearances on stage produced an effect. First, only his leg would appear through the slit of the drape in a *grand développé*, then slowly the whole white body would emerge, the long arms made even longer by long, hanging white sleeves.'

Alexandre Benois in his *Reminiscences* (1941) remembered: 'Bakst's contribution to the performance – the wonderful costumes and the clever "neutral background" of dark blue draperies – was a real masterpiece and in full harmony with the music and poetry of *Le Carnaval*.' Cyril Beaumont in *Michel Fokine and his Ballets* (1935) mistakenly recorded that the set for the first production was 'a little garden' confusing it with the first revival at the Mariinsky theatre on 6 February 1911 when the set was a park and the terrace of a country house.

Le Carnaval was so well received that it was agreed by all the members of the Ballets Russes to revive it for the opening of their season at the Opéra in Paris on 4 June 1910. According to Grigoriev in *The Diaghilev Ballet 1909–1929* (1953), Bakst at first again suggested a garden set but the idea was rejected as it was considered to be inappropriate to this small-scale ballet and 'that a simple back-cloth was all that was wanted. Bakst did not object . . .' The result was '. . . a plain green back-cloth with a wide border of stylized dull gold lilies, in front of which, to either side, stood an 1830 sofa. That was all; yet it could not have been more effective.' The ballet was repeated the following year and then revived in London in September 1918 when the colour of the set was changed back to the original. Cyril Beaumont described it accurately because this time he saw it, 'Here, then, is the ante-chamber of a ball-room conveyed simply by a deep blue back-cloth, at the top of which runs a broad black and gold frieze. The sole furniture, two quaint little brown sofas. The immense sweep of curtain and the extreme simplicity of the *mise en scène* serve both to focus the figures of the dancers and allow the eye to receive the complete impression of their every movement.' Bakst knew the effectiveness of restraint and in *Le Carnaval* he exploited to the full the theatrical force of stylish simplicity.

Earlier, before the first performance in Paris, Bakst had given one of his rare interviews on the subject of theatre design which was quoted in *Bloc-Notes Parisien*:

NUMÉRO
SPÉCIAL
CONSACRÉ
A LA
SAISON
RUSSE

LES BALLETS RUSSES

SUPPLÉMENT AU Nº DU 15 JUIN 1910 DE

COMŒDIA ILLUSTRÉ

NUMÉRO
SPÉCIAL
CONSACRÉ
A LA
SAISON
RUSSE

SAISON RUSSE 1910

L'OPERA BALLETS

Aquarelle originale de BAKST

L. VOGEL

In Russia it is the painter who inspires the material substance of a ballet or lyric drama. It is he who decides the style, the pictorial line of the whole, the colour scheme of the decor, and even the feeling of the production. When I have to design a ballet I first come to an understanding with the choreographer who brings me his choreographic ideas but who subordinates them to my ideas on design. I envisage the setting absolutely as a background which has to give the atmosphere and impression of the work; the characters costumed by me (because in Russia we design both the sets and the costumes) are treated like the final brush strokes of a painting, and the dominant note in my canvas is reserved for the principal characters. That is why it is out of the question for me to agree to change the shade of any one of the characters, because such an alteration would break both the range of my colours and the dominant note which I have chosen. Let me tell you an anecdote to illustrate the point. I designed the set and the costumes for this ballet, *Le Carnaval*, by Schumann which was performed in St Petersburg and which you are going to see danced at the Châtelet [*sic*]. I went into my colour contrasts and I arrived at what I thought was a satisfactory colour scheme. At a certain point, one of the dancers comes on stage with a flower on her bosom, a flower of a different shade to the one I had specified. A cry went up in the hall; the florist had inadvertantly provided the dancer with a flower which belonged to a similar production. And the public noticed. Need I say more?

As for me, I will tell you how I go about designing: I study the decoration of the period of the piece which I am designing; I choose the most significant element; I adopt it and I repeat it on the materials, the architecture, the jewellery. The decoration thus becomes a *leit motiv*; and I achieve a unity not only of colour but also of line. The more I work in this way, the more convinced I am that this is the only way of achieving that unity and avoiding the thousand mishaps of form and shade which can happen to a decor.

Cover of the supplement to *Comoedia Illustré*, 15 June 1910, with a reproduction of the costume design for Vassili Kissilev as Shah Zeman in *Schéhérazade*

A variation of this design is in the National Gallery of Australia in Canberra, another in the Fine Arts Museums of San Francisco

The second ballet of that evening of 4 June 1910 was *Schéhérazade*. If *Cléopâtre* had introduced Bakst's originality and splendour to Parisian audiences then *Schéhérazade* confirmed his uniqueness in their minds. Although the publicity organized by Diaghilev and Astruc was effective and persistent, the 'media', unlike today, was confined to the press, and so it was only through newspapers and by word-of-mouth that the public became aware of the extraordinary quality and sensational effect of the performances by the Ballets Russes. That public, as John Percival (1990) has commented, was 'The same mixture of business people and politicians, socialites and snobs, fans and real enthusiasts as still go to fashionable seasons in Paris, London and New York today.' Only a few thousand people had seen *Cléopâtre* at the Châtelet in 1909. A year later there was a rush for tickets but still only a few thousand would see the first performances of *Schéhérazade* at the Opéra. The effect and influence of theatrical

Vaslav Nijinsky in *Danse Siamoise* in
Les Orientales, 1910
BIBLIOTHÈQUE NATIONALE, MUSÉE DE L'OPÉRA,
PARIS

Bakst designed an accurately 'oriental'
costume for Nijinsky in *La Danse
Siamoise* which he choreographed for
himself to music by Sinding as one of the
sketches in *Les Orientales* arranged by
Diaghilev to replace *Le Festin*. It was in
this 'Siamese' costume that Nijinsky
posed for the famous portrait by
Jacques-Emile Blanche. *Les Orientales*
has often been confused with *Oriental
Fantasy* for which Bakst did the decor in
1913 for Pavlova (see pp. 166–67)

performance on artistic life, ideas, fashion and interior decoration is often out of all proportion to the very limited number of people who see the performances. The reverberations from the artistic shock waves of the Ballets Russes were so forceful that they still continue. *Schéhérazade* made 'Bakstian' an understandable adjective.

In 1910 Diaghilev took a deliberate risk in presenting only ballets. Paris waited to see what those Russian 'country bumpkins' would do. N. Kostilev, in *Apollon*, wrote: 'Merely repeating the previous year's success would not be enough . . . hundreds of pairs of eyes, among the subscribers and among the resident artists, are only too ready to say "it is just the same after all" and "they cannot do anything else."'

Schéhérazade was the ballet which proved to Paris not only that the Russians could do something else but also that no-one else could do anything like them. Bakst wrote to his wife on 18 (31) May: ' . . . We have done the fit-up for *Schéhérazade* and it's a great success with artists (Vuillard, Bonnard, Seurat, Blanche and others). Seriozha hugged and kissed me in front of everyone, and the whole company exploded in a thunder of applause and then rocked me on stage. I could hardly escape and after the dress rehearsal they threatened to rock me again. I must admit I was not expecting such a deafening success. They say that *Cléopâtre* is just childish fun by comparison.' *Schéhérazade* was new, thrilling and overwhelming. The word got round very fast. As Tugendhold reported for *Apollon*: 'It was as if an electric shock had suddenly informed the whole of France of the feverish excitement which the word 'theatre' had meant for us Russians during these last few years, and Paris somehow began to wake from its theatrical drowsiness.'

The ballet is based on the prologue to *The Thousand and One Nights*. Zobeïda is the favourite concubine in the harem of Shahriar. While he pretends to be out hunting she betrays him with the Golden Negro during an orgy. Shahriar returns unexpectedly and is so angered by what he sees that he orders the guards to massacre all the dancers. He hesitates over Zobeïda but she snatches a dagger from one of the guards, stabs herself and dies at his feet. A simple but effective libretto for a ballet, yet it caused a lot of trouble.

The stage picture was described in great detail by the critic Pierre Lalo in *Le Temps*: 'On stage, a set of extreme simplicity, reduced to its bare essentials which shows the interior of the Shah's harem: a sort of enormous tent of the most intense and magnificent bright green, a green which is dazzling yet constant, a green both violent and astonishingly sumptuous . . . Most of the costumes for the men and women are in colours which complement the set: subtle tones of red and a few greens . . . which recall the most beautiful Persian miniatures. It all combines to produce an effect of power and miraculous harmony. It is spell-binding and a constant thrill for the eye. M. Bakst, the Russian painter, who created this wonderful picture with his colours for both the set and the costumes, is a truly great artist.'

Lalo was wrong when he said the set was simple. That is how it may have appeared, and, if so, the credit is due to the designer for having successfully deceived the eye of the beholder,

Left
Costume design for a Gentleman in the
Valse Noble in *Le Carnaval*, 1910
280 × 210
SOTHEBY'S/PRIVATE COLLECTION

This is one of many similar designs that
Bakst made for 'Gentlemen' in ballets
and operas of the same period

Right
Costume design for Bronislava Nijinska
(1891–1972) as Papillon in *Le Carnaval*,
1910
380 × 270
THEATRE MUSEUM, LONDON

Vera Fokina (1886–1958) as Chiarina
and Michel Fokine as Harlequin in
Le Carnaval, 1910
BIBLIOTHÈQUE NATIONALE, MUSÉE DE L'OPÉRA,
PARIS

Costume design for a Golden Negro in
Schéhérazade, 1910
355 × 220
MUSÉE DES BEAUX ARTS, STRASBOURG

Costume design for an Odalisque in
Schéhérazade, 1910
350 × 215
SOTHEBY'S/PRIVATE COLLECTION

Vaslav Nijinsky as Zobeïda's Favourite
Slave in *Schéhérazade*, 1910
BIBLIOTHÈQUE NATIONALE, MUSÉE DE L'OPÉRA,
PARIS

but the actual design was extremely sophisticated and complex. For the first time Bakst played about with perspective. He did not design a classical, symmetrical set with a central vanishing point, but he turned the perspective on two diagonals thereby creating two vanishing points, and then he further falsified the perspective with a ceiling also on a diagonal. These tricks helped to create the illusion of space. Then, having made the space, he enclosed it with the heavy drapes hung asymmetrically and the floor cloth with painted carpets of a different colour set at another angle. The set was also properly lit; Bakst always recognized the importance of lighting as a component of the total scene. Although the available equipment then was much less sophisticated than now, very subtle effects could still be achieved. Bakst always insisted on spending a lot of time lighting a set. The result with *Schéhérazade* was an overwhelming feeling of grandeur, opulence and mystery.

The costumes were not simple either. The drawings *are* like Persian miniatures, but neither slavish imitations nor reproductions, and though small they are not miniature in their effect. Bakst's drawing is individual and recognizable, never flat, always vigorous and full of movement. No other drawings by him express the fluidity of movement in quite the same way, stopping the action of the choreography in mid flow with each character in a different pose. His designs for *Schéhérazade* are like insubstantial butterflies catching fleeting movement on paper. Although Bakst used a number of his designs for *Schéhérazade* in other productions, notably *Aladin* in 1919 (pp. 00–00), he never did anything quite the same again and yet the common misconception is that he always did the same kind of drawing. It shows what a powerful effect they had. After seeing them Huntley Carter wrote: 'He appears to be impelled by . . . [an] intense feeling for sex combined with an equally intense sense of undulating movement, impelling him to create rhythmic form . . . He has an instinct for the value of certain curves of the female body . . . He has rediscoverd the luscious female line bequeathed by the early Orientals.' Gerald Siordet, in *The Studio*, curiously thought the last sentence was meaningless, 'yet it is very true that Bakst shows a passionate enthusiasm for the flesh, for the contours of form, for strange poise and counterpoise of limb, for furious, abandoned movement, that sets an Eastern stamp upon his art.' This group of fantastic drawings with their opulent and overt eroticism represents one of the pinnacles of Bakst's career.

Benois recognized the originality of *Schéhérazade* and in his column in *Rech* on 12 (25) July wrote: 'And what of Bakst the colourist? Here indeed he found his real vocation. We see in *Schéhérazade* that Bakst can produce pictures that are truly great . . . His décor is executed with a simple and broad virtuosity in the most telling colours; the performers, too, who move against this background in Fokine's amazingly clever combinations, are Bakst's creation, and are in complete harmony with the décor. I don't think I exaggerate when I say I have *never* seen such absolute harmony of colour on the stage.'

Benois was amazingly generous with his praise of Bakst because at the time he had been very hurt. He had arrived from Russia in time for the first performance and was astonished to find, when he opened his programme in the theatre, that the libretto had been credited to Bakst instead of himself. He complained bitterly to Diaghilev who is supposed to have replied: 'What do you want? Bakst had to be given something. You have *Pavillon d'Armide* and he will have *Schéhérazade*.' The wound was very deep and the hurt was borne for a long time. It came to a head in the following year because of an episode over the production of *Petrushka* designed by Benois. The scenery for Petrushka's room had been crushed during the journey from St Petersburg and the Conjuror's portrait, which occupied the centre of one of the walls, was badly damaged. Benois could not repaint it as he had developed an abscess on his elbow, so he accepted Bakst's offer of help. Two days later, at the dress rehearsal, Benois saw a completely different portrait. Remembering the insult he had received over the authorship of *Schéhérazade* he threw a fit and left the theatre in a rage. On 28 May (10 June) 1911 Bakst wrote to his wife: 'Benois and I have broken up – for ever. You were right when you said that he was jealous of me. His behaviour towards me during these last two years and especially now in Paris has resulted in having to call (at his request) something like a court of arbitration, and unanimously Serov, Nouvel and Diaghilev said, "Benois's behaviour towards Bakst for the past year and a half has been scandalous." For what reason? He makes no effort to conceal his hatred of me, and apart from Argut[insky], with whom I have parted, they are all

Enrico Cecchetti as the Grand Eunuch in
Schéhérazade, 1910
BIBLIOTHÈQUE NATIONALE, MUSÉE DE L'OPÉRA,
PARIS

Costume design for Enrico Cecchetti
(1850–1928) as the Grand Eunuch in
Schéhérazade, 1910
355 × 220
MUSÉE DES BEAUX ARTS, STRASBOURG

Costume design for Alexis Boulgakov
(1872–1954) as Shahriar in *Schéhérazade*,
1910
355 × 220
THYSSEN-BORNEMISZA COLLECTION

positively on my side and acknowledge that my behaviour has been civil and friendly. I have put a cross on Shura [Benois], and, as always in such cases, will never return to him.' On 5 (18) June 1911 Serov wrote to his wife: 'That miserable Benois is like an hysterical woman. I don't like him. It is very wretched to witness scenes which are both frightening and off-putting. He absolutely cannot stand Bakst. I do not know the reason, unless it is that he is envious of his (deserved) glory in Paris.' On the same day he wrote to Benois: 'I still find I am under the impression of your hysterical fit (or fits) . . .

Fearing another outburst I decided not to ask you why you said to me "And, as for you, Serov, you also exasperate me."

When you have got to Lugano, quietened down, and had a rest would you be kind enough to write to me and say what the problem is. If it has to do with *Schéhérazade*, that is its authorship, then it seems to be arguable. According to those present at the meetings at which *Schéhérazade* was worked out, except for Argutinsky and Fokine (whom I will ask in London), Bakst had the right to put his name to this ballet since it was his and Diaghilev's idea to produce it.

Of course, you also played a big part.

In my opinion, it is perfectly clear that Bakst's specific artistry and inventiveness is evident here as nowhere else.

It is possible that there are other reasons why you have come to hate him so, but in any case your abusing him for his "Yiddish snout" is neither worthy of you nor, indeed, becomes you who yourself have such an outward appearance of being Jewish.

Anyway, this is not a question of Jewishness.

The important thing here is the strength of the hate, piled up over the years. I am surprised and overwhelmed.'

Benois replied to Serov towards the end of June 1911 from Lugano: '. . . Your letter is totally offensive. I am not referring to the tasteless and unworthy final passage where you remark upon my Jewish appearance, a phrase which is repulsive in its cold and caustic intent (in fact it does not affect me because I have learned to live with my ugly mug, but I mean your attitude). The intent on your part is more than just a "cliché" of abuse which is how it escaped my lips when I snapped at Bakst; we used to say it so often, and your adored Diaghilev used to say it too, indeed it was Serge who made it a cliché.

I must tell you now that I have never despised Jews, on the contrary I have a weakness for them, but I am aware of their specific defects which I hate, as with any specific defect.

Bakst is specifically Jewish in the sense that he is greedy and gentle, compliant – a combination which makes him somewhat slippery and rapacious, snake-like, that is to say repulsive.

But, anyway, that is not the point. The offence of your letter lies in the fact that you do not believe me. And I know only too well that you will not believe me now . . . But just for a matter of history, for a kind of idiotic absolutism I am compelled to tell you the facts.

The idea to produce *Schéhérazade* belongs entirely to Seriozha [Diaghilev] and to him alone. At the meeting when he announced it Bakst expressed extreme delight at the idea and thought of only two things for the production (a) to put the negroes into bags and throw them over a wall into a ditch and (b) that Scheherazade should appease the Sultan by telling him her stories.

That is all that Bakst suggested for the ballet *Schéhérazade, oeuvre du célèbre peintre Baxt* [*sic*], as is printed on all the posters. Even Seriozha understood that that would never work, and, making fun of Levushka's [Bakst's] eccentric ideas, turned to me as the specialist on libretti. At first I only made essential corrections . . . But then I refused to take any further part in the formulation of the libretto because a few days earlier Seriozha had insulted me by telling me to my face that Bakst had invented Cleopatra's entrance and indeed the whole savour of this ballet when they had been invented by me. (I suppose, you will not believe that either, but it does not change the facts.) I told him [Diaghilev] about my resentment about *Cleopatra* and he promised that he would never do anything like that again. That same day (in the afternoon) a pianist was asked to come along and he played *Schéhérazade* for me about three times in a row, after which I "visualized" her and then told the whole story to Diaghilev (Bakst was not there). In the evening I had a meeting with Fokine during which I developed the whole outline in every detail and wrote it there and then on the piano score, wrote what I alone made up and not what you, according to those liars and rogues, think of as some kind of collective work.

On my way home I told Argutinsky what I had done and why, even though I realized that my notes would have no significance in a court of law.

I needed to do this for myself especially after what happened with *Cleopatra*. Anyway, knowing a few things by then, I was anticipating further wrongs and resentments (oh, how many, how many of them piled up over 15 years "collaboration" with Seriozha, in fact his shameless exploitation throughout this time brought me, 41 years old, to the point of some kind of total withering away, total demoralization).'

My guess is that, as with all theatrical productions, *Schéhérazade* was a co-operative effort and that by the time it reached the stage in front of an audience it was no longer possible to attribute authorship precisely because the shape of the production was mostly the result of the co-operation between Fokine and Bakst. It was a case of jealousy but they all had furious tempers and it was the sad end of a long friendship. In 1959 Benois wrote to Ilya Zilberstein, theatre historian and collector, to say that he still remembered the 'sorry, stupid, unworthy story' as if it had happened the day before and deeply regretted the rupture of friendship.

Serov was commissioned by Diaghilev to paint a front cloth for *Schéhérazade*. He painted it from the end of May to the beginning of June 1911 in Matisse's old studio-workshop which

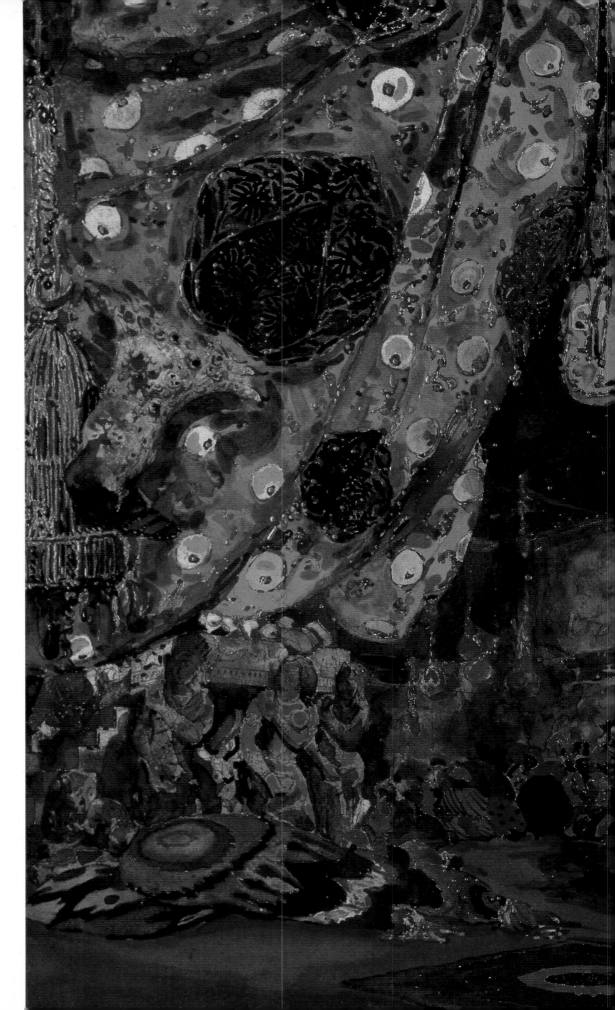

Set design for *Schéhérazade*, 1910
545×760
MUSÉE DES ARTS DÉCORATIFS, PARIS

This design was the first to be purchased
by a museum in western Europe. Bakst
made several later versions; one is in the
Robert L. B. Tobin Collection

Tamara Karsavina as Zobeïda in
Schéhérazade, 1911
BIBLIOTHÈQUE NATIONALE, MUSÉE DE L'OPÉRA, PARIS

Flora Revalles as Zobeïda in
Schéhérazade, 1916
NEW YORK PUBLIC LIBRARY AT LINCOLN CENTER

Bakst arranged to rent for him. He described it as 'rather like a Persian fresco,' and thought it would 'make a pleasant effect amongst the other bright scenery and cloths.' The cloth was first shown in Paris on 13 June 1911, on the same night as *Petrushka*'s opening. It continued to be shown until 1914 when Diaghilev said it had become too valuable to be used as a piece of scenery. (The cloth remained the property of the company. It was eventually sold by Sotheby's in 1968 along with other scenery and costumes, and is now in Russia.)

In 1915 Bakst made new versions of the set and costumes as the originals had worn out. This second version of the set was then repainted by Vladimir Polunin in 1918 who described Bakst's work in *The Continental Method of Scene painting* (1927): 'Diaghileff insisted not only that the correct harmony of tones – the blue of the ceiling, the emerald green of the walls, and the pink of the curtain – should be obtained, but also the imperceptible blending of light and shade in Bakst's design by which he suggested the character of the materials of which the scene was supposed to consist; that is to say, the colossal drapery, with its many planes, must appear to be silk; the walls, polished stone, and so forth . . . Although the painting of the back-cloth was technically rather easy, the drapery, consisting of two cut-cloths and many wings, offered considerable difficulty.'

On 24 August 1910 *Utro Rossii* (*Russian Morning*) carried an interview with Diaghilev and Bakst which revealed something of their ideas about the art of ballet. Diaghilev is quoted first: '"We do not deny a spiritual relationship with [Isadora] Duncan. We admit we are carrying on the business she began. But there is this difference between us. For Duncan dance is the sole purpose of art, and all the rest – scenery, costumes, music – are like extra accessories. Whereas in our ballet the dances are only one of the component elements of the spectacle, and not the most important." "Look, here is the hero of our ballet," cried Diaghilev seeing Bakst approaching us. And, turning to him, he added, "We are talking about the substance of Russian ballet, and I am saying that the revolution we have caused in ballet is perhaps concerned less with the special sphere of the dance but more with scenery and costume. The French were the first to be astonished to learn from us that scenery does not have to represent an exterior or an interior but has to create the atmosphere, the artistic framework for the play. Look, ask the artist." "I'll tell you what the secret of the Russian ballet and its success is," said Bakst in his slow, mocking voice, and a crooked, painful smile spread over his red-cheeked face. "The secret of our ballet lies in its rhythm. We have learned to convey, not feelings and passions as in the drama, not form as in painting, but the very rhythm of feeling and form. Our dances and scenery and costumes – everything grips because it reflects the fleeting and secret rhythm of life. Our ballet," he said, "appears as the synthesis of all the existing arts. And do you know why? Because we dare to refute decadence and return instead to a wholesome ideal. Hebe is dearer to us than Salomé. And the public at large, which is always wholesome, has responded to our call."' Bakst was forgetting; not quite *all* the arts because the libretti of most ballets are of incomparable banality.

Costume design for an Almée in
Schéhérazade, 1910
215 × 350
SOTHEBY'S/PRIVATE COLLECTION

Costume design for an Almée in *Schéhérazade*, 1910
335 × 203

Costume design for an Almée in *Schéhérazade*, 1910
340 × 220

There was no doubt in anybody's mind that *Schéhérazade* was an event of outstanding and unprecedented artistic merit, but looking at photographs of the production now it seems old-fashioned and the excitement and the enthusiasm it aroused seem incredible. At the same time, people have fastened on to *Schéhérazade* as if it were Bakst's only work and then written platitudes about his 'orientalism'. At the time everything East of Suez was called 'oriental', but the adjective was not correct in this case; *Schéhérazade* was Arabian, modified by a Russian Jew whose Arabian vision was not diluted but intensified. Furthermore Bakst's work can no more be described as being 'oriental', or 'Arabian', than 'Hellenic', 'Louis XV', 'Biedermeier', 'botanic', or whatever period or style he chose for the production in hand. Bakst has been credited with starting a fashion, but this is not true either. Péladan, in *L'Art Décoratif* (1911), called him the 'Delacroix of costume,' but Delacroix' 'orientalism' came long before Bakst, and Arabia and the East had already been discovered, explored and cultivated by a great many artists. As with all fashion, a lot of people did similar things at the same time which is why they became fashionable. Paul Poiret designed his turbans after seeing them in the Victoria and Albert Museum in London in 1908, and Louis Cartier set emeralds and sapphires together before Bakst put emerald green with sapphire blue. What is true is that Bakst was in the right place doing the right thing at the right time which is the kind of luck artists working in the theatre need. Fashion, inspired by the theatre, is something imitated by a few and then followed slavishly by those who never saw the performance in the first place. Without doubt, *Schéhérazade* acted as a catalyst for an emerging fashion. Bakst wrote to his wife on 1 (14) June 1910: 'Today is the first night of the revised *Cleopatra* and, because of the extraordinary success of *Schéhérazade*, the present series (B) of performances is like this: *Cleopatra*, *Les Sylphides* (with Karsavina, Geltzer, Nijinsky) and *Schéhérazade* again. Americans and Parisians are ordering costumes from me, and shops have issued "étoffes [material] *Schéhérazade*."' The fashion lasted for a number of years. On 21 February 1914 the *Menton and Monte Carlo News*, reported on a Futurist-Bakst Ball which had been held at the Riviera Palace in Menton: 'Just before supper, there was a distribution of banners and prizes ... The first prize went to Miss Lee, who wore a most striking and beautiful *Scherezade* [sic] costume ... Miss Norton, who was awarded the second prize, was attired in a rich and handsome Parsee lady's dress ... Miss von Scgenck, who was third, had on a Bakst costume, quaint and bizarre, but very pretty ... Mr Day was the man to carry off first prize. He represented a colour scheme, which seemed to suggest the setting sun, the sky at dawn, half-a-dozen rainbows, and a few other similar things, and was most effective. Mr Bosman, an Eastern potentate, was second, and Mr Moseley, in a Futurist costume third.' Bakst was clearly the winner of the evening.

After the Russian revolution Russian émigrés in Paris in the 1920s danced the nights through in a night-club called *Schéhérazade*, but by then Diaghilev thought the ballet so ludicrously funny that he refused to let the Ballets Russes perform it. It was revived in the 30s after Diaghilev's death by Colonel de Basil's Ballet Russe. Cyril Beaumont, who first saw

Schéhérazade in 1912, published his 'personal record' *The Diaghilev Ballet in London* in 1946: 'When I recall what I saw then and what has been recently put forward as Bakst's setting, to say nothing of the commonplace lighting, I am consumed with impotent wrath and long to stand up in the theatre and cry, "Ladies and gentlemen, I protest against this setting being attributed to Bakst, when it is only something suggested by it, a very different thing."'

With *Schéhérazade* Bakst mastered the different crafts of staging and showed himself to be a consummate artist of the theatre; but Beaumont recognized what an ephemeral art the theatre is.

The Grand Seasons before the war:
1911–1914

Diaghilev originally hoped to take the Ballets Russes to London in 1910 but because King Edward VII died on 6 May the Ballets Russes gave their first performance in London in 1911 on the eve of the Coronation of George V. The programme included *Le Carnaval* but London audiences had already seen Bakst's work in 1910 when Alfred Butt presented a *Saison Russe* at the Palace Theatre on 16 May with Anna Pavlova, her partner Michael Mordkin and 'Artistes from the Imperial Russian Ballet of St Petersburg and Moscow.' In particular, Bakst (or 'Bacst' as he was credited in the programme) was responsible for Pavlova's costume in *Les Amours de Diane* and her and Mordkin's costumes in Glazounov's *Bacchanale*.

It is a mistake to think that the so-called Russian 'seasons' in Paris were restricted to appearances by Diaghilev's Ballets Russes. Before the First World War, Russian artists frequently toured western Europe and America. In 1911, for example, there were in effect two Russian 'seasons' in Paris as well as a week of Gala performances by Ida Rubinstein in *Le Martyre de St Sébastien* at the Théâtre du Châtelet from 22 May. She had appeared twice, startlingly and brilliantly, for Diaghilev in *Cléopâtre* and *Schéhérazade*, but as she fancied herself as a dramatic actress she did not want to do any more mime parts and left him to set up on her own.

Neither Bakst nor Diaghilev was ever quite at ease with Rubinstein because she was so unpredictable. She was also frightening and brave. In between her productions and gala performances she would disappear for weeks on end on hunting expeditions to Africa. Fond of panthers she kept one as a pet. Bakst told of once coming into her flat and terrifying the beast. It sprang into a waste-paper basket to hide and then rolled round the room in it unable to escape. Ida chased the waste-paper basket and when she hauled out the panther her arms were scratched to ribbons and bleeding, but she calmly put it into another room and carried on with the conversation as if nothing had happened. On another occasion Bakst and Diaghilev came to see her, Diaghilev was so frightened by the sight of the panther that he scrambled on top of a table and spent the whole time whimpering with fear while the panther, equally frightened at the sight of Diaghilev in a morning coat, growled gently in a corner.

The first 'season', beginning 2 May at the Théâtre Sarah-Bernhardt, was a packed programme of Russian opera with singers from the Imperial Theatres. The second Russian 'season' was of Diaghilev's Ballets Russes beginning on 6 June at the Châtelet. The ballet was more glamorous than the opera as this note from *Comoedia Illustré* (1 May 1911) testifies: 'Paris belongs to the Russians, that is an undisputed fact. After their caviar, their samovar and their Tolstoy they have conquered us with their music, their designers and finally their incomparable dancers. The Russian seasons continue as always and Parisians flock to them more and more enthusiastically and in ever greater numbers.'

The three and a half years from 1911 to the summer of 1914 were the busiest of Bakst's career. In 1911 he designed three ballets for Diaghilev, a play for Ida Rubinstein, various sets and costumes for operas, a number of individual costumes (mostly for the opera singers

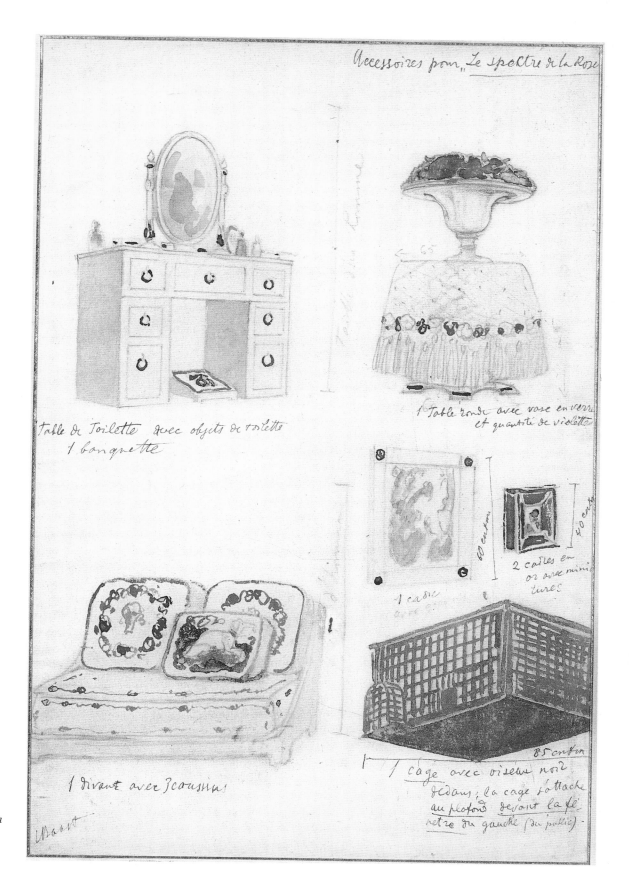

Props and furniture for *Le Spectre de la Rose*, 1911
390 × 260
SOTHEBY'S/PRIVATE COLLECTION

Props and furniture for *Le Spectre de la Rose*, 1911
398 × 265
THEATRE MUSEUM, LONDON

Maria Kousnezoff and Dimitri Smirnov); costumes for fancy-dress balls, and had his first one-man show in Paris. In 1912 he designed five ballets for Diaghilev, two plays for Rubinstein, more costumes, again mostly for Maria Kousnezoff, and had his first exhibition in London. In 1913 he designed a ballet and an opera for Diaghilev, an opera for Covent Garden, a play for Rubinstein, a ballet for Pavlova, a revue for London, still more costumes and exhibitions in Berlin and the United States. In 1914, before the war began, costumes for Diaghilev, sets for Covent Garden and costumes again. And then he cracked. He went into a deep depression for several months.

In April 1911 Bakst wrote from Paris to his divorced wife: 'Working with Seriozha will be much more tedious because he makes no attempt to extol his artists but is very keen to be successful. He is not at all happy that I have established myself here, but his poster exploits my name disgracefully. Think, five out of eight ballets this season are mine. I feel bad about it.' Bakst's ballets were revivals of *Le Carnaval*, *Schéhérazade* and *L'Oiseau de Feu* as *L'Oiseau d'Or*, and two new ballets *Narcisse* and *Le Spectre de la Rose*. Bakst was not quite right with his figures as eight ballets were not presented.

The programme, due to begin in April in Monte Carlo and in June in Paris, was not settled until a few weeks before. Diaghilev's plans originally included *Le Dieu Bleu* and *La Péri*, apart from *Daphnis and Chloë*, and the first ballet choreographed by Vaslav Nijinsky, *L'Après-midi d'un Faune*. As Ravel had not finished composing the music for *Daphnis and Chloë* and as Diaghilev was nervous of losing Fokine as choreographer, who might have left in a huff, so a new 'Greek' ballet, *Narcisse*, was devised to replace *Daphnis and Chloë*, and *Le Spectre de la Rose* replaced *L'Après-midi d'un Faune* which was not ready. Bakst designed them all.

Jean-Louis Vaudoyer, the poet and critic, had on impulse put at the head of a piece he had written about the Ballets Russes for *La Revue de Paris* in 1910 two lines of a poem by Théophile Gautier:

> 'Je suis le spectre de la rose
> Que tu portais hier au bal'
> ('I am the spirit of the rose
> You wore at the ball last night')

The lines had been inspired by a *pas de deux* in *Le Carnaval*. He then suggested the idea of a ballet to Bakst using Weber's piano piece *L'Invitation à la Valse* orchestrated by Berlioz. The suggestion was remembered when Diaghilev and the company began to think about a replacement for *L'Après-midi d'un Faune*.

Le Spectre de la Rose, called 'a graceful trifle' by Benois, was first performed at Monte Carlo on 19 April. It is eight minutes long. A young girl (Karsavina) having returned from a ball, falls asleep in a chair. In her dream, the rose which she holds in her hand becomes a spirit (Nijinsky), who kisses her and disappears at daybreak. The less story, it seems, the better. The

Portrait of Vaslav Nijinsky as the Rose
in *Le Spectre de la Rose*, 1911
400 × 285

Romola Nijinsky described the costume:
'It consisted of a close-fitting, fine elastic
silk jersey, into which Nijinsky was
sewn, covering his entire body, except
part of his breasts and arms, where
bracelets of silk rose-petals bound his
biceps. This jersey was stitched with
rose leaves, which Bakst would colour
as they were needed. Some were ragged,
as from a dying flower; others were stiff
and firm; while still others curled even
from his thighs ... On his head he wore
a close fitting helmet of rose-leaves, and
the whole effect was an extremely close
blending of different reds, rose-violet,
pink, and purple, shading one into
another, which is the essential
indefinable tint of the rose.
Nijinsky's make-up was conceived to
personify a rose. His face was like that of
a celestial insect, his eyebrows
suggesting some beautiful beetle, which
one might expect to find closest to the
heart of a rose, and his mouth was like
rose-petals.'
During performances Nijinsky used to
shed some rose petals and the story goes
that his Russian valet, Vasili, sold them
as souvenirs to admirers and quite soon
was able to build himself a house on the
proceeds which became known as
'Château du Spectre de la Rose.'
This design has been copied by Bakst
and others

Left
Tamara Karsavina and Vaslav Nijinsky
in *Le Spectre de la Rose*, 1911
Photograph by Bert
BIBLIOTHÈQUE NATIONALE, MUSÉE DE L'OPÉRA,
PARIS

Right
Vaslav Nijinsky in *Le Spectre de la Rose*,
1911
Photograph by Bert
BIBLIOTHÈQUE NATIONALE, MUSÉE DE L'OPÉRA,
PARIS

ballet was produced very quickly by Fokine and immediately became very popular. Prince Lieven wrote: 'Perhaps the very speed with which the work was done gave it that character of extraordinary freshness and unity... It took the form of a *pas de deux* which fused together with the subject, scenery, and music in one potential entity.'

Bakst's scenery for the young girl's bedroom (p. 108) was one of his most charming creations in the Biedermeier style. Cyril Beaumont described the set: 'The walls were covered with a bluish-grey paper, flecked with white blossoms; the window frames, skirting, and dado were all white. The french windows – in the background – reached from dado to skirting. Two of the windows were open, that on the right revealing a glimpse of the garden, which showed a rose-bush overhung with a deep blue sky ... The room was bathed in a sentimental moonlight which cast yellowish-green shadows on the floor.' He noticed the lighting, always so important to Bakst, and elsewhere described the furniture and props (pp. 103, 104) which defined the period and fixed the atmosphere. Karsavina in her memoirs, *Theatre Street* (1954), remembered Bakst fussing: 'Unheralded by quarrels, demure as it should be, the *Spectre de la Rose* gently passed over the agony of the first night. That night there was no fuss on the stage – Diaghileff benign; only Bakst moved about helpless, agitated, carrying a canary cage. The cage was a feature of the scenery from his point of view, a nuisance from everybody else's. He had installed the canary over a window from where it had been banished; Nijinsky had to appear through it, and the other window was to be free for Nijinsky's famous leap. 'Levoushka, for God's sake, chuck the canary, the public is growing impatient. Oh, don't be ridiculous; canaries don't stand on the chest of drawers.' – 'You don't understand, Serioja; we must give the atmosphere.' Bakst protracted the interval alarmingly, but he gave the atmosphere by finally hoisting the canary high up under a cornice. In further travel the cage, with its stuffed bird, was maliciously lost.'

Karsavina refers to Nijinsky's 'famous leap'. Bakst's set was as essential an ingredient as Nijinsky's muscles for making that leap so famous. The illusion of great height was created by making the window stretch 'from dado to skirting', and although Nijinsky only had to jump a few inches, the space seemed vast. He came in through one window but, in order not to worry about falling, he leapt out of the other on to a mattress. The old theatrical trick always works because audiences believe what they think they see and not what they really see.

To dress a man like a rose in a serious ballet must have been risking ridicule even then, but to dress him like a rose, outside of pantomime, and get away with it is theatrical genius. Bakst indeed created the spirit of a rose in human form for Nijinsky's costume (p. 106) but it was the dancer who carried it off convincingly. Indeed, critics who have seen many different

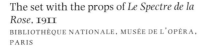

The set with the props of *Le Spectre de la Rose*, 1911

Scene in *Narcisse* from *Comoedia Illustré,*
15 June 1911
Photograph by Bert

dancers in the part have said that only Nijinsky was able to give the role its necessary ethe-real and sexless quality.

When it became obvious that Ravel would not finish the score of *Daphnis and Chloë* in time, Bakst persuaded Diaghilev to mount a ballet based on the theme of Narcissus and Echo simply called by the short title *Narcisse,* and a score was commissioned from Tcherepnine who worked closely with Bakst on the libretto. The substitution annoyed Fokine because he had been developing his ideas for *Daphnis and Chloë* and now found that he had to adapt them hurriedly for *Narcisse,* a ballet for which he had no particular enthusiasm. 'What angered me greatly,' he wrote, 'and seemed to me most inartistic was Diaghilev's use in *Narcisse* of the Bakst scenery designed for *Daphnis and Chloë.* All the paraphernalia I need for *Daphnis* – the green meadow, the grove with the statues of the three nymphs; wreaths; sacrificial offerings of the shepherds – were all in *Narcisse.* The nymphs played an important part in *Daphnis* but had no relation whatsoever to the story of *Narcisse.'* Bakst's design for *Daphnis and Chloë* with the nymphs, Daphnis, Chloë and a herd of sleepy sheep was reproduced in *Comoedia Illustré* on 15 June 1911 with the misleading caption 'Décor de Narcisse'. One can sympathize with

Costume design for a Minor Deity in
Narcisse, 1911
339 × 200
ASHMOLEAN MUSEUM, OXFORD

Costume design for a Boeotian in
Narcisse, 1911
400 × 273
MUSEUM OF THEATRICAL AND MUSICAL ARTS,
LENINGRAD

This design is one of the series of
original sketches (unsigned) which
Bakst made for Fokine and which he
himself copied later

Fokine's annoyance and he was right to accuse Diaghilev of being inartistic; but Bakst should not have agreed to being Diaghilev's accomplice.

The scene on stage was a 'sylvan glade overhung with a dense mass of foliage.' Inexplicably, there was a band of monsters at the beginning and end of the ballet. Although they were irrelevant to it they gave Bakst an opportunity to design an entirely new kind of costume using grotesque masks as the main decorative element. He successfully anthropomorphized the monsters by strongly exaggerating the bestial quality and proportion of the costume so that the human appearance became insignificant. Monsters and other animals also occur in later works such as *Le Dieu Bleu* and *Orpheus* (pp. 135 and 175). His drawings for these costumes are weird, grotesque and repulsive. His other costume designs for *Narcisse* (pp. 30, 111, 114 and 115), are again a unique set of drawings in a style peculiar to this ballet. The turbulence about the half-naked figures with their swirling scarves radiates an extraordinary erotic energy. The dancers in their diaphanous dresses with Greek inspired patterns in blues, greens, reds and oranges, revealing thighs, arms, naked feet and pubic hair are all larger than life and almost spill over the edge of the paper. These drawings show Bakst escaping from the frame and miniature effect of *Schéhérazade*. Some of them became very popular because he copied them several times, and some so popular that other people have copied them often.

Cyril Beaumont made an interesting observation about those scarves: 'Then there was Nijinska as the Bacchante . . . She danced . . . sometimes holding a red and blue scarf which she held extended between her raised hands, or allowed to curl gracefully in the air. Years afterwards, while watching from the wings, I saw Sokolova perform the same dance. When she came off, she asked me to hold the scarf for her. I was astonished to find that the material I had thought to be light as chiffon, was, on the contrary, quite thick and heavy.' Bakst understood that a thickish material was naturally easier to control and manage by a dancer than something thin and light which would tend instead to be controlled by the draught created by her movements.

Bakst always saw the make-up as part of the dancer's costume. For Nijinsky as Narcissus he invented a new tone. Instead of the usual sun-tanned look he gave him a lemon-coloured make-up with a dash of ochre which covered his whole body, including his face. His eyes, eyebrows and lips were only lightly lined. His whole appearance was illusory, like another flower.

Narcisse was only moderately successful. Benois was still smarting from the recent rows with Serov and Bakst and therefore what he wrote in *Rech* on 22 July 1911 is reasonably honest and even generous: 'What can I say about Bakst's staging? I have to admit that I do not like it. The effect of unity and the "mythological" atmosphere was broken up . . . It is an old, innate fault of Bakst's. This talented man does too many things at once, too many different things and thinks he can do everything. He is matchless in those things which call for fashionable refinement, beauty, elegance, but on the other hand poetic reverie or a generally noble tone are beyond his means and powers in spite of an "ambitious inclination" towards them.' But this was by no means a universal opinion either of *Narcisse* or of Bakst's work. N. Minsky in *Utro Rossii (Russian Morning)* 11 July 1911 thought that *Narcisse* was 'the pearl of the season . . . I would never have believed that in a ballet, over a period of ten minutes, such depth of thought and feeling could be expressed just by movement and a combination of costumes.'

More problems were caused by the two new ballets, *La Péri* and *Le Dieu Bleu*, which were not produced in 1911 than by the two which were. As far as Diaghilev was concerned most of the fault lay with Bakst because of his agreement to design simultaneously *Le Martyre de Saint Sébastien* for Ida Rubinstein.

Diaghilev intended to revise the story of *La Péri* and had commissioned Paul Dukas to compose a new score. He was the first non-Russian composer to be commissioned as a first step in Diaghilev's plan for the Ballets Russes to become more international. As part of the deal Dukas insisted that his mistress, Natasha Trouhanova, should dance the part of the Péri. Diaghilev and Fokine both knew, however, that she had no real technique and both agreed that she was much too fat to be a spritely peri. As they could not say so openly to Dukas without causing deep offence they prevaricated endlessly until he withdrew his score. But Diaghilev, in his dealing with Astruc, mischievously also used Bakst as an excuse for not getting on with *La Péri*. Bakst was busy in Paris and had every intention of finishing all five productions that he was working on: *La Péri*, *Le Dieu Bleu*, *Le Martyre de Saint Sébastien*, *Le Spectre de la Rose* and *Narcisse*, and he was coping. During April and May a flurry of telegrams and letters went between him, Diaghilev and Astruc. Bakst is much the most impatient of the three, but justifiably so.

15 April, Bakst letter to Diaghilev, Riviera Palace, Monte Carlo: 'I have sent you a sketch for *La Péri* on which I have drawn two costumes, but as I work on them I change them, as I change everything. But remember, when you receive the sketch, send it back to me within three hours so that I do not, as now, have to ask everybody – you, Shura [Benois], Fokine – a hundred times to send me the staging [*mise-en-scène*] for *Dieu Bleu* . . .'

16 April, Bakst letter to Diaghilev: 'Much as I should like to, it is out of the question for me to leave Paris even for an hour. I am torn apart on every side and every moment is vital, I am afraid lest everything should collapse. Besides I just have a blind fear of not finishing the huge amount of work. *Narcisse* and *Rose* are finished with detailed plans and models, etc. Please ask Shura to do the lighting, and he would also do a wonderful plan for *Dieu Bleu*. I wrote to Fokine that I must have a full libretto (with instructions for the designer) as soon as possible for *Dieu Bleu* because without it and without the names and measurements of the dancers which you promised to send me I cannot order a single costume or prop. It really is dreadful

Costume design for a Boeotian in
Narcisse, 1911
400 × 273

how you organize things. Dreadful. I have minimum time for the maximum amount of work, you have no idea . . . I can send you the sketches for *La Péri* and *Dieu Bleu* to Monte Carlo but it seems to me that I might be trusted. You did not see *Rose* at all. *La Péri* is done and finished, but *Dieu Bleu* is not quite finished but it needs most time and, actually, I have put it to the end of my schedule. Don't forget the libretto for *Dieu Bleu*.

Of course, your endless changes (I received four different orders for your rhapsody and four changes) are really upsetting and I think that anyone else in my position would have given up long ago and done what is 'fixed'. In any case, I am warning you that I am doing *La Péri* and that if you order a fifth variation I will not do it.

I consider the productions of *Narcisse* and *Rose* in Monte Carlo to be like rough drafts. In Paris I will make them more complex and more refined according to my taste, but in fact I think you are trying too hard for all those half-drunk gamblers, and that riff-raff is not worth all the effort.'

17 April, Diaghilev telegram from Beausoleil to Astruc: 'If Rubinstein is here from 24 to 30 April my contract with Blanc is broken. Foresee the consequences. Is not Bakst's treachery who has announced to me his absence from the first night of *Narcisse* enough for you?'

(Ida Rubinstein was due in Monte Carlo earlier in order to dance in *Schéhérazade*.)

23 April, Diaghilev telegram to Astruc: 'Help Bakst send with Rubinstein this evening sketches for *Péri* and *Dieu Bleu*. Ask Rubinstein not to forget scarves.'

22 May, Diaghilev letter from Rome to Astruc: 'First *Péri*. Up till now I still have not received the contract signed by Trouhanova. And besides, you have informed me that there are still several points of disagreement between us. You must understand that I cannot begin to carry out a business deal which is not founded upon a sound basis . . .

You have observed my work for five years now and you know well enough the principle upon which it is based. I do not play the impressario and my strength lies in the collaborative work of painters, musicians, poets and performers.

One of these components – and the most indispensable – until now was Bakst, my childhood friend and collaborator in all my projects; he owes his whole reputation in Paris to the Russian seasons which as you know have cost me a superhuman effort.

This year I entrusted him with four productions of which one, *Narcisse*, we worked out and agreed together. As for the second, *Le Spectre de la Rose*, Bakst followed the rehearsals in St Petersburg and saw it developed choreographically. Therefore he adapted his set to a completed work. As for *Dieu Bleu* and above all *Péri* we have had a few vague ideas, a few idle sketches, that is all, not even a pencil drawing. I believe that the set of *Dieu Bleu* has to have a temple but I do not know where or how it is positioned. I do not know if it is the interior of a temple or an open space around it. I do not know where the pool or trap door required by the scenario are placed. In other words I know not only nothing about the construction of the set

Costume design for a Nymph in
Narcisse, 1911
400 × 268
MUSÉE DES BEAUX ARTS, STRASBOURG

but also nothing about the ideas behind it. And it is under these conditions that Fokine, Benois and I are supposed to devise a production?

As far as *Péri* is concerned the situation is becoming absolutely ridiculous, because we simply do not know whether the action takes place in a palace, on a mountain, or in the clouds – and this two weeks before the first night. Bakst claims that we lack confidence in his work, but I must say I have never seen such a tremendous lack of the most elementary artistic and aesthetic principles as he has shown with regard to us. When Bakst undertook the production of *St Sébastien* he swore to me that it would not interfere in any way in our work together which he said meant more to him. I can see now that we have been sacrificed completely to the work of Rubinstein and d'Annunzio and that we are reduced to paying the price of too great a trust . . . But now thanks to you and Bakst, after such a long wait, we are forced to abandon the production of these two ballets for the season which begins two weeks from now, and this is to inform you that you must bear the consequences. I do not have to tell you that in giving up the public dress rehearsal of *Dieu Bleu* we lose about 100,000 francs. But what distresses me most is not to be able to show Paris the whole artistic programme that was planned, for you know that that is what I particularly care about.

I leave it to you to judge upon whom the responsibility falls for what happens. It is not for nothing that I went out of my way to go to Paris to implore Bakst to come to Monte Carlo if only for two days. Now, here I am in the most difficult position with regard to Dukas and above all Reynaldo Hahn [the composer of *Le Dieu Bleu*] who put himself out to come to St Petersburg. I beg you to sort this whole business out and explain to them the reason for this delay. In any event I am suffering too much from the financial and moral loss which Bakst and you have caused.

P.S. Copies of this letter have been sent to Bakst and Reynaldo Hahn.'

Diaghilev was being his usual foxy self and covering his tracks.

23 May, Bakst letter to his wife: '. . . I am very scared by the amount of work I have to do and all the responsibility; I am afraid that I will not have time to do it and will do it badly because of the rush. And besides, neither Diaghilev nor d'Annunzio wants to hear about replacing me. And Seriozha has also given me a new (wonderful music) ballet by Paul Duca [*sic*] – *La Péri*. Would you believe it, I go to bed at 10 o'clock, get up at 7.30 in the morning and work the whole day without stopping until I am absolutely exhausted, completely worn out (!!). I go to bed feeling totally beaten and several times a day I lose my courage, I want to leave it all and run away somewhere. Astruc has surrounded me with five assistants – but just think, in two months, I have had to design eight sets! and make about 200 costume designs, not counting the props.'

Bakst made at least three costume designs for *La Péri* and two set designs. The scenery was made because we know it was used, inappropriately, for *Cléopâtre*, after its scenery was burnt in South America. The costume designs, marvellously evocative masterpieces, are the quintessence of Bakst's work for the theatre, unsurpassed in refined eroticism. The Peri's costume was made but Trouhanova was indeed no sprite and the erotic effect was pathetically unfulfilled. It is ironic that Bakst's most famous drawing was for a ballet which was eventually performed with someone else's designs. Although Diaghilev used Bakst's work on *Le Martyre de Saint Sébastien* as an excuse for not being ready, Bakst finished *La Péri* and would have finished *Le Dieu Bleu* in time. *Le Martyre de Saint Sébastien*, however, must have taken the longest time to do.

'150 Actors, 350 Performers, 500 Costumes.' This was the sensational banner line on the poster, the major selling point for *Le Martyre de Saint Sébastien*, more important than the names of Ida Rubinstein and Gabriele d'Annunzio the author. He had first seen her in *Schéhérazade* and had instantly fallen in love with her, especially her legs. She wanted to further her career as a dramatic actress and needed a suitable play. He had wanted to write a play for some time about St Sebastian and his martyrdom at the hands of the Emperor Diocletian's archers and he recognized in her apparent sexual ambiguity the ideal incarnation of his vision of the Saint. She encouraged him and saw that his play could be the ideal vehicle with which to storm the Parisian stage. The play, in five acts or 'mansions' as d'Annunzio called them, was ready in March 1911. The greatest theatrical talents of the time were engaged to bring this masterpiece onto the stage: Debussy was commissioned to provide the music, Fokine the choreography – Rubinstein did not entirely forsake the dance as she had a scene dancing frenetically on hot coals which turned to white lilies – and Bakst was asked to design the five sets and all the costumes. There was a painted curtain for the prologue; the first act was the 'Courtyard of the Lilies'; the second act was the Prefect's residence; the third act was a room in the Emperor's palace, 'The Council of False Gods'; the fourth act was a sacred grove, 'The Wounded Laurel', which transformed for a few moments for the fifth act into 'Paradise'.

This was the largest and most complicated production in Bakst's career so far. In an interview with Rose Strunsky which was published in the *New York Tribune* on 5 September 1915 (but which must have taken place much earlier) under the title 'Léon Bakst on the Modern Ballet' he explained his method and his symbolic use of colour:

> I have often noticed that in each colour of the prism there exists a gradation which sometimes expresses frankness and chastity, sometimes sensuality and even bestiality, sometimes pride, sometimes despair. This can be felt and given over to the public by the effect one makes of the various shadings. That is what I tried to do in *Schéhérazade*. Against a lugubrious green I put a blue full of despair, paradoxical as it may seem. There are reds which are triumphal and there are reds which assassinate. There is a blue which can be the colour of St Madeleine, and there is a blue of

Natasha Trouhanova in the costume of the Peri from the cover of *Comoedia Illustré*, 15 June 1911
THEATRE MUSEUM, LONDON

There is very little connection between the delicate but erotic Persian sprite and the stout dancer

Opposite
Costume design for Natasha Trouhanova as the Peri in *La Péri*, 1911
680 × 485
MR AND MRS N. D. LOBANOV-ROSTOVSKY COLLECTION

This is a later and larger version of the original drawing, as is the design for Nijinsky (see p. 120). They were both so popular that they were made into lithographs. Two editions were made of the design for the Peri herself, one of 100 during Bakst's lifetime and one of 50 after his death. Neither the size nor the date of the edition of the design for Nijinsky is known

Right
Poster reproducing costume designs for minor characters in *Le Martyre de Saint Sébastien*, 1911
130 × 400
SOTHEBY'S/PRIVATE COLLECTION

Messalina . . . It is in line as well as in colour that I make my emotions . . . Sometimes I bring out the purely mystic in the stage setting, as in d'Annunzio's *St Sébastien*, which I produced last year. Because the subject matter was essentially Christian, I used the cross in a thousand variations, for the basis of my linear ornamentation, not only disguised and hidden in the costumes and accessories and ornaments in the beautiful play of d'Annunzio, but even in the lines of the landscape and buildings of the scenery. My method is generally to take a simple motif and vary it indefinitely, so as to create a harmony of colour and line.

The motifs which he took were based on his previous studies; groups of characters were identified by having costumes with the same, or similar, motif but in varying colours. He again established a standard figure for each group of characters and then decorated each one differently; it was like painting by numbers, and, presumably, much of it was done by the assistants he referred to in his letter quoted earlier (p. 116). In any event, it was impossible for him to produce all the required drawings by himself in the time available, and yet he skilfully managed to avoid drawing a set of dull uniform costumes. It was a race against time as there were so many to produce and they had to be of high quality. Madame Muelle wrote to Astruc on 9 May that 'Mr Bakst wants costumes to be in silk and very beautiful.'

The public dress rehearsal on 21 May had to be cancelled because M. Bertaux, the Minister for War, was killed in an air crash so the first public performance was on 22 May. Louis Schneider, in *Le Théâtre*, was aware of Bakst's intentions: 'We were filled with admiration not only by the richness of the decor and the costumes but by the perfect harmony which made them, as it were, sing in unison. Their realization is due to the master of decor in Russia, the painter Léon Bakst who has for three or four years had the most favourable influence in the world on theatre art in France. He has made scenery the servant of the drama, and costume the servant of scenery. He has synthesized and simplified outlines, stylized and generalized the periods he has to represent; without lingering over detail and seeking to exteriorize

N.TRUHANOVA

BAKST
1911

Opposite
Costume design for Vaslav Nijinsky as Iskender in *La Péri*, 1911 (1922)
660 × 510
THE METROPOLITAN MUSEUM OF ART, NEW YORK, GIFT OF SIR JOSEPH DUVEEN

A porcelain dish using this design was made by the Lomonosov factory in 1925 as a tribute to the artist. [See note to caption on p. 118]

Judith holding the head of Holopherne, 1922
Oil on canvas, 460 × 535
SOTHEBY'S/ROBERT L. B. TOBIN COLLECTION, MARION KOOGLER MCNAY ART MUSEUM, SAN ANTONIO

A third design for *La Péri*, a *suivante*, was reproduced in *Deutsche Kunst und Dekoration* in October 1912. This is identical, except for the head of Holopherne and the necklace, to the painting above which Bakst made specially for the exhibition. The addition of the head and the exclusion of the necklace makes this drawing gruesomely erotic where the original was charmingly sensual. All three designs for *La Péri* were exhibited at the Musée des Arts Décoratifs in 1911; the later one called *Judith* and the new version of the design for Nijinsky were exhibited at Knoedler & Co. in New York in 1922

The scene in Act I of *Le Martyre de Saint Sébastien*, 1911

trivia,' and then in another article in *Comoedia* he emphasized the crucial point about Bakst's stage technique, '... simplicity does not exclude sumptuousness. M. Léon Bakst has wanted to use construction as little as possible and to achieve all his effects through the use of the paint-brush alone ... The colours of all the characters, although appearing to be variegated all carefully harmonize with the background ... the painter has also used lighting effects discreetly and with great aesthetic care; there is not a single instant of crude or violent lighting, all the effects are successful and are designed to change the scenery gradually to match the change in the feelings of the characters.'

Robert de Montesquiou, poet, aesthete, 'Prince of Decadents' and the model for Proust's Baron de Charlus, was besotted by Ida Rubinstein and was in ecstasy over her as the Saint. He exalted her performance in *Le Théâtre*: 'I have seen many things, many beautiful things, but in my experience, I have never seen anything to compare in beauty with what this artist disclosed to our gaze during the whole of the first act and most of the third.' Most critics did not go so far but were warm in their general praise. A few, like François de Nion, were not deceived: '... I do not know anything quite so woefully and pretentiously boring as these five

Set design for Act I of *Le Martyre de Saint Sébastien*, 1911
420 × 573
SOTHEBY'S/PRIVATE COLLECTION

Left
Costume design for Ida Rubinstein as
Saint Sebastien in *Le Martyre de Saint
Sébastien*, 1911
695 × 405
SOTHEBY'S/PRIVATE COLLECTION

Right
Costume design for Ida Rubinstein in
Act 5 of *Le Martyre de Saint Sébastien*,
1911
445 × 275
SOTHEBY'S/PRIVATE COLLECTION

Opposite
Costume design for Ida Rubinstein in
Act 2 of *Le Martyre de Saint Sébastien*,
1911
280 × 210
ISABELLA STEWART GARDNER MUSEUM, BOSTON

acts which are dragged along incomprehensibly by screeching chants.' Whichever critic was nearest the mark it is clear that the effect of Bakst's work was a successful feast for the eye which obscured the ostentatious piffle of the text.

By 1911 Bakst's reputation was sufficiently well established for the Musée des Arts Décoratifs in Paris to be the first museum to mount an exhibition of his theatre designs. Jean-Louis Vaudoyer in his introduction to the catalogue wrote: 'In general, and often with good reason, it is found not to be necessary to exhibit hurried and sometimes clumsy sketches in a gallery which the costumier has to make up into costumes for characters condemned to develop in a setting devised by another artist; the one is often not in keeping with the other. This absence of harmony cannot be held against the Russians because the same artist is always entrusted with the design of both the set and the costumes ... Of all these artists M. Bakst is perhaps the one who experiences most and makes us also experience most profoundly the poetry of the subject entrusted to his talent.' There were 85 exhibits and the museum was astute enough to snap up the set design for *Schéhérazade*. This design more than any other has become almost a symbolic illustration not only for Bakst but for any survey of theatre design or history of the Ballets Russes (pp. 94–95). He felt honoured and was pleased by the exhibition. Above all he was thrilled by the financial success. He wrote to his friend Valerian Svetlov: 'Have a look at my exhibition at the Louvre, Pavillon Marsan.

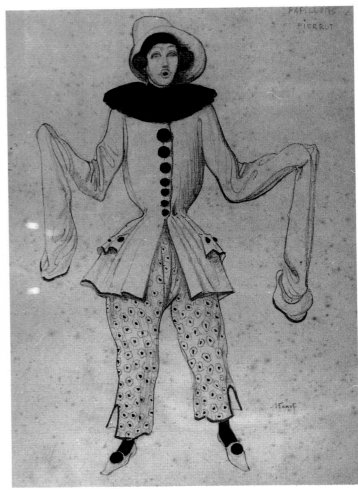

About 120 objects. Simply a wild success. Just think, only about 20–25 objects from the whole lot have not been taken, that's all! That's a "foreigner" for you! I can see your smile – I assure you that the minimum price is 400–450, but the large costume designs are 1,000 francs – and that amounts to quite something.'

As soon as the exhibition had started he went to Algiers for a holiday and a rest before starting a heavy programme of work in the autumn. He seemed to lose heart a little at this time. In the Montesquiou papers in the Bibliothèque Nationale, amid the bright confetti of postcards and thank-you notes, there is a melancholy letter from Bakst written on 18 October after his exhibition had finished on the 15th: '. . . And now that the exhibition has closed I am once again working on a new and urgent project; the theatre is a terrible and relentless art where one always has to hurry, and I always regret the slow and peaceful life of a landscape painter or even a painter of "battle scenes". I feel sad; at the end of the day I linger by the darkened windows of my studio – it's a bad sign for the state of mind . . . huge canvases for *Dieu Bleu* are laid out before me and I am splashing the immaculate white background with colours which will dumbfound the English, because London is going to see this ballet on 20 November.'

Costume design for Girl in yellow and
brown in *Papillons*, 1912
270 × 180
SOTHEBY'S/PRIVATE COLLECTION

London did not see *Le Dieu Bleu* in November 1911. The Ballets Russes, in London from October to December, repeated the previous repertoire, added a number of other ballets but no new productions. As Pierre Monteux, the conductor for the whole season, wrote to Astruc from London on 28 October 1911: 'Diaghilev is parading all the old chestnuts of his repertoire so that he can keep the good things for the spring season. That is why I am conducting *Giselle*, *Le Pavillon d'Armide*, *Les Sylphides* (some works by Chopin orchestrated), Tchaikovsky's *Sleeping Beauty* which is musically horrid, so awful that I am refusing to conduct it!!' Instead of *The Sleeping Beauty* there were performances of *Swan Lake*. London would have to wait another ten years for its first *Sleeping Beauty*.

As a prelude to his own hectic season of work in Paris Bakst designed *Papillons* for Fokine for a charity performance at the Mariinsky Theatre on 10 (23) March 1912. Using Schumann's music of the same name *Papillons* was a continuation of *Carnaval*, a group of young girls make fun of Pierrot who imagines them to be butterflies. Bakst designed romantic costumes of the early Victorian period for what A. Pleshe'ev of *Novoe Vremia* called 'an insignificant trifle, not worth pausing over.' Bakst did not pause too much over this production either because his scenery was not painted in time, and the dancers had to make do with scenery from stock. *Papillons* was revived in Monte Carlo in 1914 with a symmetrical set by Mstislav Dobuzhinsky while Bakst's delicate and romantically feminine costumes were used again. This ballet became popular but it was really too slight and too fragile to make a strong impression in a large theatre.

The 'good things' which Diaghilev planned for Paris in 1912 were four new productions as well as the most popular ballets already shown. They were included in what came to be known as *La Grande Saison de Paris*, in effect a festival or a continuous programme of events organized by Gabriel Astruc. In 1912 the programme included from 1 to 10 May six performances of *Hélène de Sparte* with Ida Rubinstein; from 13 May to 10 June, fifteen performances by Diaghilev's Ballets Russes (eighteen were announced); and from 11 to 20 June, six performances of *Salomé* also with Ida Rubinstein.

Diaghilev could not have been too pleased that his season of ballets was framed by Rubinstein's Gala weeks in the same theatre. He was jealous, too, that Bakst was also the designer of both Rubinstein productions. The whole programme was a great strain on Bakst, although the fact that he was responsible for mounting all four new Diaghilev ballets must have made fit-ups, get-outs and rehearsal schedules at the Châtelet easier to organize. Stravinsky had other doubts as he wrote to Benois: 'So many commissions should not be given to Bakst alone (however talented he is). Why ruin the artist and his work? . . . in a single month he has put on three Greek productions which consist of 6 sets: *Helen of Sparta* (3), *The Faun* (1), *Daphnis* (2).' Stravinsky did not include the costumes of which there were over a hundred.

Verhaeren's play *Hélène de Sparte* takes place after the sack of Troy when Helen returns to Sparta.

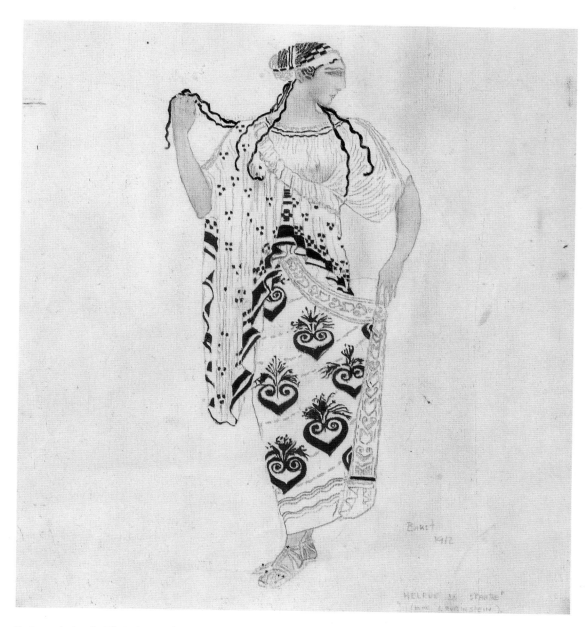

Costume design for Ida Rubinstein as
Helen in Act 2 of *Hélène de Sparte*, 1912
270 × 200
SOTHEBY'S/PRIVATE COLLECTION

Ida Rubinstein as Helen in Act 2 of
Hélène de Sparte, 1912
BIBLIOTHÈQUE NATIONALE, MUSÉE DE L'OPÉRA,
PARIS

Above
Set design for Acts 1 and 3 for *Hélène de Sparte*, 1912
Oil on canvas, 1320 × 1870
MUSÉE NATIONAL D'ART MODERNE, CENTRE GEORGES POMPIDOU, PARIS

This is a later and slightly larger copy of the original design in pencil and watercolour in the Musée des Arts Décoratifs, Paris; there is also another version in the Fine Art Museums of San Francisco

Right
Ida Rubinstein as Helen in Act 4 of *Hélène de Sparte*, 1912
BIBLIOTHÈQUE NATIONALE, MUSÉE DE L'OPÉRA, PARIS

Opposite
Costume design for Ida Rubinstein as Helen in Act 4 of *Hélène de Sparte*, 1912
270 × 196
THYSSEN-BORNEMISZA COLLECTION

Left
Costume design for Edouard de Max
as Pollux in *Hélène de Sparte*, 1912,
reproduced in the Souvenir Programme

There is a later version of this design
used for 'Greek' characters

Right
Portrait of Ida Rubinstein as Helen in
Hélène de Sparte, 1912, reproduced in
the Souvenir Programme

This is a portrait of Rubinstein in the
part, not a costume design.
Unusually for this period Bakst
signed it in Russian; it was probably
made specially for Ida Rubinstein
and as an illustration for the
programme

Below
Characters in *Hélène de Sparte*, 1912,
from the Souvenir Programme

The caption bottom right is right for the
actor but wrong for the role. Roger Karl
played Castor

"HÉLÈNE DE SPARTE"

Costume design for Desjardins as
Menelaus in *Hélène de Sparte*, 1912
260 × 240
PARMENIA MIGEL EKSTROM COLLECTION, NEW
YORK

Bakst crossed out the original title and
used this design also for three brigands
in *Daphnis and Chloë*, 1912. The figure,
apart from the left arm, and the
costume, apart from the decorative

detail, are similar to the design for
Pollux. The motifs in both cases are
based on Bakst's archaeological
research.

Bakst described his scenic ideas in an interview with René Chavance which was published in *Gil Blas* on 4 May, the day of the first performance:

> I have known it for a long time because it was translated into Russian long before it was published in France. In my sets I have tried to show the Homeric world as I see it. I did my research in Crete, in the labyrinth of Minos. And, I must admit, I found what I had hoped to find there. In fact, I have always thought that early Greek art which corresponds to the same Egyptian period did not have that lack of colour which is generally ascribed to the classical period. Statues and monuments were all multicoloured, and I found traces of those vivid, even brutal, colours which I had imagined. But I hate the dryness of an archeological note-book.
>
> Therefore I merely got my inspiration from this art, and transposed it in the way I wanted.
>
> First, I tried to express the ruggedness of a warlike kingdom; then the charm and melancholy of a lonely place where one likes to feel at home; and finally the strangeness of a pantheistic set where all the forces of nature aspiring to Helen unite.
>
> I consider that choice of colours and their combination can be made to express feelings just as words and music do, and therefore I have harmonized both the choice and the combination in each of the acts.

He tried to create an impression of prehistoric Greece with a series of painted cloths. It is not necesssary to understand the symbolism of an artist's colour scheme to be affected by it. The first and third acts, with decorative details which Bakst had seen in Crete at the Palace of Minos, represented the *agora*, or main public place, of Sparta with its ramparts, and high above, palace of King Menelaus. The second act, in contrast, was the simple, tranquil, modest abode of Menelaus based on the houses he had seen near the palace. The fourth act was classical and 'pantheistic', as Bakst said, with massive columns on either side bounding a forest of trees, statues, mountains and rivers 'where dryads, naiads, satyrs, and centaurs lust after Helen. This set is like a Paradise where everything sings of love and beauty,' wrote Louis Schneider in *Le Théâtre*. The production did not kindle a flame for the season, indeed its reception was quite cool. Félix Duquesnil wrote that 'this useless performance seems to me to have been given above all to produce Madame Ida Rubinstein on stage who is more of a mime artist than an actress.' And Robert de Flers in *Le Figaro* was of much the same opinion: 'But why does Mme Ida Rubinstein speak? Her accent is disagreeable and her diction is incomprehensible. One is tempted to say to her, only slightly changing Baudelaire's line, "Be divine and be quiet!"' Bakst's work had a mixed reception. At one end of the scale, there were critics like Robert de Flers: 'Everyone will come to see the curiously polychrome sets by M. Léon Bakst who ... also designed the many picturesque and warm-coloured costumes. There is something about the general effect which is sumptuously barbaric, the last word in over-

Characters in *Le Dieu Bleu*, 1912, from the Souvenir Programme

refinement.' But others had their own ideas of a rather colourless classical Greece and doubted that Bakst's designs were based on reality. A Russian critic, E. Pann, in *Studia*, summed up the general view: 'I do not know if Léon Bakst's decorative Bacchanalia correspond to the Ancient Greek ideas of colour (in an interview which I had with Bakst he assured me that he found unmistakable traces of Greek polychromy in the labyrinths of Crete), but the production gave off a whiff of spicy Oriental paganism, and the interplay of colours echoed Verhaeren's tempestuous verses.'

Le Dieu Bleu, the ballet which began the Ballets Russes season and followed *Hélène de Sparte*, was described as a 'Hindu ballet' and although it was indeed oriental, its spice did not greatly appeal. This production had caused Bakst endless problems. He worked on it for a very long time and complained bitterly to Diaghilev in the letter (already quoted, p. 113) of (15) 28 April 1911 that he had still not received the libretto

Monsters in *Le Dieu Bleu*, 1912, from the Souvenir Programme

. . . without which I am not prepared to do any more work. Apart from a few arbitrary and vague instructions you gave me when the priority was to work on *Thamar* and *Après-midi d'un Faune*, I have received nothing – no libretto, no number of characters, nor number of scenes, no definite budget, no cast list. I repeat (but I may as well be singing to the wind) that the whole essence of my way of designing for the theatre is based on the most calculated arrangement of patches of colour on the background of a set with costumes which correspond directly to the build of the dancers. Even so, I am doing a lot on *Le Dieu Bleu*, but blind, not knowing what band of colour will come out of it. It's terrible . . . I have already told you more than once I cannot design the settings in one country, travel to another to help with the staging, and then to a third to do all the lighting and make adjustments to the scenery. It's too much. Every second here is dear to me, and you should know from my parcels of *Rose* and *Narcisse* how conscientiously and honestly I concern myself with the productions, and that I can be trusted more than a little, especially as every artist can only work in his own characteristic manner and style. Once again I remind you that Muelle needs the exact measurements of the dancers, those who have not been cast as well as those who have, and, most important, the shoe sizes for Crait. Once again I ask you to send me without delay the libretto for *Le Dieu Bleu* because I cannot work in uncertainty. It will have fatal consequences on the work. Ask Serov, he'll tell you how much I am working for you – and therefore I ask you to help me a little, and not sit back indifferent to what I am doing here. After all, it is for you. Once again, I repeat, that the costumes of the main characters appear dominant, like flowers on the bouquet of the other costumes. If my backgrounds remain uncertain then I cannot finish the work. It is pointless to go on repeating 'send me, send me *Le Dieu Bleu*', when I am obstinately refused the rudiments of my work.

Left
Vaslav Nijinsky as the Blue God in
Le Dieu Bleu, 1912
BIBLIOTHÈQUE NATIONALE, MUSÉE DE L'OPÉRA,
PARIS

Right
Tamara Karsavina as the Fiancée in
Le Dieu Bleu, 1912, from the Souvenir
Programme

The slippers have been touched in after
the photograph was taken

Set design for *Le Dieu Bleu*, 1912
558 × 780
MUSÉE NATIONAL D'ART MODERNE, CENTRE
GEORGES POMPIDOU, PARIS

Opposite
Costume design for the Young Rajah in
Le Dieu Bleu, 1912
285 × 210
SOTHEBY'S/THEATRE MUSEUM, LONDON

This design is dated 1911. Bakst copied
the figure, in an enlarged version
(490 × 325), for the costume of
M. Clemenceau as the Grand Vizier in
Aladin ou la Lampe Merveilleuse in 1918.
The pattern on the coat was different
and the basic colour was changed to
green

Bakst's pleading had been to no avail, and it was not until the end of May 1911 that Diaghilev accepted that *Le Dieu Bleu* would not be ready. Having been postponed for a year, the first performance finally took place at the Châtelet on 13 May 1912. The libretto, by Jean Cocteau, which had caused so many problems was simple if not trite but was obviously thought to have all the necessary appealing elements suitable to a ballet.

Diaghilev set great store by it, lavished a huge budget on it and hoped that it would give Nijinsky another sensational role and run successfully in the repertoire. Although it was far from disastrously received it was only performed for one season in Paris and one in London. All the inspiration seems to have evaporated during the long preparations. Diaghilev's usual acumen deserted him, or perhaps they had merely all got bored, as can easily happen in the theatre. The choreography, considered to be uninspired, owed its origin to the Siamese Dances Fokine had seen when the ballet troupe of the Royal Siamese Court had performed in St Petersburg in 1900. Bakst had also seen a performance and had been sufficiently affected to have painted the Siamese Dancers in the Lantern Dance. Cyril Beaumont thought that the best thing about *Le Dieu Bleu* was the setting 'in which Bakst proved that while he could evoke all the cruelty and voluptuousness of the East, as in his setting for *Schéhérazade*, he could also, by a different combination of colour and design, conjure up the mystery and sense of awe produced by the East in a mood of religious exaltation.' Robert Brussel in *Le Figaro* called Bakst's setting 'the pinnacle of decorative art,' but Svetlov was unimpressed, '*Le Dieu Bleu* is a failure in every sense of the word, – in subject, in musical composition, in setting and stage management.' And he was supposed to be a friend.

The set was an orange-coloured cliff silhouetted against a deep blue sky with a group of huge heads hewn out of the rock jutting from the cliff, symbols of deity worshipped by the priests, identified by Nicoletta Misler (See Baer, 1988) as being derived from the sandstone faces that decorated the towers of the Bayon Temple of Angkor Thom in Cambodia. Against this background the dominant colour of the costumes was white. This is the most difficult colour to use on stage but Bakst often used it as an incidental or decorative highlight. In *Le Dieu Bleu* he reversed his usual practice and set other pure or primary spots of colour against a base white which gave an effect of jewelled lightness to the costumes. Because of the delay in mounting the production Bakst had to copy a number of his own drawings as the originals had become dispersed, but the copies lacked spontaneity.

Thamar, first performed on 20 May, was intended to be another *Schéhérazade* but never quite achieved the same popularity. Bakst suggested both the theme, taken from a poem by Lermontov, and the music, Balakirev's symphonic poem of the same title. Thamar, Queen of Georgia, in her castle on the precipitous heights of a gorge entices passing travellers and after making love to them, stabs them and has their bodies thrown over the mountain side. After visiting the Caucasus specially to research, Bakst designed an unusual and disproportioned set. Bakst's play with the perspective made it appear as if the room was

3 BAÏADÈRES avec paon
DIEU B.

BAKST
1911

Costume design for Tamara Karsavina
as the Fiancée in *Le Dieu Bleu*, 1912
210 × 280
SALLIE BLUMENTHAL COLLECTION, NEW YORK

Opposite
Costume design for a Temple dancer in
Le Dieu Bleu, 1912
430 × 280
SOTHEBY'S/MUSÉE NATIONAL D'ART MODERNE,
CENTRE GEORGES POMPIDOU, PARIS

This design was reproduced on the
cover of the Souvenir Programme of the
seventh season of the Ballets Russes. A
variation, dated 1922, in different
colours is in the Robert L. B. Tobin
Collection

"DIEU BLEU"
PELERIN

BAKST
1911

Costume design for a Pilgrim in *Le Dieu Bleu*, 1912
282 × 228
THYSSEN-BORNEMISZA COLLECTION

This design is dated 1911. Bakst sold this design at the Fine Art Society and had to make another before the ballet was ready

indeed perched on top of some great height, and the crude, garish colours straight away suggested the fierce and furious passion of the action.

In 1916 when the Ballets Russes company returned from their tour of America in the *Dante Alighieri* to Cadiz, a case containing the scenery of *Thamar* fell into the harbour. According to Grigoriev, 'by the time it was fished out of the sea, water had soaked all the canvas and ruined it beyond repair.' But Polunin described salvaging it: ' . . . when the scenes were unfolded in the studio they not only proved to be damp, but the whole area of the back-cloth and a part of the cut-cloth were seen to be covered with enormous spots from two or three yards in diameter. The scene for *Thamar*, like nearly all the settings designed by Bakst, consisted of minutely patterned cloths which added considerably to the difficulty of removing the blemishes mentioned. All the tones had to be renewed step by step, irrespective of their durability. When *Thamar* was lighted, the reflection from a fire-place reached the silver setting of an ikon, producing a beautiful effect which caused Diaghileff to remark that what Bakst had sought for so long had at last been found.'

But as with so many revivals of Diaghilev's ballets, especially after his death and long after Bakst had any control over them, Beaumont (1946) found by the late 30s a depressing lowering of artistic standards in their production. 'Those who have seen only the post-War [he means the First World War] performances of *Thamar* will have little idea of its first tragic beauty. Like so many revivals of Diaghilev ballets, it has shed its original atmosphere. Nowadays, there seems to be a vulgar clamour for more and more light, and so the setting is shown in a crude glare unknown to the Diaghilev Ballet of pre-War years. That glare banishes every suggestion of the drama and mystery so essential to certain ballets.'

No-one is definite about whether it was Diaghilev, Nijinsky or Bakst who first thought of making a ballet from Debussy's *Prélude à L'Après-midi d'un Faune* to the eclogue by Stéphane Mallarmé. As with a number of other ballets (and as with so much in the theatre) the genesis for this one was probably conversations between the three of them discussing various ideas. What is clear, however, is that Diaghilev, having become disenchanted with Fokine as choreographer, was hoping to replace him with Nijinsky. Furthermore, Diaghilev was never an impresario who relied exclusively upon safe and tested productions but was, on the contrary, always restless to experiment and promote new artists. *L'Après-midi d'un Faune* was pivotal for the Ballets Russes.

Debussy, approached about having his prelude adapted for the stage, said 'Why?' but he agreed. Nijinsky first began to work on his ballet in the autumn of 1910. So-called 'unofficial' rehearsals (to keep them a secret from Fokine) began in Berlin in January 1912 and then continued in Monte Carlo. Igor Stravinsky in his *Autobiography* (1936) sounds plausible about the ballet's creation: 'Diaghileff made up his mind that year that he would spare no effort to make a choreographer of Nijinsky . . . his idea was to make Nijinsky compose, under his own strict supervision, a sort of antique tableau conjuring up the erotic gambols of a faun importuning

4ᵉ ANNÉE.- Nᵒ 17   1ᵉʳ JUIN 1912   NUMÉRO EXCEPTIONNEL de 60 PAGES. 8 HORS-TEXTES en COULEUR. PRIX: 2 FRANCS

Comœdia Illustré

Mᵐᵉ KARSAVINA et Mʳ BOLM dans   THAMAR.

Trichromie Comœdia Illustré   Costumes dessinés par Léon BAKST.

Opposite
Tamara Karsavina and Adolph Bolm in
Thamar from the cover of *Comoedia
Illustré*, 1 June 1912

nymphs. At the suggestion of Bakst, who was obsessed by ancient Greece, this tableau was to be presented as an animated bas-relief, with the figures in profile. Bakst dominated this production. Besides creating the decorative setting and the beautiful costumes, he inspired the choreography even to the slightest movements.'

According to Nijinsky there were 60 rehearsals for the ten minute work, Bronislava Nijinska said there were 80, Romola said 120. She generally exaggerated but in this case her arithmetic was supported by Arnold Haskell and Walter Nouvel. Before the first performance on 29 May, Diaghilev said to Bronislava Nijinska: 'I have never seen Bakst so enthusiastic. Levushka said the *L'Après-midi d'un Faune* is a "super-genius" creation and that we are all fools not to have understood it.' The programme note, by Jean Cocteau, read: 'A faun dozes,

Characters in *Thamar*, 1912 from the
Souvenir Programme

Set design for *Thamar*, 1912
740 × 860
MUSÉE DES ARTS DÉCORATIFS, PARIS

Bakst copied his own design later. It was the first Ballets
Russes ballet that Cyril Beaumont saw and he never
forgot his first impression: 'I can still recall the mood
established by that scene. It was just as though some
terrible menace had been halted, leaving behind a
perceptible tenseness which suggested that the threat
was about to be renewed . . . That scene has always
remained in my mind as an object lesson of the immense
value of restraint, for, used with taste and skill, there are
few qualities so telling in a ballet.'

Costume design for Maid-Servants in *Thamar*, 1912
270 × 255
SOTHEBY'S/PRIVATE COLLECTION

Bakst gave this design to Gabriel Astruc, the French
impressario, who first presented the Ballets Russes in
Paris. The note specifies that the veil should be of fine silk

Scene in *L'Après-midi d'un Faune* from a double page spread in *Comoedia Illustré*, 15 May 1912

Nymphs tease him. A forgotten scarf satisfies his dream. The curtain descends so that the poem can begin in everyone's memory.' The final moment of the ballet, when Nijinsky as the Faun made love to the scarf, scandalized the audience. At the first night Diaghilev mistook the boos for cheers and ordered the ballet to be repeated immediately.

The set (p. 150) was a painted cloth of a Grecian landscape in autumnal colours, described by Louis Schneider in *Comoedia* as 'something like a primitive tapestry, rather than a realistic evocation ... With rare good fortune M. Léon Bakst has realized that atmosphere which brings out the 'thickly wooded sleep' of the Faun ... he has imagined the "beautiful country" perfectly. In this deep forest where we know that the burning light of mid-day has made its mark, there is something better than colour, there is reverie, rhythmic clarity, an exact transcription of the spoken word into the language of sounds.' Nijinsky was apparently not pleased with the scenery thinking it too oppressive but Diaghilev and Bakst disagreed. The problem was that at first the cloth was hung only two metres back from the proscenium arch which created difficulties for the dancers who had hardly any room for their movements.

Nijinsky's costume for the Faun was an extraordinary creation. Nothing could be further from the animal and yet Bronislava Nijinska thought that the whole effect was 'the very image of an adolescent faun, a young being half animal, half human. In the costume, as in Nijinsky's expression, one could not define where the human ended and the animal began.' Once again Nijinsky somehow managed to imbue a simple costume with supernatural powers, but at the same time Bakst knew that he could and therefore kept his costume simple.

There were seven Nymphs. They wore no tights and were naked under their costumes. Modelled on the Greek peplum, the costumes were sleeveless diaphanous dresses of finely pleated gauze bordered at the hem with tiny squares or wavy lines of blue or dull red, the white overskirt being decorated also with wavy lines, bands of ivy leaves or dots of the same colour as the squares. The motifs were variations on the standard decoration developed by Bakst for his 'Greek-style' costumes. The Nymphs also wore tightly fitting wigs made of cord painted gold with Grecian locks falling to their waists. Bakst made a number of different costume designs for the Nymphs but they do not all correspond to the photographs of the finished costumes of which there were three matching pairs and a single different one for Nelidova, the First Nymph. Bakst was again most particular about the make-up of the dancers, designed it for them, told them how to apply it and even painted their eyes himself whitish-pink to look 'like those of a pigeon'.

Diaghilev had not only got bored by *Daphnis and Chloë*, the last new production of the season, but seemed to want to obstruct Fokine, the choreographer, in every way. Fokine bitterly recalled in his memoirs that Diaghilev did everything to cancel *Daphnis and Chloë*, first by saying that the old *Narcisse* costumes had to be used, then by interfering with rehearsals, and finally by scheduling the first performance as a curtain raiser starting half an hour earlier than usual. Indeed, the first night was postponed from 5 to 8 June but, after a furious row with Diaghilev, Fokine managed to persuade him to change the running order so that *Schéhérazade* came first and *Daphnis and Chloë* was not performed to an empty auditorium. The ballet, in three scenes, was the first act only of the same ballet which Fokine had written in 1904. The first and third scenes were the same, an idyllic grove of cypresses sacred to Pan and his Nymphs; the second scene, in a completely different colour scheme, was the pirates' camp in a clearing surrounded by orange-brown rocks. Louis Schneider in *Comoedia* thought that the sets did not 'summarize the action, but determined the meaning, the atmosphere and the character; and, what is more, the one was in contrast with the other. Thus the painter with his palette has realized the tryptych dreamt of by the choreographer and the composer.'

Critics, unaware of the behind-the-scenes row which was going on between Fokine and Diaghilev, probably made matters worse by praising the production.

In spite of favourable notices Fokine resigned from the company immediately after the curtain came down and *Daphnis and Chloë* was only performed twice in 1912. Fokine revived it with his own company at the Opéra in Paris in 1921; Diaghilev revived it with a new costume for Daphnis designed by Juan Gris in Monte Carlo in 1924; Bakst's set for scene one was used by Diaghilev for *The Gods Go A-Begging*, the ballet to Handel's music, in 1928.

Bakst's last production in 1912 was *Salomé* for Ida Rubinstein. Without the censor and without the interference of the church she was finally able to perform the words of Oscar Wilde's play although, by all accounts, her performance would again have been more

Set design for *L'Après-midi d'un Faune*, 1912
750 × 1050
MUSÉE NATIONAL D'ART MODERNE, CENTRE GEORGES POMPIDOU,
PARIS

Vaslav Nijinsky as the Faun and Bronislava
Nijinska as a Nymph in *L'Après-midi d'un
Faune*, 1912
BIBLIOTHÈQUE NATIONALE, MUSÉE DE L'OPÉRA, PARIS

Portrait of Vaslav Nijinsky as the Faun in
L'Après-midi d'un Faune, 1912
400 × 270
WADSWORTH ATHENEUM, HARTFORD, ELLA GALLUP
SUMNER AND MARY CATLIN SUMNER COLLECTION

This was used for the cover of *Comoedia Illustré*,
15 May 1912. There is a photograph of Bakst
painting a larger version of it in about 1922. A
lithograph was also made at about this time

Costume design for Shepherdesses in
Daphnis and Chloë, 1912
265 × 210

Here Bakst is economizing with his
drawings. The two girls were first drawn
for *Daphnis and Chloë* as is testified by the
names of the dancers Choklova,
Bonietska, Ezerska and Banetska written
on the back. In fact their costumes,
reminiscent of those for *L'Après-midi
d'un Faune*, were nothing like this design
and, with total economy, were never
made. Bakst subsequently used the
same design, as can be seen from the
inscription, for two Maid-servants in
Phaedre in 1923. He also copied both
figures, especially the figure on the left,
several times for other designs.
Sometimes the figures are mirror images
of each other. All the copies and
variations have the same shorthand in
face, no hands, and big toe widely
separated from the rest of the curious
foot

effective had she not spoken them. At the first performance some of the audience began to tit-
ter and de Max, playing Herod, approached the footlights and, according to a report by Ves-
tris in *Comoedia*, said: 'Ladies and gentlemen, Miss Rubinstein and I are going through an
awesome moment and we cannot continue if there is any more imbecilic laughter.' De Max
silenced the audience.' Evgeny Tugendhold, in *Studia*, deeply moved, dwelt on Rubinstein's
appearance: '. . . Her thin, pale face and thick, black curls and large pearl ear-rings and oriental kaftanesque costume, into which the whole talent of Bakst was poured, her thin legs,
naked to the waist, her snakelike grace, and the very timbre of her voice – all this was amazingly distinctive.' One wonders sometimes if people have seen the same show.

Newspapers and magazines of the time devoted much more space to theatre criticism
than now, but even so, many critics, when reviewing productions designed by Bakst, generalized about his work and persisted in using adjectives like 'sumptuous' to describe it. The
daily newspaper *Comoedia* was an exception even then, devoting more than a whole page to
the different aspects of a production. A regular feature was Louis Schneider's serious column
'La mise en scène et les décors' ('Staging and design'). After describing Bakst's work for
Salomé he wrote that the most remarkable thing was that: '. . . he does not limit his realism to
a simple materialisation, to colours only for an outward appearance; his lines, colours and
shapes express a profound thought, the inner aspect of a period and people . . . He cares less
for an accuracy of detail than for a general exactitude. A work which is based on too strict a
documentation becomes a study picture, a valuable piece of information, but it ceases to be a
work of art . . . M. Léon Bakst instinctively possesses inexhaustible resources of evocation; it
seems as if he must recall having once lived in some voluptuous Orient; it seems as if the ves-
tiges of some primitive spirit reside in his contemporary heart and he continues to see the
mysterious dazzlement of ancient suns.'

Schneider knew what Bakst was trying to do but not every critic or writer was either so
understanding or so flattering. Edward Gordon Craig, philosopher of the theatre with revolutionary ideas about theatre design some of which he was about to put into practice with
Stanislavsky at the Moscow Art Theatre in a production of *Hamlet*, was the editor of the
periodical *The Mask* and wrote most of it himself under sixty-six pseudonymns. His was one of
the very few voices at the time almost perversely condemning the Russian Ballet and Bakst.
In 1912, as John Balance, Craig 'contributed' an article to *The Mask* in which he wrote: 'M.
Bakst has a pretty knack of drawing coloured supplements and covers for the illustrated papers. Although the designs are ugly they are only ugly enough to shock Parisians. . . Bakst is
ugly on account of his clumsy sense of the sensual. All his women . . . are drugged and in a
kind of sofa orgy. They seem to hate ecstasy and they adore a good wriggle.

Bakst has a passion for beads, and his evidently sincere devotion to thick lips and flat
noses enables him to indulge in a ring or two now and again.

The women he draws protrude; therefore when he attempts to suggest something Indian

Costume design for Tamara Karsavina
as Chloë in *Daphnis and Chloë*, 1912
285 × 510
WADSWORTH ATHENEUM, HARTFORD, ELLA
GALLUP SUMNER AND MARY CATLIN SUMNER
COLLECTION

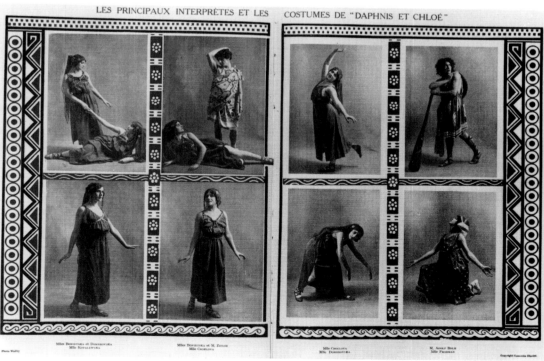

Characters in *Daphnis and Chloë*, 1912
from *Comoedia Illustré*

Set design for scenes 1 and 3 in *Daphnis
and Chloë*, 1912
740 × 1035
MUSÉE DES ARTS DÉCORATIFS, PARIS

Opposite
Costume design for a Maiden in *Daphnis
and Chloë*, 1912
270 × 226
PRIVATE COLLECTION

BAKST
1912

Left
Edouard de Max as Herod in *Salomé*,
1912, from *Comoedia Illustré*

Right
Costume design for Roger Karl as
Iokaanan in *Salomé*, 1912
270 × 180
SOTHEBY'S/PRIVATE COLLECTION

Below
Characters in *Salomé*, 1912, from
Comoedia Illustré

LES INTERPRÈTES ET LES COSTUMES DE "SALOMÉ"

Photos Waléry   Esclaves
Esclaves d'Hérodias   Le page d'Hérodias (M. DALT)
Juifs   Hérodias (Mme Odette de FEHL)
Esclaves   Ambassadeurs de César
Soldats   Copyright Comodia Illustré.

or Chinese (and Russian Ballets are wedded to the East), he gets curiously confused. Indians and Chinese hate that which bulges. Bakst adores bulge; . . . it helps his beads so much. In short Bakst is vulgar . . .

On the stage Bakst is not vulgar, he is simply lost.

His designs for *La Péri* and *Narcisse* are charming in the magazines; in actuality they are non-existent. No one has seen them on the stage. This is an oversight on his part for which he can hardly be held responsible for he has the misfortune to be an amateur, and in amateur theatricals these accidents always happen.

Many of his designs for costumes have lately been published, but to his eternal undoing photographs of these same costumes have been published at the same time. These photographs give M. Bakst away, for the designs and the photographs are unlike each other, and the stage with which he has merely flirted opens its artificial arms for a last embrace. M. Bakst is dead.

The stage does not like philanderers . . . and M. Bakst was a philanderer. R.I.P.'

But Gordon Craig was alone. Bakst was certainly not dead but by the end of the season he was exhausted and wrote to his wife: 'It is a tumultuous, complicated and confusing season. I am sick and tired of everything, and I do not even read what they write about me. I just wish everyone would leave me alone, and let me spend three or four months in total silence and monotony . . . I want to sketch, sleep ten hours at a time every day, and not rush anywhere!'

But by the end of the year Bakst had recovered for on 24 December 1912 he wrote to his wife: 'Diaghilev and Nijinsky have arrived and I am going with them today to Debussy who will play us his new ballet *Les Jeux* . . . I am pleased that I have arranged Steinberg's ballet with Seriozha. I do not know when he will put it on. It has not been decided. Diaghilev has entrusted me with the Polish part of *Boris Godunov*, *Les Jeux* by Debussy, *Danse Oiseuse* [*The Firebird pas de deux*] by Tchaikovsky and a lot of other things.' In the end, Bakst only designed *Jeux* and the Polish scene from *Boris Godunov* in 1913; 'Steinberg's ballet' *Midas* was postponed for a year.

The Ballets Russes 1913 season in Paris took place in the newly built Théâtre des Champs-Elysées, the ceiling of which had been decorated by Maurice Denis, one of Bakst's heroes. Diaghilev had impatiently over-burdened Nijinsky with the responsibility of choreographing two new ballets, *Jeux* and *Le Sacre du Printemps*, whose French title had been suggested by Bakst and always preferred by Stravinsky as being closer to his meaning than the English *The Rite of Spring*. Nijinsky paid more attention to *Le Sacre du Printemps* than to *Jeux* even though it began the season on 15 May. A Young Man (Nijinsky) in curious tennis clothes runs on to the stage chasing an unnaturally large tennis ball. He is followed by two Young Girls (Karsavina and Schollar). They flirt, and play hide and seek. Suddenly another tennis ball arrives. For some reason it frightens the trio and they run away. The scene is a garden at dusk next to

Set design for *Salomé*, 1912
459×625
ASHMOLEAN MUSEUM, OXFORD

Opposite
'Fantasy on a Modern Costume', 1912
445×280
SOTHEBY'S/PRIVATE COLLECTION

Bakst said: 'A woman's dress is my most cherished dream. In spite of my many productions for the theatre, every morning, when I wake up, I create one or two dresses with which I adorn, sometimes in my imagination, sometimes in actual fact, elegant women with beautiful bodies.' He made a series of drawings

called 'Fantasies on Modern Costume at the end of 1912, beginning of 1913. Exquisitely drawn, delicately sensual, these pretty pin-up girls with modest sex-appeal dressed in adaptations of contemporary fashion were gentle fantasies and were given the names of Greek godesses and nymphs, 'Nike,' 'Atalante,' 'Alcyone' or fashionable seaside resorts like 'Deauville.' The dresses were made up by Madame Paquin, the hats by Camille-Roger, the footwear by Hellstern and the ensembles were launched at the end of March 1913

a tennis court and the action is supposed to take place in the near future, in 1920. The first idea included an aeroplane moving across the back of the stage. It was not a romantic garden, but one full of a sense of foreboding before a storm, larger than life. Nijinsky had wanted something not so overpowering. He had wanted to confine this ballet within a smaller space but the dancers had to fight unnecessarily against the weight of the set. Bakst's costumes were his only attempt at futurism and they were obviously not successful as Marie Rambert remembered in her memoirs *Quicksilver* (1972) : 'Nijinsky leapt on to the stage wearing Bakst's idea of the sports costume for a tennis-player: hideous long shorts almost down to his knees and making his legs look very thick (we were used to tights which softened the line), thick socks half way up his legs, and to top it all ... a red wig.

Diaghilev was appalled, and started shouting at Bakst, "He can't go on like that, Lyovushka!"

And Bakst shouted back, "How dare you say he can't go on, Seryozha? It's designed, and it's made, and it's going to go on."

And so they went on slanging one another ...

"I won't alter a stitch, Seryozha," yelled Bakst.

Set design for *Jeux*, 1913
Pencil on paper laid on canvas,
740 × 1040
ROBERT L.B. TOBIN COLLECTION, MARION
KOOGLER MCNAY ART MUSEUM, SAN ANTONIO

In his pencil drawing, with the tiny figure holding the ball against the backdrop of the massive trees and anonymous building, Bakst created a most threatening atmosphere

Vaslav Nijinsky in *Jeux* by Léon Bakst
BIBLIOTHÈQUE NATIONALE, MUSÉE DE L'OPÉRA, PARIS

A portrait of Nijinsky in practice clothes, but Boris Kochno identified it as Nijinsky in the ballet and Marie Rambert's story about the costumes substantiates the identification

"All right, Lyovushka," replied Diaghilev. "But they are not going to appear in these costumes."

So he sent the women ... to Paquin, the great couturier, who made them very pretty white skirts and jerseys. And for Nijinsky, Diaghilev simply said that he should wear his own hair, a white shirt with the sleeves rolled up, and trousers caught at the ankles and leaving the foot free, such as were used at the Mariinsky for classes and rehearsals, only made of white cloth instead of black.' Diaghilev got his way but Bakst made a spirited sketch of Nijinsky in practice clothes. Diaghilev's efforts at modernity and his fostering of Nijinsky as choreographer were unrewarded. The originality of *Jeux* was dismissed as being 'mere stupidity.' Stupid criticism, however, is a hazard all artists suffer, but fortunately ignore.

After the enormous success in 1908 of Chaliapin in the title role in *Boris Godunov*, Diaghilev decided to bring a new production to Paris. For his set for the Polish scene Bakst used the monumental sculpture of Neptune by Giambologna from the park of Pratolino, the estate outside Florence which belonged to the Demidoffs and which Bakst must have visited. The costumes, as usual, were described as being 'sumptuous'. They were more than that. Costumes for opera are different from costumes for ballet. As they do not have to be danced in, they can be richer, heavier and many-layered. Bakst used this production to display an opulent medievalism.

During the period 1910–14 Bakst made many designs for the opera singers Dimitri Smirnov and Maria Kousnezoff in which they appeared in various productions in Russia and France. A completely designed opera production was still something of an innovation. Actors and singers often travelled with large trunks of their own costumes, armour, props, and wigs.

A completely different opera from *Boris Godunov* was *Il Segreto di Susanna* which Bakst designed for the Royal Opera House, Covent Garden. The set was a simple room on a diagonal perspective. (He repeated the formula for the set of Stravinsky's *Mavra* in 1922.) Although it was not a very important commission for Bakst it was an imaginative one for the management of the opera house. It showed that they were prepared to go to some trouble and expense to produce as well as they could a work which was not the primary attraction of the evening. As *The Times* noticed on 21 May 1913: '... *Il Segreto di Susanna* was being sung and acted with delicious froth and freshness by Signor Sammarco and Miss Nielsen ... *Il Segreto di Susanna*, moreover, was furnished with a new scene by M. Léon Bakst, a beautiful triangular room in blue and white; but all this was merely a prelude to the event of Signor Caruso's reappearance in a part in which he first made his mark here in 1904, that of Canio in *Pagliacci*.'

For her Gala performances at the Théâtre du Châtelet in 1913 Ida Rubinstein staged another play by d'Annunzio. She again gathered round her the most distinguished theatrical talents in order to ensure maximum publicity and success for her enterprise: Meyerhold as director, Fokine as choreographer, Bakst as designer. She also commissioned a score from Ildebrando

BOTIS GODOUNOU
POLONAIS

Opposite
Costume design for a Polish Officer in *Boris Godunov*, 1913
263 × 210

Set design for the Prologue of *La Pisanelle ou La Mort Parfumée*, 1913 from *Comoedia Illustré*, 20 June 1913

This set, with minor changes, was also used for Act 3
(see p. 165)

Décor du 1er Acte. — Le Port de Famagouste, maquette originale de M. Léon BAKST

Set design for Act I of *La Pisanelle ou La Mort Parfumée*, 1913 from
Comoedia Illustré, 20 June 1913

The scene in Act I of *La Pisanelle ou La Mort Parfumée*, 1913 from
Comoedia Illustré, 20 June 1913

Set design for Act 2 of *La Pisanelle ou La Mort Parfumée*, 1913
268 × 400
MUSEUM OF FINE ARTS, BOSTON, GIFT OF
L. AARON LEBOWICH

The scene in Act 3 of *La Pisanelle ou La Mort Parfumée*, 1913 from *Comoedia Illustré*, 20 June 1913

Pizzetti (or Ildebrando da Parma as d'Annunzio called him) and engaged Inghelbrecht to conduct it. There were 212 actors in the cast including her regular leading man Edouard de Max. The public dress rehearsal was on 10 June and there were ten performances. The publicity was colossal, the success was doubtful and Ida Rubinstein underwrote the deficit of a quarter of a million francs.

Meant to be a comedy with a serious theme of redemption through Christian love, *La Pisanelle ou La Mort Parfumée*, turned out to be another ludicrous extravaganza. The action takes place in Cyprus in the Middle Ages. Bakst set the atmosphere of the play and maintained the decorative continuity with a series of curtains behind a permanent, decoratively painted, false proscenium which acted as a constant visual frame for the changing sets behind, and which he had already used for *Le Martyre de Saint Sébastien* (p. 122). A patterned and painted floor cloth was also a permanent fixture, even, incongruously, for the exterior set of the port of Famagusta. The first curtain was black and gold with decorative medallions and the Greek word 'ichtys' (symbol for Jesus Christ). This was followed by a purple curtain which opened to reveal a set for the Prologue with dark blue shining, as if enamelled, walls painted with indistinct figures of saints, like icons with Byzantine faces clothed in emerald and gold. At the back of the stage, through an arch, there was a view into a vineyard. The scene for Act One, in distorted perspective, monochrome but bathed in crimson light as if predicting doom and blood, was the port of Famagusta. The scene for Act Two was a convent. The calm of the scene was expressed by a flat, grey-green wall across the whole of the stage, broken occasionally by small windows, with the height being emphasized by the stylized trunks and leaves of tall trees. The action was concentrated round the focal point of the well, centre stage. Act Three was in the same set as the Prologue but with different, gaudier lighting. During an orgy of dancing and singing, Pisanella is suffocated under a mass of blood red roses.

Bakst had to achieve some cohesion out of this pot-pourri and managed it with sets and costumes that were applauded by the audience when the curtain rose. He matched the drawing of his set designs to the mood he wanted to create: the design for the Prologue and Act Three (p. 163) is rich and colourful whereas the designs for Acts One and Two (pp. 164 and 165) are pencil drawings for the monotone backdrops where colour was achieved by light. He also had to make a great many costume designs for this production and although they are mostly in his characteristic sketchy style they are very positive and show how the costumes should be made but only by a costumier who was used to working from his drawings.

Félix Duquesnel in *Le Théâtre* thought it was all too much: 'The production undoubtedly cost a lot of money. It is clear that no expense was spared on the sets and costumes. I heard choruses of approval, but I cannot add my voice to them. Their general effect is not as harmonious as for example those of *Kismet*. As for the sets, they are of the new school, and I must say that I prefer the old.' So much for Bakst, but at least, according to M. Duquesnel, Ida Rubinstein had nearly lost her Russian accent which made her performance bearable.

Costume design for Anna Pavlova in
Oriental Fantasy, 1913
480 × 330
THEATRE MUSEUM, LONDON

BALLET HINDOU
POUR A.PAVLOVA

BAKST
1913

N6

Although the audience, unlike this critic, applauded the sets and costumes, that was obviously all there was to applaud because this ridiculous play was never revived.

In the autumn Bakst renewed his collaboration with Anna Pavlova by designing for her the ballet *Oriental Fantasy* which was first performed at the London Opera House on 6 October. There were echoes in this ballet of both *Thamar* and *Schéhérazade*, and Pavlova intended to profit herself from their popularity by having her own version of an 'oriental' ballet in her repertoire. Bakst was the obvious choice for designer. He did not let her down and produced a thrilling variation of his *Schéhérazade* set in shades of yellow ochre, blue and silver, with great cushions, carpets, hanging lanterns and drapes festooned from the ceiling enclosing the space to make it like a claustrophobic lair. Bakst had written to his friend Svetlov about Pavlova's partner, Novikoff that he 'advised against letting [him] out more often because he is rather clumsy and, more important, not of a very attractive build.' But the audience loved it all.

After London Pavlova went on a tour of the United States and just as London had first seen Bakst's work in Pavlova's *Les Amours de Diane* and *Danse Bacchanale* in 1910 so now America first saw his work at the Metropolitan in New York in *Orientale* (as *Oriental Fantasy* had been retitled for the American tour). This ballet is also sometimes confusingly called *Les Orientales* and Bakst himself, to add to the confusion, titled some of his costume designs for it *Ballet Hindou*. Bakst's great reputation had, however, already crossed the Atlantic. He designed the cover of *Harper's Bazar* for October 1913, and on the contents page there was a photograph of him with an announcement about *Orientale* and the first exhibition of his designs the following year in New York. May Tevis, reviewing the exhibition for *The Theatre Magazine* wrote perceptively: 'One of the most observable things . . . is his dependence for his most striking effects on schemes of three strong colors, such as red, blue, and yellow.

And though these schemes are diversified by more or less intricate details in the use of ornaments and the patterning of fabrics, such details are always carefully subordinate to the main impression.

This main impression, moreover, is not merely intensified by simplicity, but made more salient by deliberate *exaggeration*.

Thus Bakst proves himself, in spite of his careful historic studies, a true son of his own era, and strongly influenced by the tenets of Post impressionism.' It is always too easy to attach labels. Bakst's combination of colours is his own.

Vaslav Nijinsky married Romola de Pulsky on 10 September 1913 in Buenos Aires. The news was a devastating blow to Diaghilev who, later using the excuse of Nijinsky's non-appearance in Rio de Janeiro, had a telegram sent to him saying that his services were no longer required. Nijinsky now signed a contract with Alfred Butt, the owner of the Palace Theatre in London, to appear there with his own company for a period of eight weeks in the spring of 1914. He immediately approached Bakst to design scenery and costumes. But Bakst refused to work for Nijinsky. Although Bakst, too, quarrelled with Diaghilev and was often infuriated by him because he was so unreliable, he now maintained his first loyalty, and besides he must have thought it would be safer working for him than for Nijinsky. Events, however, did not turn out as he thought.

On 27 November 1913 *Teatr* published an interview with Diaghilev when he announced that the 1914 season in Paris would include two new ballets, *Joseph and his wife Pentephria*, as it was then called, composed by Richard Strauss with costumes designed by Bakst, and *Metamorphoses* (based on Ovid's poems) composed by Maximilian Steinberg with set and costumes, as well as the libretto, by Bakst. Diaghilev said that Bakst's intention was not to present the Greece of classical tragedy but the Greece of the present day with 'a hint of humour'. Diaghilev had to find a new choreographer to replace Nijinsky and eventually persuaded Fokine to return to the company.

The year 1913 ended for Bakst on 23 December at the London Hippodrome with the first performance of the revue *Hullo, Tango!*. Bakst designed only the striking costumes, not quite fashion, not quite fancy dress, and this was his one production in a contemporary setting (p. 170). It was generally acknowledged that to have engaged him was a coup. *The Tatler* (7 Jan) which reproduced four designs reported that 'The Hippodrome paid a very large figure to secure his services, and the result has justified its enterprise', and that the drawings show the method adopted by Bakst 'which is elaborated by very precise and detailed notes as to colour, cut, and material.' It was Albert de Courville, one of the co-authors and producer of the revue, who had the imagination to engage Bakst for this unique production of his career. Although he probably did not expect the costumes to cost as much as they did he remained impressed, as he wrote in his memoirs *I Tell You* (1928), both by Bakst's methods and by his firmness in defining the financial basis of the engagement: ' . . . he designed the whole of the costumes for my second revue, *Hullo, Tango!*, and . . . charged the highest prices for his designs. Not only did he charge as much as £50 for a design for a dress, but he also insisted on his sketches being returned after they had been executed, because his paintings had a value of their own and fetched big prices.

Another condition he made was that every costume should be made by a special dressmaker in Paris, who, he said, was the only one who understood his peculiar type of work.

He took more trouble than most designers, for he went over to Paris, picked out all the materials and arranged in the actual workshops how the costumes were to be made. The result was extremely satisfactory.'

The press, too, applauded the results. The critic of the *Daily Graphic* wrote: 'The dresses are more than gorgeous, and M. Léon Bakst has brought his taste for bizarre arrangements for primary colours to bear on some of them . . . This revue is certainly topical, and is the most genuine form of the new invasion that has yet been seen in London.'

Right
Costume design for Ethel Levey in the
Cake Walk in *Hullo, Tango!*, 1913
280 × 235
SOTHEBY'S/PRIVATE COLLECTION

The design is dated 1914 and is therefore
presumably a copy of a previous
drawing because Ethel Levey was
wearing the costume by the time the
show opened on 23 December 1913

Below
Ethel Levey in *Hullo, Tango!* from
The Tatler, 7 January 1914
BRITISH LIBRARY

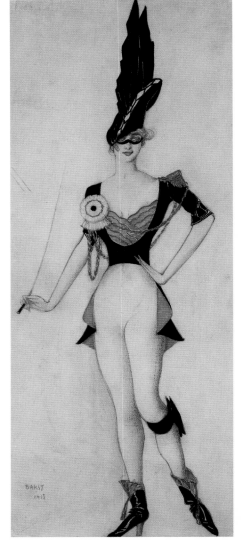

Above
Costume design, 'Costume Eccentric', for *Hullo,
Tango!*, 1913
437 × 184
SOTHEBY'S/PRIVATE COLLECTION

Opposite
Costume design for Maria Kousnezoff as
Potiphar's wife in *La Légende de Joseph*,
1914
482 × 330
THE FINE ARTS MUSEUMS, SAN FRANCISCO

Bakst could always dazzle. The costumes were an extension to the 'fantasies on modern costume' (p. 159) he had done earlier in the year. But he was not a fashion designer and, contrary to the headline in *The Tatler*, Bakst was not at his best here.

The Legend of Joseph was the only ballet Bakst worked on in Diaghilev's 1914 season and he only designed the costumes. Louis Schneider began his description in *Comoedia*: 'Léon Bakst's costumes are a true discovery: a symphony of mauve, green and blackish-brown singing in the decor.' It was the first ballet composed by Richard Strauss and marked the debut of Léonide Massine. Diaghilev had high hopes for it. With choreography by Fokine it was first performed after a revival of *Papillons* on 14 May 1914 at the Opéra in Paris. The 'legend' was the biblical story of the contrast between the opulence of Potiphar's court and the pastoral simplicity of the life led by the shepherd Joseph. The critics liked it, but Diaghilev was disappointed by it as were the audiences; there was more mime than dancing and the public was beginning to tire of over-lavish luxury. In January Bakst had published an article in *Peterburgskaya Gazeta* expressing his view of contemporary theatre that 'no-one wants to listen any more, everyone wants to see,' and although he was really referring to the anticipated take-over of the theatre by the silent cinema he still thought that the theatre should be truly spectacular. That is probably why *The Legend of Joseph* was set incongruously in the Venice of Paolo Veronese in about 1530: the designers adopted that artist's convention of depicting biblical scenes in luxurious style. The set, which appeared to be made of gold, was by the Spanish painter José-Maria Sert, husband of Diaghilev's great friend Misia. Bakst's costumes in blazing, undiluted colours were the most ostentatious he ever designed but the two designers obviously did not plan their work together because the costumes did not harmonize with the setting as perfectly as when Bakst was himself responsible for both. In London, Karsavina, wearing extra built-up Venetian clogs, played the role of Potiphar's wife (p. 171). Charles Ricketts gave a vivid description in a letter to Gordon Bottomley: 'If the Russians had not been the inspired interpreters of the thing, it would have been intolerable and fatuous. Karsavina as Potiphar's wife was superb. A creature of gold and marble at the start, her sinister repelling of the begging dancer was evil but passionless; it suggested the avoidance of something unclean. When she strangled herself with her pearl necklace, the act was spontaneous and spasmodic like a moth meeting a flame.' After London, Diaghilev withdrew the ballet from the repertoire, but when it was performed from time to time in Germany and Austria Strauss would send Karsavina 'dictatorial telegrams to come and play the part.'

Metamorphoses, retitled *Midas* in 1914, was to have been a new production for Bakst but because of illness he was replaced by Mstislav Dobuzhinsky. This ballet, too, met with no success and was withdrawn after its performances in London. But Bakst did accept the commission from the management of Covent Garden to design the sets for Boito's *Mefistofele* which was performed on 26 June. The management was praised for its enterprise, although the *Westminster Gazette* wrote that a 'difficulty about the Bakst scenery in the case of ordinary operas is that it requires the Bakst costumes and accessories if the total effect is to be free from incongruity.' Critics then were more perceptive about whether opera productions were congruous or incongruous than the audiences who seemed neither to notice nor to care very much. The anonymous critic of the *Pall Mall Gazette* devoted a whole paragraph to the settings and stage atmosphere created by the lighting: 'Mr Bakst ... displayed a new side of his art, for he gave us very little of his fantastic and abroad style, but surprised us with beautiful detail work. We did not appreciate his painting for the prologue; it suggested the North Pole rather than warmer regions; his lovely garden scene reminded us of a Claude Monet in its open-air quality. The Brocken was the sombre Bakst which we know something of already, while the shore of Peneus was in purest classic style, the whole being a study in misty grey and blues, with a real moon shining over it all. It was the first natural stage moon we have seen, and its brilliantly pure silver radiancy must surely be another discovery of Mr Bakst.' The critic does not describe how the effect was achieved technically but it must have been more subtle than with the crude use of colour filters and shows Bakst's inventiveness and persistent devotion to getting the best result.

The strain of so much work over such a long period was too much for Bakst. He collapsed into a nervous depression for several months but before shutting himself off from the world he managed to summon his sister from Russia to look after him. She arrived with her three daughters, one of whom remembers seeing Bakst sitting motionless in silent gloom in his studio staring into nothing. He was tenderly nursed into recovery, but then on their way back to Russia his sister and nieces were stopped in Germany by the outbreak of the First World War and returned to Paris. With Stravinsky's help Bakst found them somewhere to live in Switzerland and, by the end of the year, he was back in buoyant mood. He wrote to Misia Sert from Geneva: 'I am trying as hard as I can to avoid that filthy exploiter whose name is Serge.

Among other things, do you think he has paid me? Not on your life: he has only given me back what *I lent him*. But both he and his money disgust me. Especially after having sold a good many pictures in America during the summer (think of it!!!) I am in a position to throw money in his face!'

The exhibition in New York in 1913 and its subsequent tour of American cities during the first months of 1914 had been such a commercial success that a second exhibition was arranged in October. *The New York Times* defined the difference between painting pictures and working for the theatre: 'He still is working for the stage, however, still building up flat patterns on paper of what in his own mind he sees as three dimensional space hung with colored fabrics and enlivened by moving figures weaving in and out of light and shadow in a flow of rhythmic lines. The artist who works thus for the stage creating scenes that must be fulfilled by living men and women is in direct contrast to the artist who sees his subject made to his hand and may copy and select and recompose at will. The task of the former requires

Costume design for two negroes
in *La Légende de Joseph*, 1914
325 × 413
SOTHEBY'S/PRIVATE COLLECTION

This design, unsigned, was illustrated in
the Souvenir Programme for 1914 when
the red was very bright. It is one of the
rare examples of designs which Bakst
signed later and, uncharacteristically here
added his initial 'L', and the later date 1920

174

Costume design for Monsters in *Orphée*,
1914
245 × 310
PUSHKIN MUSEUM, MOSCOW

the kind of imagination that finds outlet in the field of higher mathematics.'

The realization of a successful theatre design is often like finding the solution to a mathematical problem and to a logistical one. But for Bakst 1914 was more a year of moral and physical problems.

The war, 'The Sleeping Beauty', the revolution: 1915–1918

1915 was also a lean year. No one thought the war would last. For the first time since 1909 there was no Ballets Russes season in Paris and there would not be another until 1917. In December 1915, however, Diaghilev arranged the only two performances that year in Geneva and Paris with two new ballets. Bakst wrote to his wife on 26 November (8 December) 1915 from Paris: '... Diaghilev is in a state. He is giving a gala performance at the Opéra on 28 December – in aid of the British Red Cross. There will be a new *Schéhérazade* (I have designed it rather differently – richer, stronger), then *The Enchanted Princess* – a short ballet to Tchaikovsky's music [*The Firebird pas de deux*] (my set and costumes) and *The Snow Maiden* (dances) – sets and costumes by Larionov. After the gala they are going to America (New York) from Bordeaux. I will not be going now, probably only at the end of February for two months.' On 26 December 1915 (6 January 1916) Bakst again wrote to his wife: 'The gala at the Opéra went off brilliantly. My new *Schéhérazade* and the new Indian set for the short ballet were a huge success. They dragged me on to the stage and gave me an ovation.' But Ilya Erenburg, writing in *Utro Rossii* (*Russian Morning*) on 12 January in his 'Letter from Paris,' had a different impression. He thought that *Schéhérazade* was boring and said that a sigh of relief went up in the audience 'when the 'Muscovite savage' Larionov replaced the European Bakst.' This was the first murmur of taste changing. Bakst had been thought 'savage' only a few years earlier but was now beginning to appear tame.

The war forced Diaghilev to make other plans for his company and he decided to take the Ballets Russes to America in 1916. The advance publicity was impressive and effective. Bakst, 'the real genius of the Ballet Russe', was the focus of attention by copywriters and journalists. The company was in the United States from 17 January until 29 April 1916, visited New York City twice and sixteen other cities. It went with fourteen ballets in its repertoire, eight of them designed by Bakst, but he did not travel across the Atlantic for fear of being torpedoed by submarines.

The Sleeping Beauty had haunted Bakst for years. In 1915 he was commissioned by James Rothschild to paint mural panels for his new house in Park Lane. Bakst could select the subject. His choice was significant for he chose *The Sleeping Beauty*. He was twenty-four when he first saw the ballet but his memory of seeing it is as if he was still a small boy:

> The ardently expected dress rehearsal of Tchaikovsky's *The Sleeping Beauty* fell upon a murky and cold November afternoon ... Before entering the auditorium, already swarming with people, custom ordained a visit to the stage-manager's room, where he – a veritable pasha, with his Methusalem-like white beard and a Persian cap on his head – smoked and drank his perpetual glass of tea in this club, wherein gathered the stars of the opera and the ballet...
>
> This visit has remained in my memory all my life ...

At the end of the sumptuous, Persian-carpeted room, through the crowd of dancers in daintily puffed-out skirts, I saw in outline two central figures, and, from the respectful distance kept by the artists, I gathered that they were personages of importance.

One of them – tall, slightly bent, with an aquiline nose, and a smile at once affable and sly, wore the Star of the Vladimir order on the left breast of the blue uniform he wore as director of the Imperial Theatres . . .

The other gentleman was shorter. His hair and beard were white, his complexion very pink, his manner shyly amiable. He appeared very nervous, but was making a visible effort to control himself.

'Who is it?' I sought to catch the eye of my old friend, who at last saw me (I was then far from tall), hemmed in among the frothy mass of fluttering ballet-skirts.

'Lovushka (Little Léon), come here and let me introduce you to our glory and pride, Piotr Ilytch Tchaikovsky.'

Blushing with emotion in my tight uniform as a student of the School of Fine Arts, but wearing white gloves – so smart, I thought – with my carroty, close-cropped hair, I must have looked funny. Boldly escaping from my pleasant prison, without hesitating, I stepped forward and held out my hand to the famous musician.

'Here he is,' continued the old regisseur 'this youngster adores the theatre and is already painting scenic designs. The other day, whilst telling some friends at tea about your *Sleeping Beauty*, he improvised scenery in his own way . . .'

'Ah! You already know my ballet?' laughingly said Tchaikovsky with surprise . . .

Unforgettable matinée! I lived in a magic dream for three hours, intoxicated with fairies and princesses, splendid palaces flowing with gold, in the enchantment of the old tale. My whole being was as if swayed in cadence to the rhythms, the radiant flow of refreshing and beautiful melodies, which were already friends . . .

That evening, I believe, my vocation was determined.'

Bakst's recollection of the dress rehearsal at the Mariinsky Theatre on 2 (15) January 1890 (not November) was printed in the programme of Diaghilev's production in 1921. This is often thought to be the first production outside Russia and Bakst's designs for it the zenith of his career. Not so. There had been a few performances at La Scala, Milan in 1896, and in 1916 Bakst designed *The Sleeping Beauty* for Pavlova in New York which because of its similarities to his later version was like a dress rehearsal for the 1921 production.

On 28 June 1916 the *New York Times* reported that Léon Bakst had accepted an offer from Charles Dillingham, the manager of the Hippodrome Theater in New York, to design the scenery and costumes for his next production scheduled for 4 September. On 30 July the same newspaper reported that Bakst 'will design the Hippodrome decorations in his Paris atelier and forward them by mail to be executed here.' It also said that 'the genius of this Slavic artist has done as much as any one agency to give impetus to the new decorative movement in the theater,' and forecast that 'perhaps by midwinter all Manhatten will be wearing bizarre costumes of ultra hues, reclining on mottled couches in vivid green, cerise and yellow rooms, smoking Russian cigarettes the while.'

New Yorkers had seen Bakst's work during the Ballets Russes tour so what did they imagine he was going to design for *The Sleeping Beauty*? Did Bakst realize that Charles Dillingham was producing something called *The Big Show* and planning to live up to the title? Dillingham's policy at the Hippodrome, with its capacity of 5,697 seats, was to produce 'the biggest show in the world at the lowest prices.' The first performance of *The Big Show* was on 31 August. There were two performances a day at 2.00pm and 8.15pm. The show was in three acts. Act One finished with The Mammoth Minstrels ('400–Count'Em–400'). Act Three was *The Merry Doll*, a new ice ballet from Berlin. Act Two was *The Sleeping Beauty*. It was forty minutes long.

A detailed anonymous scenario in French survives in the Dance Collection of the New York Public Library. Probably by the choreographer, Ivan Clustine, it both summarizes the action and is a precise brief to the designer. The whole production was to be 'in the pronounced style of Louis XIV' and it was 'highly desirable to retain the character of the children's fairy story, that is to say that the style should not kill the fantasy.' The set for the Prologue representing the interior of the Royal Palace 'must not be complicated. On the left there is an entrance for the King and Queen, and on the right, near the wall, there is a raised platform on which is the cradle with a canopy above.' The description is followed by a list of the characters taking part in the scene with a note that 'the Seven Good Fairies' costumes should be again fantastic or appropriate to their special character. The number of Fairies was later changed to eight with each having a symbolic colour: Beauty – Pink; Gracefulness – Lavender; Cleverness – Grey; Wisdom – Blue; Gentleness – Yellow; Goodness – Gold; Contentment – Rose; Happiness – White. The one Bad Fairy embodying jealousy, envy and malevolence, was green. The brief continues with Act One which should represent 'a sumptuous garden which goes right up to the steps leading to the Palace' which is on the right and the detail that 'we see only a terrace with steps down into the garden … in the style of the gardens of Versailles … Given that the dimensions of the stage are vast it is possible to have great depth and have several fountains playing water, and avenues of trees pruned as at Versailles. [The Hippodrome stage was half the size of a football pitch, 160 feet wide.]

On one side of the stage there should be something like a grotto, with water falling from above, forming a kind of curtain, behind which hides the Good Fairy to appear when the water stops flowing.

At the end of the act, when everyone falls asleep under the spell, the Good Fairy makes a forest grow which rises from different parts of the stage floor to cover the set.'

Anna Pavlova in *The Sleeping Beauty* in *The Big Show*, 1916, from the programme

Set design (preliminary drawing) for Act 5 in *The Sleeping Beauty*, 1916
240×425
SOTHEBY'S/PRIVATE COLLECTION

The final design, dated 1916, which was used both for *The Sleeping Beauty* in New York and *The Sleeping Princess* in London is in the Musée des Arts Décoratifs, Paris

The note about costumes includes a reminder that sixteen years have gone by: 'Also, the Four Princes should be dressed differently, one as an Oriental, the others as a Spaniard, Italian and Frenchman, and that as the French Prince has to dance he must have a more tight-fitting costume which does not interfere with his movements; and Princess Aurora, who dances classical steps, has to have a short dress.

Act Two was to be 'a huge forest ... lit by the setting sun. Soon the lighting changes. Moonlight.

(It has not yet been definitely decided, but maybe during this scene we will show a vision of the Princess asleep through the forest. In that case part of the forest will have to be made transparent which can easily be done by painting that part of the set on gauze. Behind the gauze we will therefore have to have a little set of the bed for the sleeping Princess around which there should be a huge bush of variously coloured roses forming a canopy over the bed.)

At the end of the act there is a Panorama which unrolls from one side of the stage to the other showing the different landscapes seen from the boat carrying the Fairy and Désiré.

At the end of the Panorama we see a corner of the Palace, and the sleeping hunters, horses, dogs, etc.

At the final moment, clouds come to cover the whole set giving time to change the scenery.

The costume for the vision of the Princess should be fantastical, in the nature of a long shirt in some silver material falling below the knees.

Act Three or Apotheosis: When the clouds disperse we see the Good Fairy and Désiré enter a dark room in the Palace covered with cob-webs.

The King, the Queen and all the Courtiers are sleeping in different positions on the furniture.

At the back of the room there are a few steps leading to an alcove.

The Good Fairy leads Désiré up to the steps and tells him to go in and wake the Princess.

As soon as Désiré touches the Princess the spell breaks.

There is a moment of darkness.

The curtains which represent the room go up and the stage shows a magnificent hall in the Palace or a garden full of flowers.

We will decide this later on.'

They decided on the 'magnificent hall' which Bakst preferred as a complement to the set for the Prologue. Bakst's brief was clear; in two months he had to do a lot of work. As well as five sets with all the extra scenic effects and props he had to design all the costumes and send the drawings to New York in time for them to be built and made. There were eleven principal

Costume design for Natalie Dagwell as the Queen and her Page in *The Sleeping Beauty*, 1916
300 × 455
SOTHEBY'S/PRIVATE COLLECTION

This is the original version of a design copied several times and adapted later for *The Sleeping Princess* (see pp. 210–11)

Set design for Scene I (Prologue) in *The Sleeping Beauty*, 1916
840×725
EVERGREEN HOUSE FOUNDATION, BALTIMORE

(See also p. 206) The similarities between the designs, sets as well as costumes, for *The Sleeping Beauty*, 1916, and *The Sleeping Princess*, 1921, have led to confusion. The earlier production is little known and the designs for it have been wrongly ascribed to the later and more famous one

Set design for the drop curtain of the Enchanted Castle in *The Sleeping Beauty*, 1916
660×520
EVERGREEN HOUSE FOUNDATION, BALTIMORE

Opposite
Costume design for M. Hubart as the Oriental Prince and his Page in *The Sleeping Beauty*, 1916
483×330
EVERGREEN HOUSE FOUNDATION, BALTIMORE

characters and 25 other named dancers, but the stage was so huge that every scene had to be filled out with crowds of extras. Bakst wrote to his wife on 2 July about 'the gigantic ballet in the mad style of Louis XIV with 400 people taking part.' Bakst did not choose the style but he exaggerated a little, there were about two hundred extras. He was greatly influenced by the theatrical designs of the Bibienas, especially Ferdinando (1657–1743) for the architectural scenery and Jean Bérain the elder (1640–1711), Jean-Baptiste Martin (1659–1735) and Louis Boquet (1717–1814), designers at the French court, for the seventeenth- and eighteenth-century costumes. A number of his designs at first glance appear to be copies of their work, but a second look reveals that Bakst has not imitated the original sources but interpreted them in his own grandiose fashion while remaining faithful to the spirit of the period (pp. 000 and 000). Many of the costume designs were subsequently refined and carried through to the later production of *The Sleeping Princess*.

His work as usual was not unappreciated although for the first time the full effect of Bakst's costumes against sets was dwarfed by the sheer size of the theatre. Heywood Broun wrote in the *New York Tribune* on 1 September: 'It is noteworthy that, for the first time, beauty has invaded the mammoth playhouse. There has been much that was novel and striking in various effects produced at the big theatre in previous years, but it has remained for Bakst to bring the beautiful. Strangely enough, not the scenery, but the costumes, are the triumphant feature of the work which the Russian artist has contributed to the Pavlova ballet.' The *New York Times* was much harsher. While generally liking the show, praising the minstrels and the pageant on ice, the critic wrote: 'The Pavlova ballet is a grievous disappointment. The quest of entertainment that will have a broad enough appeal to please 60,000 persons every week is a difficult quest, but if this ballet proves a weak spot in *The Big Show* it will not be because it is too rare for the multitude. It will be because it is not good enough ... The Bakst costumes – if not all the backgrounds – are brave in colour and lovely in design, but the ensembles are miscellaneous and undistinguished. The lighting is atrocious, the whole ballet sprawled without focus over an absurdly large area ... Perhaps it would be better to pitch *The Sleeping Beauty* into the scrap basket and let Pavlova and Volinine dance on a narrowed stage before one beautiful setting.'

The advice was taken. This *Sleeping Beauty* was both before its time, and in the wrong place. The stage was much too large even for such a grand spectacle. But the production also suffered because Bakst did not go to America to supervise it. The ballet was first cut to eighteen minutes, and then on 27 November, two months before the end of the engagement, replaced by a 'Program of Request Numbers' selected from Pavlova's repertoire of divertissements.

The Big Show was in between two Ballets Russes tours. The second, a 'coast-to-coast' trip, was from 16 October 1916 until 24 February 1917. Bakst as designer of Diaghilev's ballets continued to arouse comment. On the principle that all publicity is good publicity both Bakst and

Left
Tamara Karsavina as Mariucca in *The Good Humoured Ladies*, 1917
BIBLIOTHÈQUE NATIONALE, MUSÉE DE L'OPÉRA, PARIS

Right
Léonide Massine as Leonardo in *The Good Humoured Ladies*, 1917
BIBLIOTHÈQUE NATIONALE, MUSÉE DE L'OPÉRA, PARIS

Diaghilev must have smiled when they read the syndicated article which appeared in the *New York Review* on 20 September under the headline 'De Diaghileff Gave Bask Her First Opportunity.' It credited Bakst's work with having 'lately earned him the Nobel Prize,' and called Diaghilev 'a wealthy Russian nobleman, with a penchant for the arts' who 'dabbled somewhat into the art of the theater, and then had a sort of coterie of pseudo-Bohemians about him.' Other journalists were better informed and produced more thoughtful articles about Bakst's work and his wider influence. 'Barbaric' began to replace 'sumptuous' as a favoured descriptive adjective. Hermine Edelstein in *Musical America* wrote: 'His return to what we call the "barbaric" is just the shock that we needed and, indeed, anything less mild would not have aroused us. I do maintain, however, that his work as well as that of his school of artists is but a stepping stone to a future decorative art that, as I said, would not have evolved but for the return to the primitive of our modern wizards of color.

And, when we come to think of it, the return of modern art is not so much to the "barbaric", the "primitive", as we like to call it, but rather to the *vital*, the *fundamental*, for we had become weak, anaemic, degenerate in our art. We needed to be stirred, shocked!'

1916 was a significant year for Bakst in another way. He met and was befriended by Alice Warder Garrett. She was the wife of an American career diplomat, John Work Garrett. They were from Baltimore, but at that time Mr Garrett was in Paris for the Red Cross and later became the American ambassador at The Hague. She was interested in the arts, fancied herself as a singer, and was rich. She and her husband soon began to play host to literary and

Set design for *The Good Humoured Ladies*,
1917
410 × 591
SALLIE BLUMENTHAL COLLECTION, NEW YORK

This is the design for the second version

artistic Paris; she became a patron of the Ballets Russes, and a particular and vital patron of Bakst.

After America Diaghilev and the Ballets Russes found refuge in Spain and Italy. The war was still on. The February 1917 revolution in Russia was welcomed by Bakst, in a letter to his wife, as a 'great liberating turn-around,' and he told her how pleased he was by 'the bright dawn beginning to flame up gloriously over our people.' Diaghilev, with his 'headquarters' in Rome, prepared a new and revolutionary season for Paris. Bakst was the only member of the 'old guard' left and they discussed a new revised production of *The Fairy Doll* to be called *La Boutique Fantasque*, but plans to produce it were postponed. Diaghilev did ask Bakst, however, to design *The Good-Humoured Ladies* which he wanted to present in Rome before taking it to Paris. Based on Carlo Goldoni's play, *Le Donne di Buon Umore*, with music by Domenico Scarlatti, it was first performed on 12 April at the Teatro Costanzi. But Diaghilev was determined that the Ballets Russes should change course again and, according to Grigoriev (1953), thought that Massine, as choreographer, was 'capable of becoming the very incarnation of all that was modern in art and of putting Diaghilev's own ideas into practice.' He then commissioned Picasso to design his first work for the theatre, *Parade* by Erik Satie and Jean Cocteau, a Cubist ballet. This was rehearsed in Rome but first performed in Paris at the Châtelet on 18 May 1917.

Bakst had no intention of ceding his place as innovator in design for the Ballets Russes. As if to make a stand about himself he contributed an introductory article to the 1917 Souvenir

Left
Costume design for Josephine Cecchetti
as Silvestra in *The Good Humoured Ladies*,
1917
485×330
ROBERT L.B. TOBIN COLLECTION, MARION
KOOGLER MCNAY ART MUSEUM, SAN ANTONIO

Right
Costume design for Enrico Cecchetti as
Luca in *The Good Humoured Ladies*, 1917
445×290
SOTHEBY'S/PRIVATE COLLECTION

This is the original design dated 1916.
There is another version dated 1917

Programme with the title 'Choreography and Settings of the New Ballets Russes'. He discussed the choreography of Massine and the design by Larionov for *Midnight Sun* and *Russian Tales* before introducing Picasso's *Parade*. 'This great painter,' he wrote, 'has found another branch to his art. He is also a theatre designer. He is guided here as elsewhere by his feeling for the limits of possibility.' He then introduced his own work for *The Good-Humoured Ladies*:

The reconstruction of an epoch on the stage is a fiction. I do not think that one should be able to undertake such a task without incurring the risk of being accused of parody. That is the reason why I preferred, instead of imitating Italian eighteenth century stage decoration, to offer a personal interpretation of the Goldoni epoch. I had to emphasize the farcical character of the 'Guignol', and Italian gaiety, which abounds in the Venetian master's work (and often in Scarlatti's music). Besides that, in order to emphasize the characters and make them stand out, I tried to design a setting (in fairly dark tones) as if it were seen through a hemispherical glass so popular in the eighteenth century. The optical effect I managed to achieve gave me great pleasure (is that the only respectable point of departure for an artist?) in that it distorted the lines of perspective so that concentric curves emphasized the vertical axes of the

Costume design for Princess Volkhova
in *Sadko*, 1917
673×485
SOTHEBY'S/PRIVATE COLLECTION

Costume design for 8 Boyars in *Sadko*, 1917
490×330
SOTHEBY'S/PRIVATE COLLECTION

Sadko, the opera by Rimsky-Korsakov, was a project
planned for the Opéra in Paris, but it did not take place.
There is no record of Bakst having designed any sets for
the production. Bakst used Russian folk art motifs
extensively in these costume designs. As well as being for
the theatre, they may have been intended as illustrations
to the story, as were the designs (pp. 190–91) which
follow for *The Firebird*

characters. Massine, in turn, in his singularly attractive choreography sought to emphasize the burlesque nature of the piece.

The scene represents a square in a small town near Venice enclosed by the false proscenium of a green and white curtain. The first sketch was much too extreme; the convex distortion of the perspective did not work at all and the trick appeared to be merely pointless and ludicrous. Bakst was asked to make another drawing (p. 186) and, for the performances in Rome and Paris, the distortion of the buildings was only slight. The style of the costume designs (p. 187) was again new for Bakst. Influenced by, or rather, attempting a 'cubist' approach to drawing, the figures are flat and angular with exaggerated hands, legs and feet in awkward positions like marionettes. The drawings were so appreciated for their colour and amusing liveliness that Bakst later made copies of several of them. No one, however, much liked or was ready for what was thought to be quirky scenery but, otherwise, the ballet was considered to be great fun. When the Ballets Russes came to London in 1918, their first visit since 1914, Diaghilev asked for the setting for *The Good-Humoured Ladies* to be redesigned and repainted so that the buildings appeared to stand straight.

Vladimir Polunin, engaged by Diaghilev to paint the new scenery, described his work (1927): 'To transfer a design by Bakst into suitable proportions for the stage proved to be a difficult task, for he often painted his effective designs with more regard for their pictorial effect than for the use of the scene painter, and so it was in this case. If his design were to be transferred to the prepared canvas in the same proportions, the nearest houses of the back-cloth would have appeared so small that the heads of the dancers would have been on a level with the roofs, which would have destroyed the veracity of the effect. On the other hand, if the buildings were to be of normal size, the top of the tower would have been cut off by a sky-border.'

Polunin was right. In this case Bakst was more concerned about painting a picture than designing a set.

During 1917 Bakst undertook several projects most of which remained unrealized. He made a number of costume designs for the opera *Sadko* for Jacques Rouché, director of the Opéra in Paris. The designs for undersea monsters continued the angular 'Baksto-cubist' style, others were naturalistic and a few showed a new development. He was probably thinking about the events taking place in Russia because he went back to his Russian roots for decorative ideas; he certainly emphasized the Russianness of *Sadko* in his designs. The costumes of the large, fat, flat figures are covered with bold, colourful, intricate Russian peasant and folk-art patterns (p. 188). At this time he also made a unique series of drawings for *The Firebird*, unique because of the peculiarly two-dimensional, angular style of drawing, the exaggeration of limb and cheeks rouged with spots like dolls (p. 191). For the most part they are also uniquely grotesque and hideous. The Firebird herself looks more like a plucked chicken

Opposite
Costume design for the Firebird in
The Firebird, 1917
674 × 490
MUSEUM OF MODERN ART, NEW YORK, JOAN
AND LESTER AVNET COLLECTION

Costume design for the Tzarevna in
The Firebird, 1917
670 × 485
PARMENIA MIGEL EKSTROM COLLECTION, NEW
YORK

The undated costume designs in this
style have previously been thought to
have been made in 1913. Bakst did
design new costumes for *The Firebird* in
1913 and his illustration for *Harper's
Bazar* in 1915 was still in the same vein
as the original designs he made in 1910.
There is nothing else in his work to
suggest that these designs were made
before 1917

than a bird of fire. The colours are strong, almost crude, and the patterns are also based on Russian folk motifs. These drawings are undated, which is unusual, and have been attributed to 1913. However, their style, the manner of drawing the letters of the titles and a similar signature place them at about the same time as the drawings for *Sadko*. While *Sadko* was originally intended for production both sets of drawings in this genre may have been a project for an illustrated book of Russian fairy stories.

In the summer of 1917 Ida Rubinstein gave a charity matinée performance of act four of Racine's *Phèdre* with costumes designed by Bakst. It has always been wrongly assumed that designs dated 1917 and titled *Phèdre* are for d'Annunzio's play *Phaedre* which Rubinstein finally produced in 1923 and that Bakst worked on the production for six years. However, when Bakst came to design *Phaedre* he used, economically, many of the designs he had made in 1917.

After the October revolution Bakst wrote to his wife on 4 November 1917: 'We will see each other some time. I will then at last have the great joy of seeing you all serene and happy, I believe in the happiness and future of Russia.' Like so many others, Bakst was at first optimistic about the future of Russia; the revolution seemed like a great liberating force for the arts, but the optimism was quickly stifled.

Innovation, tradition, America:
1919–1924

La Boutique Fantasque (*The Fantastic Toyshop*, although always called by its French title) was a long time in preparation and, from Bakst's point of view, led to nothing except a valuable set of drawings. He worked on the production during the early part of 1918. A design for the set and 31 costume designs were exhibited in The Hague from 19 May. Frits Lapidoth wrote in *Nieuwe Courant* (*Art Chronicle*): 'I regret that I am not permitted to mention the name of the young lady ... whose initiative we have to thank for the fact that Leon Bakst consented to allow some of his works to come to our country; but we must concur with her opinion: "We are here concerned with the genius of Bakst and with that alone."' The 'young lady' was Mrs Garrett whose husband had by then been appointed American ambassador to The Hague. Lapidoth went on: 'You will certainly laugh heartily at his enchantingly droll ideas which he has converted into dolls and people in the *Boutique Fantasque* in which one sees puppets and shop assistants and all sorts of customers, large and small, rejoicing in their dolls or walking away with them in an awfully awkward manner.' The drawings are reminiscent of the early *Fairy Doll* designs (p. 37) but not so delicate. And there is a sinister touch of cruelty rather than humour in the way Bakst shows the dolls struggling in pain while being gripped by smiling humans.

While Bakst was trying to exploit his designs as fine art drawings there was silence from Diaghilev about the production of the ballet until the spring of 1919 when he suddenly asked for all the remaining designs. Diaghilev may have thought that Bakst had done no work on the ballet so that the rush which he now imposed upon him would force him to refuse and allow him to commission someone else without offending Bakst. Diaghilev's deviousness had its desired effect, but Bakst also had his tongue in his cheek when he protested to Diaghilev on 24 March 1919 (from a French translation of the original Russian letter in the Bibliothèque Nationale) that he 'beat all thoughtlessness and disorderliness' with his sudden demand.

> But that is not the point, the main thing is that I do not have the time, not one free moment, to go on working on the set design, nor on the unfinished costume designs. As usual, I have imagined everything on a grand scale, and can tell you that the set for the Galeria in Naples in 1852 is one of my most brilliant and important creations, and the first and second sets *will* be the same. But if I have to produce all this now in a hurry (each costume drawing takes at least a week...), it will all go to the devil, and I do not accept. First of all, copies have to be made of all my costume drawings (there is a huge number of them and they are all different) because, in fact, these drawings are *my only capital asset*, the fruit of my strenuous labours, and I cannot run the risk of having them stained, covered with shit, or damaged as is usually the case with all designs entrusted to the Diaghilev Management. (You have already made me lose 12,000 francs because you did not return a set design even though I telegraphed you in Rome begging you to send it back.) The work of copying these drawings will probably

take about two or three months, which is not entirely my fault, because when you commission me to design a ballet once a year, or every two years, I take the greatest trouble over the drawings, and copying them takes a lot of time.

Now, a question of the utmost importance: *when the copies of my drawings have been done* who is going to make the costumes? If it is Muelle, then that is all right, because the whole secret of the success of my costumes lies in the fact that it is I who see to their making, by inventing each time a new and particular interpretation for the way they are made. . . . If you get the costumes made in London, leaving the English costumiers the freedom to act as they want, they will produce something trite, or ''Bakstian'' which is exactly what must be avoided in *Boutique*. Obviously, following your instructions, Polunin would paint the set well or even perfectly, but my decor is so complicated, it is so full of curious, charming and folksy detail, that *I cannot and will not* rush my design. Since you are in such a hurry, ask another designer to design this production for you. Perhaps he will cook something up for you quickly. As for me, I will be left with the consolation of having done something important which, in time, I will publish under the title of *Boutique Fantasque* or *Reveries of Naples 1852*. It is sad that the years have not taught you to have a little consideration for a painter, a chum, and that you spit on him when he is not useful to you. As for me, I am becoming in my way, selfish, and I wish Massine's ballet well. The whole secret of the success of the way I design productions is that I take to heart every one of them and finish off the work of the choreographer or author of the ballet. . . It is laughable to want to produce this ballet now because I do not have a single minute in which to draw breath, and all day my flat is stuffed full of actors, actresses, writers, costumiers . . . [working on *Aladin*] This fairy story has a monstrous spread with a lot of sets (12 or 14, it hasn't been decided yet), and costumes. I have no time at all. Say hello to Massine.

Diaghilev at once took Bakst's suggestion of approaching someone else seriously and, pursuing his new policy of commissioning contemporary Western artists, asked Massine to talk to André Derain. The production, then designed by Derain, was given its first performance at the Alhambra on 5 June. Bakst, according to Massine, was 'hurt and indignant' at having had his suggestion accepted and did not speak to Diaghilev for nearly two years.

At the time he wrote to Diaghilev he was, as he said, very busy with the final preparations for *Aladin ou la Lampe Merveilleuse*. In the end, this fairy story, written and produced by Rip, was in three acts and eleven scenes. The first performance was on 20 May 1919 at the Théâtre Marigny in Paris; it was postponed from 11 May because of a strike by tailors and embroiderers, but whether this was on account of Bakst or not we do not know.

Rip, or Georges Thenon which was his real name, was taking advantage in *Aladin* of the continuing vogue for 'orientalism', east of Suez rather than east of Calcutta, and the new

Costume design for a Grandee in *Aladin ou la Lampe Merveilleuse*, 1919
485 × 325
SOTHEBY'S/PRIVATE COLLECTION

This is a copy, in different colours, of the costume design for a Eunuch in *Schéhérazade*

Caricature of characters in *Aladin ou la Lampe Merveilleuse*, 1919
(in an unidentified newspaper)
BIBLIOTHÈQUE NATIONALE, DÉPARTEMENT DES ARTS DU SPECTACLE, PARIS

This clearly shows the variety of characters and costumes there were in this production – from tutu to samurai. The only missing type was the Bakstian 'Greek'

Set design for Act I scene I in *Aladin ou la Lampe Merveilleuse*, 1919
320 × 480
SOTHEBY'S/PRIVATE COLLECTION

Costume design for a Page in *Aladin ou la Lampe Merveilleuse*, 1919
285 × 165

This drawing is not by Bakst but the handwriting is. The bottom left hand corner of the drawing has been cut off. Still visible on the bottom line is the letter 'c' and the beginning of the letter 'o'. The line used to read 'copie d'après Bakst' but someone was careless with the cutting. This is not a fake but a working drawing made by assistants. This particular figure became a standard 'Page' figure for a number of productions. Bakst first used it for *The Sleeping Beauty* in 1916 (see p. 181), then for *Aladin* and later for *The Sleeping Princess* (see pp. 210–11). One of the *Aladin* pages was reproduced in Levinson's book on *The Sleeping Princess*. Sometimes, assistants' copies are intact except for the words 'copie d'après' which have been painted out white and leaving the signature to fool unsuspecting buyers

vogue for the Russian revolution. During an interview reported on 17 May he said that *Aladin ou la Lampe Merveilleuse* was a modern fairy story with the action taking place during the present day and that 'The transformations brought about by Aladin's lamp make very varied transitions possible. Here and there I have introduced some current jokes. Revue is an extendible art form which fits in well with fairy stories. In *Aladin* there is a scene on music, another on fashion, and another on bolshevism. We will see the bolshevist Signoret claiming the right for all workers to be millionaires, and the beggar Albert Brasseur suddenly in charge of a fortune which he doesn't know what to do with.' The story was modish but thin although the transformations were far fetched enough to be highly entertaining.

In this production Bakst continued his scenic innovations, but in a completely different direction from *The Good-Humoured Ladies*. For the set designs (pp. 196 and 198–99) he used a 'pointilliste' method of painting for the first and only time. Some of them are thought to be variations of designs for *Schéhérazade* or *Thamar*, but their style rather than date provides the real clue that they were made for *Aladin*. He reduced the scenery to eleven flat back-cloths painted with all the architectural details, furniture, props and any other decorations. The cloths were like eleven primitive paintings. The stage was left bare except for token stylized tables, chairs and props made out of unpainted wood necessary for the action. Critics found this method of staging a scene unconvincing and disconcerting but agreed about the effectiveness of the transformations. They all praised the costumes as usual and yet Bakst this time took much less trouble over them than over the sets. He had to design 300 costumes and there was a limit even to Bakst's imagination about the number of variations he could give to an 'oriental' costume and so he reused and redrew many of his designs for *Schéhérazade* and *Le Dieu Bleu*. As these drawings are imitations of earlier ones their date, rather than the style, provides the clue for identifying the production for which they were intended. One of the scenes was a fancy dress party in the style of Louis XIV. Bakst used some of his designs for *The Sleeping Beauty* and also made many new designs, some of which are often attributed to the later *Sleeping Princess* (p. 201). No-one noticed the similarities. Bakst again provided the management and the public with the costumes if not the sets they wanted. At any rate, Louis Schneider was taken in and thought that 'the genie of this Aladin's magic lamp was Léon Bakst.' Since then critics and writers have largely ignored *Aladin* as if it were an embarrassing episode in Bakst's career and more designs have been attributed to the original Ballets Russes productions than he could ever have drawn for them. But Bakst clearly enjoyed the challenge of designing a complete revue as it was a medium in which he could experiment with his scenic ideas. It was fun but it did not work.

Bakst did not go to America when Mrs Garrett arranged the 'transfer' of his exhibition from The Hague to New York in April 1920 although she hoped that he would. His reputation as an original theatre designer had been established before the first visit by Diaghilev's Ballets

Set design for Act 2 scene 5 in *Aladin ou
la Lampe Merveilleuse*, 1919
211 × 295
MUSEUM OF MODERN ART, NEW YORK, GIFT OF
JOAN AND LESTER AVNET

Russes, but it had become a little tarnished during the tour because a certain sloppiness in
production was remarked upon, a sloppiness, incidentally, which Bakst would never have
allowed had he travelled with the company. Mrs Garrett and he must have hoped,
therefore, that the exhibition would completely restore his name and, by all accounts, it did.
On 11 April the *New York Times*, in its column 'Art Notes' reviewed the exhibition: 'All America knows, or thinks it knows, Russian stage decoration ... We think of it as blazing and raw
and slashed with sinister greens. Bakst's colour is deep and mellow and without insistence. It
is color that draws the eyes to it, not color that pushes out into the room. It is an excellent
thing to see these beautiful originals with their rollicking humour of design and their serious
art ...'

Mrs Garrett not only wrote the foreword to the catalogue herself but also wrote an article
(signed only with her initials) which was published in *Vanity Fair* in which she tried to
redress the balance in the general opinion about Bakst as an artist: 'We have been so busy in
acclaiming Bakst as the greatest living colorist, that we have passed by, almost unperceived,
other great qualities of his art ... For many years now, all over the world people have been
trying to invent "Bakst" colour schemes. But draperies at the bargain counters in our best
department stores are of as much consequence, artistically speaking, as these so-called Bakst
costumes, Bakst rooms, and Bakst stage decorations.... He should be acclaimed far more
widely than he has been, as a great draughtsman ... Bakst was *born* a great colorist, but he

198

became a great draughtsman. He searched for and found the line which would express the soul of a person or thing – as he drew it. His work is free from all self-consciousness or affectation. With perfect freedom he varies his style in all of his drawings. He seeks ardently to reveal, not himself, but the inner consciousness of the thing he draws; to reach beyond – to make the outer envelope give up the secret of the spirit which it encloses.' She was a true friend: she not only praised him but also understood what he tried to do.

After his initial euphoria over the revolutionary dawn breaking over Russia Bakst began to learn the terrible truth and to receive snippets of uncertain but disturbing news about his wife. He fell into another deep depression. An old friend but one who had quarrelled with Bakst in 1911, Prince Argutinsky-Dolgorukoff, managed to escape from Russia and went to see him. Prince Lieven, who jumbled time, recorded Argutinsky's impressions: 'Bakst gave the impression of being half crazy. "You know, I am nearly blind; I cannot look at the light" . . . Upon hearing the story of his wife's sufferings he became very agitated, walking up and down the room and repeating: "No, no . . . don't tell me . . . it is so awful." Bakst then somehow managed to arrange to send his wife a thousand francs a month and he slowly came out of his depression. He recovered and began another year of intensive work.'

In February 1921 rumours that Bakst had gone blind reached America, but, as reported by Alexander Woollcott in the *New York Times* on the 13th, Bakst himself strongly denied the rumours and was quoted:

The story is made out of whole cloth. My sight was never so good. I can even descry the individuals to whom this *canard* would be profitable and I can even see the tiny springs which direct the flight of so brazen a tale. That's sighting them pretty well, isn't it? I am busy now in London with the decorations of a magnificent house – that of Lord Rothschild. It tells a fantastic story, a fairy story, painted a little in the spirit of the Italian primitives of the fourteenth century with Lord Rothschild's family portraits worked in, here and there, among the characters of the story. This interests me enormously just now – perhaps to the detriment of the theatre. Not that I am giving up the theatre. But more than ever it seems to me that the art of the theatre is so fleeting, of its vast display only my roughest sketches remain. More and more, I think, I shall do murals and portraits.

But of course Bakst could not desert the theatre and was already preparing a revival of *Daphnis and Chloë* intended as a come-back for Fokine and his wife, Vera Fokina, at the Opéra in Paris after their year in America. Fokine had arranged for Bakst to design some costumes for *Mecca*, yet another 'oriental' style extravaganza in New York in 1920. Bakst was instrumental in making the arrangements with Jacques Rouché, for the Fokines to appear in Paris. Bakst, responsible for the scenery, costumes, and props based on the earlier designs, fussed most of all about the lighting as we can read from the following extracts from previously unpublished letters (written in French).

> *From Bakst to Rouché, 17 May 1921:* 'I am writing to you – very early – to beg one thing which will greatly contribute to the beauty of the staging of *Daphnis and Chloë* – that is to give me (really, a lot of advance notice) one *evening* for me alone to do the lighting of the two sets. If, as is usual, the evening set aside for lighting takes place *at the same time as an orchestra rehearsal* for *Daphnis* then, as always happens in cases like this, I will get in the way of the orchestra and vice-versa. The result: appalling lighting. In my long experience I have come to the conclusion that a set which is lit in peace, *meticulously*, is three quarters of the success, even when the set is well painted! . . . I am writing to you early so that you may have the means to arrange a whole evening (from 8 – midnight) – which is not long for two such important sets, with "miracles", transformations and changes.
>
> Two more things. I have agreed with M. Fokine that all the dancers should have wigs made of glued together *threads* (my idea) – this will give them that striking *archaic head* which the painters liked so much in *L'Après-midi d'un Faune*. Muelle knows the process very well and so we will be able to avoid those burlesque heads, half-modern, half-"conventional-Greek" of *former* stagings! The stuff is very cheap and the gluing which I taught the prop makers at Muelle is very crude – the result is *very beautiful and very artistic . . .*

I should also like to have *one day* with Fokine to choose the props from your store at the Opéra (you have a lot and it will be unnecessary to order special ones). It might be necessary to repaint (by Paquereau) some of them according to my instructions in order to stay within the spirit and *colour range* of my two sets, but it is only a small matter of a couple of days.'

'Meticulous' was the word; Bakst had to battle.

From Bakst to Rouché, 8 June 1921: 'Tomorrow, probably, all the sets for *Daphnis* will come to the Opéra. Can you arrange *one whole afternoon* (after Sunday) for the lighting of the sets? I am in a hurry to carry out this task of prime importance for the sake of the beauty of the show. Therefore, do me the kindness, when you have arranged the afternoon (and I agree to any in advance) to call Mr Fokine and Mr Paquereau (and I count on *not having* the orchestra which will be resting) and the whole team of electricians with all their projectors (and lenses and colour filters), as well as the whole team of stage-hands.'

There is a note in pencil at the top of the page, presumably by Rouché: 'Tuesday evening 8 o'clock'

From Bakst to Rouché, 17 June 1921: ' You now have in your hands a magnificent work with your dancers *transformed* – I tell you that between you and me, with all my heart. But do not spoil this beautiful creation by a detail which can *kill everything*: that is the absence of setting the lighting *to suit the choreography*. The electrician did not have time to rehearse this and it could have a disastrous result on the triumph of this ballet – because *triumph* it should. . . .

We need a complete rehearsal, in peace, *without orchestra*, where everything will be settled, because the first act has *not been adjusted* as there was no time – this must be done in your interests . . .'

The first night was on 20 June 1921. The production was of no particular significance to Bakst; it was nothing new but, always the professional, we see that he cared enormously about the result. He wrote an ironic note to Rouché on 19 August: 'How can I get what the Opéra owes me for *Daphnis and Chloë*? Should I send an invoice, where to and when? Forgive me my inexperience!'. As if he did not know.

In 1921 Bakst made his final come-back with Diaghilev and the Ballets Russes with *The Sleeping Princess*. In March 1911 Diaghilev had written to *The Times* when he was criticized for not bringing something specifically Russian: '. . . as for *The Sleeping Beauty*, this interminable ballet on a subject taken from a French fable, composed on French themes, does not possess a single national element which might justify the idea of presenting this Franco-Italian fairy story in London.' Furthermore, having developed the one-act ballet where all the elements

Opposite
Cover of the Souvenir Programme for *The Sleeping Princess*, 1921

Reproduced is the costume design for 4 porphyry carriers to the King and Queen. A similar design is in the collection of the Museum of Modern Art, New York. The programme was printed in France and the editor did not spot the mistake in the title of the ballet

Right
Mural painting on the theme of *The Sleeping Beauty*: 'The Awakening'
Oil on canvas, 2100 × 820
PRIVATE COLLECTION

This is panel 7 of seven panels Bakst painted for James de Rothschild's London house between 1915 and 1922. Each panel represents an episode of the fairy story *The Sleeping Beauty* which Bakst had chosen as his theme. The figures in each of the panels are also portraits of the Rothschild family and their friends. There are forty-three portraits altogether, including three of the Baroness Maurice de Rothschild, two of Mrs Eugene Pinto, a self-portrait, two dogs and a cat. This panel shows James de Rothschild kneeling in front of the Baroness Maurice de Rothschild, and 'Muffin', Mrs James de Rothschild's papillon. The only similarity between the murals and the productions is the canopy for both the prologue and 'The Awakening'

Below
Design for the cradle in The Prologue of *The Sleeping Princess*, 1921
473 × 320
THEATRE ARTS COLLECTIONS, HARRY RANSOM HUMANITIES RESEARCH CENTER, THE UNIVERSTITY OF TEXAS AT AUSTIN

Bakst specified an unbreakable baby

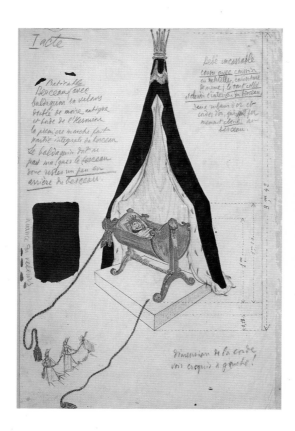

A L H A M B R A   T H E A T R E

4 Porteurs de la
porpyre du Roi
et l Reine 5 acte

BAKST
1921

A L H A M B R A   T H E A T R E

SOUVENIR : THE SPLEEPING PRINCESS

were considered to be of equal importance he rather despised the full-length 'classical' ballet of Petipa. By 1921, however, everything was different. It was after the war and after the revolution. Diaghilev and his team were stranded in the West like 'displaced persons' unable or unwilling to return to Russia. At first he, too, had been enthusiastic about what was happening to his country, and in performances of Stravinsky's *The Firebird*, that specifically Russian ballet, he had replaced the emblem of the double-headed eagle with a star. But not for long. Diaghilev felt that he and his company were not just the Russian Ballet but that they had become the symbol for the art of ballet. He therefore felt he had a duty to maintain the classical tradition which should no longer be despised but even glorified. At the same time he had to regroup the company which was difficult then as he was without a choreographer and had to find and train new dancers who were not Russian. A crucial consideration was also a financial one. Diaghilev thought he could imitate the long running success of a show like *Chu-Chin-Chow* by mounting one hugely spectacular ballet and making enough money to guarantee the continuity of the Ballets Russes. With Stravinsky's eager support Diaghilev chose Tchaikovsky's *The Sleeping Beauty*, the most 'classical' of ballets, the pinnacle of Petipa's art. Diaghilev is supposed to have retitled the ballet *The Sleeping Princess* because he did not think that any of his dancers was a beauty, but the more probable explanation is that he did not want his production to be confused with a Christmas pantomime. Diaghilev's first thought for designer was Alexandre Benois but he was still in Russia. He therefore turned to Bakst (they could never quite get out of each other's hair) because he knew that he would design the kind of grand and gorgeous spectacle that was needed. In June 1917 there had been an exhibition of 22 designs for Pavlova's *The Sleeping Beauty* at The Fine Art Society in London. Diaghilev must have known about Pavlova's *The Sleeping Beauty* in New York but he may not have seen the exhibition in London. It is unlikely, however, that Bakst kept either event a secret inspite of the tiffs between them. In his luxuriously produced book *The Designs of Léon Bakst for 'The Sleeping Princess'* (1922), André Levinson does not mention the Pavlova production and exaggerated when he wrote: 'In less than six weeks . . . Léon Bakst composed, or, rather, improvized the six scenes and the three hundred costumes . . . which the ballet contains. A less bold, more timorous worker, seeking the exact historical document, nosing about in portfolios, compiling dossiers, would have succumbed to the difficulties. Bakst, above all else an imaginative artist, triumphed.' Bakst actually had longer than six weeks and in any case had done his 'nosing about' several years earlier when he designed Pavlova's *The Sleeping Beauty*, but from a letter written towards the end of July to Georgi Lukomsky, who was trying to arrange an exhibition, we also know that the production took much longer than six weeks and that Bakst continued to be irritated with Diaghilev:

> What can one do about Diaghilev – he has been like that all his life. He does not answer letters, he leads people by the nose, he is always in a hurry, he is always busying

The scene in Act I of *The Sleeping
Princess*, 1921
BIBLIOTHÈQUE NATIONALE, MUSÉE DE L'OPÉRA,
PARIS

himself with one thing or another. Everyone always complains about him. Alas!
I have nothing to exhibit. I do not have the right to exhibit any *Sleeping (Beauty)*
designs before the first performance in Paris at the Opéra, and anyway I do not want
to. Thank you for the invitation but I will not be exhibiting anything before 1923. To
hell with exhibitions! I never liked them and never went to mine.

Bakst quite often indulged in this kind of false modesty while actually needing to sell his
designs. From the first, Diaghilev planned to take the production to Paris after London. On
4 October Bakst wrote to Diaghilev:

You must remind your directors in London that they took a year and a half to stage
this ballet at the Imperial Theatres and yet I, in two months, between 10 August and
10 October, have to do with my own hand more than two hundred designs for costumes and sets, not counting the props, wigs, shoes, armour, jewellery, etc., that
makes about four watercolours a day, work beyond human and creative strength . . .
the fact that we are mounting *The Sleeping Princess* in two months is certainly a record
for energy and speed which has never been seen in the theatre before.

Right
Set design for Act 2 of *The Sleeping Princess*, 1921, reproduced in the Souvenir Programme

Below, right
Set design for Act 3 scene 2 of *The Sleeping Princess*, 1921, reproduced in the Souvenir Programme

Below
Set designs for Anna Pavlova's *The Sleeping Beauty*, 1916, reproduced in the programme for *The Big Show* for comparison

For Act 1 of *The Sleeping Princess* Bakst 'opened up' the centre stage and painted a huge staircase with figures receding to give added depth to the scene (see p. 205). The garden has been made less formal by avoiding a symmetrical set, the castle has an added romantic tower. The last scene was the same

THE GARDEN OF KING FLORESTAN
Scene of the Second Act by Leon Bakst

Copyright by Leon Bakst, 1911

Castel in the forests where the Princess sleeps.   Design by Léon Bakst for the second scene of the third act.

Set design for Act 4, 'The Awakening' of
The Sleeping Princess, 1921
480 × 668
THYSSEN-BORNEMISZA COLLECTION

This set was not used in the final
production as the 'truck', with Aurora
protected by the hovering eagle, proved
to be too cumbersome to move on and
off stage easily, and an alternative had
to be designed quickly

Alternative set drawing for Act 4 of *The
Sleeping Princess*, 1921 on Savoy Hotel
writing paper
BIBLIOTHÈQUE NATIONALE, MUSÉE DE L'OPÉRA,
PARIS

Bakst was not telling all the truth. Although he based many of the designs on his previous flamboyant work for *The Sleeping Beauty* and *Aladin*, he did have to do a great deal of new drawing in a short time, and so he employed a number of copyists. More copies were made for *The Sleeping Princess* than for any other production and the same figure, differently coloured for separate costumes, was used several times. Accurate attribution is a problem because many of the designs have notes written on them written by Bakst. It used to be assumed that the presence of notes meant that Bakst had done the drawing, then it was thought that he would only have written on a copy because he needed to keep a 'clean' drawing for exhibition or sale, but in fact he sometimes wrote both on copies and on his own drawings. It is of some help that he sometimes signed copies with 'Copie d'après Bakst' (Copy after Bakst).

The Sleeping Beauty and *The Sleeping Princess* were essentially the same with the same libretto except that Diaghilev was presenting a full length version of over three hours instead of Pavlova's curtailed version of forty eight minutes. The main scenic difference, affecting the whole scale of the production, was in the size of the stage, the Alhambra's being less than half the size of the Hippodrome's. Bakst's sets were more suited to the smaller stage because the scenery and props were less cluttered and the special effects were easier to achieve (p. 206). The only set that was significantly different was the second scene, the garden. Instead of the formal, symmetrical garden *The Sleeping Princess* had a more romantic one with a colonnade and a sharp perspective. The first and last sets were almost identical except for their size, and the castle in London had a touch of Bavarian Neuschwanstein added to Tuscan fort. There were problems over the painting of the scenery as Polunin described: 'The numerous acts . . . had been prepared in Paris; some of the scenes were painted there and others in London. Bakst, like a field-marshal, sent out from his headquarters in Paris his instructions to various studios. Those intended for us arrived by air mail, but his explanations were frequently contradictory. Three acts fell to our share but, as Bakst was not present, it was often difficult to fathom his meaning so that his work had to be held up pending explanations.' But Bakst was present at the fit-up, the dress rehearsals and the lighting, and this made a big difference to the final staging and appearance. Cyril Beaumont was allowed to attend a rehearsal and wrote his impressions for *The Dancing Times*: 'The auditorium is without lights, empty, cold, gloomy – altogether cheerless. Seated in the stalls are at most a dozen people. You will recognize the broad back of Diaghileff; to his right, Léon Bakst, dapper, keen, leaning forward with his chin supported on the back of the fauteuil in front of him; to his left Stravinsky, coat collar turned up and felt hat pulled over his eyes . . . Each dancer finds in his dressing room his costume and the original drawing mounted on card and protected by a sheet of talc. [The drawing was almost certainly a copy. Bakst would not have left his drawings lying about in dressing rooms.] When dressed he walks upon the stage and hands the design to the director, who compares it with the realization. Nothing is left to chance. The dancer is required to perform

Costume design for a Court Dignitary in *The Sleeping Princess*, 1921
450 × 300

Several costumes in different colours were based on this figure

Costume design for the Queen and her Page in *The Sleeping Princess*, 1921
295 × 450

This drawing is probably by one of Bakst's assistants (see also *The Sleeping Beauty*, p. 181 and *Aladin* p. 201) but the notes are in Bakst's handwriting. Bakst's design, with his 'optional dog', was reproduced in the Souvenir Programme and also in Jacques-Emile Blanche's article in *L'Illustration* where the page was also in blue. This copy is very fine but Bakst made the face of the Queen more regal

such and such a 'variation'. Does the costume prevent free movement of the arms? Does its weight prevent the execution of such a step? Notes are made and orders given for the necessary alterations.'

The result was impressive, lovers of the ballet flocked to the production, and went many times. It was all more wonderful than they had ever imagined. There is practically no-one left now who saw that production but it remains the stuff of dreams. In the smaller theatre Bakst was able to realize more effectively and successfully his scheme of arranging groups of costumes in blocks of strong, bright contrasting colours in front of pale, almost monotone sets. He successfully solved the problem of inventing different kinds of costumes for the mime parts and the dancing parts. He certainly got the credit as in 'Notes on Decor' in *The Dancing Times*: '*The Sleeping Princess* is an example to all producers of theatric decor. It possesses originality to the extent of genius, it preserves unity between costume and set, and it creates that most difficult of all decorative results, a sense of rhythmic perfection.' Bakst's designs for *The Sleeping Princess* were neither original nor exactly new but, precisely because he was able to refine previous work, the production was paradoxically generally considered to be his crowning theatrical achievement. But *The Sleeping Princess* was a disaster for Diaghilev. Ernest Newman in *The Sunday Times* thought it was 'the suicide of the Russian ballet.' And so it was, for a time. While 'balletomanes' went mad over it (Cyril Beaumont 'saw it night after night for some three months') English audiences, on the whole, were not ready for Petipa's ballet; they did not want to see dancing displays of technical wizardry however pretty; they did confuse it with the pantomime *The Sleeping Beauty*. At the same time no classical ballet had been performed in London before for 105 consecutive nights. Diaghilev had spent the original £10,000 advance made to him by Sir Oswald Stoll, the producing manager, and a further two payments of £5,000 so that only full houses for the whole run scheduled for six months would show a profit. *The Sleeping Princess* lost money and was taken off early. Stoll sequestered the scenery and costumes. The transfer to Paris was out of the question. Instead, Diaghilev took the last scene only, calling it *Aurora's Wedding*, with the set and some costumes from *Pavillon d'Armide* designed by Alexandre Benois, and some new costumes designed by Nathalia Gontcharova.

The Sleeping Princess was the last production which Bakst designed for Diaghilev. The simple explanation for their final break is that Diaghilev, having promised him the responsibility of designing Stravinsky's one act opera *Mavra*, broke his 'contract' (even though Bakst had already made a drawing for the set) and commissioned Leopold Survage instead. Though true, this was not the whole reason. It was only the final straw, and a tiny straw at that, which broke the back of their long friendship. They were often infuriated with one another and perhaps Diaghilev blamed Bakst a little for the expensive failure of *The Sleeping Princess*. Contrary to general belief they maintained some contact with each other. Professionally Diaghilev moved on but for Bakst the end of the collaboration meant that he

Costume design for Errol Addison as Puss in Boots in *The Sleeping Princess*, 1921
483 × 325
ROBERT L.B. TOBIN COLLECTION, MARION KOOGLER MCNAY ART MUSEUM, SAN ANTONIO

no longer stretched himself artistically. He did not stop work as the continuing activities of the Ballets Russes acted as a goad but, with one exception, he now tended only to repeat himself.

When he complained to Diaghilev about the amount of work he had to do on *The Sleeping Princess* Bakst was covering himself because he was also busy on other projects though none of them was so huge. The first to reach the stage was the *Spectacle d'Art Russe* on which he collaborated with his old friend Maria Kousnezoff at the Théâtre Fémina in Paris in April–May 1922. This was a half-serious, half-lighthearted revue, with short sketches, playlets, songs, some of them funny, some not. Kousnezoff stated her policy in the programme: 'What I have wanted to do is to create and bring to life an absolutely new theatre in which the whole range of human feeling, from the maddest gaiety to the most horrible suffering, is concentrated into very short scenes. . . .' There were two programmes – Bakst shared the design of both with Sergei Soudeikine. (They also designed together, Bakst the costumes, Soudeikine the sets, a production of Henry Bernstein's *Judith* at the Théâtre Gymnasse in October.)

The most important sketch for Bakst, which he described as a mime-drama, was his *Lâcheté (Cowardice)* postponed from the first programme to the second. While the story was conventional the staging was not. Set in an open space in front of a hostel in Petrograd in 1916 it told of the triangle of love between a student labourer and two girls, the inevitable jealousy and his death by stabbing. Bakst's idea, as he explained in *Journal*, was original but also the result of having developed an interest in folk dancing: 'I came to long for a choreography that would hammer on the stage and give up trying to evoke sylphs.' He therefore invented symbolic characters not usually associated with either ballet or mime, and, instead of a crowd or 'corps de ballet', the actors were dressed and behaved like puppets. '*Lâcheté*,' said Bakst in an interview for *Comoedia*, 'is a mime-drama initiating a completely new technique of staging. It is a first step towards discovering how to treat crowd scenes in the theatre. I think you have to symbolize a crowd rather than represent it.' The set, a distorted background painting of houses and rooftops (p. 215), was done as a projection with the crowd-puppets, larger-than-life, arm in arm, dangling on wires moving constantly in front of it. They must have been a severe distraction from the main action which took place in front of them. 'I heard someone in the audience behind me say', a reporter noted, 'that they were symbolic and that this hateful and entangled nightmare represented the German-Bolshevik alliance. Well, maybe.' Bakst's originality, for once, was mis-cast although this critic read more into the piece than was intended.

The *Spectacle d'Art Russe* was an entertaining but serious diversion for Bakst, but in addition to *The Sleeping Princess* his major work continued to be several simultaneous projects for Ida Rubinstein. She commissioned Bakst to design the interior of her house and the garden as a kind of personal stage set. Stravinsky later remembered in *An Autobiography* (1936) the clever idea that Bakst arranged the flower beds 'so that all the flowers were in trays and

Costume design for Nicolas Kremneff as the
Chinese Mandarin in *The Sleeping Princess*,
1921
405 × 252

Set design for *Lâcheté* a 'mime drama' by
Bakst in *Spectacle d'Art Russe*, 1922

The design was made into a projection –
a scenic innovation

Set design for *Adoration* in *Spectacle d'Art
Russe*, 1922
320 × 490

the whole garden could be changed every few weeks.' Bakst made even gardening into an ephemeral art.

Rubinstein wrote to Robert de Montesquiou on 2 November from the 'source of the Nile' that before she had left on her travels she had agreed to dance a new ballet in April called *Diane Troublée* (the goddess was later called by her Greek name Artemis), that the libretto was to be by Bakst and that she would be an eighteenth century Diana dancing in pink slippers to choreography by Fokine who would come from America. She also wrote to say that in June she would be reviving *Le Martyre de Saint Sébastien*. This is not consistent with what Bakst had written to Rouché on 16 September: 'I have worked a little with Mr Paray [the composer of *Artemis Troublée*] and it seems to be working out; at least he is very satisfied. On the question of Fokine I have to say that Madame Rubinstein suggested to me that she would prefer Massine . . . [as] I do not think that Madame Rubinstein would want to bring him over specially. As for our ballet with Fokine and Vuillermoz [*La Nuit Ensorcelée*] – that's just waiting for Fokine's arrival! Why don't you invite one party, Massine (2 months), then 2 months Fokine? They would both be exhilarated by the rivalry!' In the end, neither Fokine nor Massine was the choreographer of *Artemis Troublée* but Nicolas Guerra.

On 29 December 1921 Bakst wrote to Rouché after he was commissioned to do the sets and costumes for *Artemis Troublée* and *Le Martyre de Saint Sébastien*:

> I am sorry but I cannot accept your conditions as for *Daphnis and Chloë* – that is 1,000 francs for a set and 25 francs for a costume. That price would not even cover my incidental expenses, necessarily tied to my work, which consists not only in having to make new designs for the sets and costumes, but also to supervise (with the care that I believe is required) the costumiers, the wig-makers, the shoe makers, the prop makers, my scenic assistants; and then the many rehearsals, where I am forced to be involved with everything; the extras, the movements on stage, the lighting, the choreographic rehearsals, in fact the whole staging. In practice I have discovered that in my productions I have also had to be the director. You may answer that that is someone else's business; but that is just the *essential factor* which gives a production its artistic unity; a kind of individual will on the work which subconsciously imposes itself on the audience. I accepted *Daphnis and Chloë* as a concession to Fokine, to try and give him work in Europe . . .
>
> Unfortunately, I have to 'live' as they say, and also keep alive those dependent on me. I cannot accept any of your conditions; the only solution is to propose to you a price as a friend, that is to say the prices which Mr Diaghilev, my childhood friend, pays me, who, besides, is known for his abstemiousness when it comes to paying artist-painters. The contract for *The Sleeping Princess* was to pay me – in total – for each act (set and costumes included) five thousand francs, that is 25 thousand francs.

Also recognizing that I will lose time ('time is money' [in English in original text]) he added three thousand francs on to the contract for travelling – that is 28 thousand francs. I accepted these conditions, so moderate compared with the English proposal (15,000 francs for each act), because I considered the work as helping a childhood friend. I propose the same conditions to you, knowing that a great friend Madame Rubinstein is involved in both these productions. That is all I can do – nothing more. Please let me know if I am to consider my time engaged from now till spring, or not.

There was further haggling between them and although they reached a partial agreement about *Artemis Troublée* at the end of February they did not agree about the revival of *Le Martyre de Saint Sébastien* which was scheduled for June. On 2 April Bakst wrote refusing 1,000 francs per set and 25 francs per costume and prop and 'furthermore supervizing the sets, the rehearsals, the staging which I will have to do if I accept your conditions.' On 5 April he wrote that he wanted 25,000 francs and that 'no force in the world, and no law, would force me to work if I do not accept the desired fee.' But then he warned Rouché that even if his terms were accepted it would be too late to do a proper job and 'how is it, after all I have done for fifteen years for Madame Rubinstein, that she puts me into this inextricable position, knowing full well that I am asking a normal fee.' On the same day Rouché agreed to Bakst's fee and on 10 April Bakst sent him 'the designs and ground plans for the animals, dogs and deer, which will be painted and cut out to be chased by Actaeon who will be killed by Artemis.'

The first performance of *Artemis Troublée* was on 28 April 1922 following a performance of Verdi's *Falstaff*. Bakst's scenario was on the theme of the classical Greek fable of Aretmis and Actaeon. The setting and costumes were not in Bakst's 'classical Greek' mode but, unexpectedly, in his seventeenth-century style. Although his staging was unconventional for such a ballet at the time, Bakst repeated many previous ideas in his designs and did not particularly stretch his imagination. He explained his motives and his ideas in an interview with André Rigaud published in *Comoedia* on the day of the first performance:

> I consider that music follows such mysterious rules that the mind is capable of conceiving an infinity of dreams in any particular musical theme. In my adaptation of this mythological and passionate subject I was inspired by mythology as it was thought of in the 17th century, that is to say an impression of passion. The choreography by Mr Nicolas Guerra while keeping to this note of passion is nevertheless inspired by the great choreographic traditions of the time.
>
> The decor was conceived in the spirit of 17th century rustic paintings and hunting scenes which is why I have not hesitated to put a tent in the style of Louis XIV in the middle of the set. This is not inconsistent with the decorative tradition of that period.
>
> The costumes were inspired by the ballet costumes of the Sun-King. I consider that

Costume design for *Lâchete* in *Spectacle d'Art Russe*, 1922
330 × 245
SOTHEBY'S/PRIVATE COLLECTION

This design was for two non-speaking characters in the background who were like marionettes as if moved by strings from the 'flies'. Their incessant movement proved to be an irritating distraction

THEATRE FEMINA

BAKST
22

MARIA KOUSNEZOFF
dans "L'Adoration"

Opposite
Programme cover for *Spectacle d'Art Russe*, 1922 at the Théatre Fémina, Paris with a reproduction of a costume design for Maria Kousnezoff in *Adoration*

One of Bakst's last variations on the 'oriental' theme, but a long way from *Schéhérazade*

Costume design for Mme Leontowitch in *Moscou d'Autrefois* in *Spectacle d'Art Russe*, 1922 (1923)
480 × 320
SOTHEBY'S/PRIVATE COLLECTION

A careful enlargement for exhibition

Costume design for *Artémis Troublée*,
1922
420 × 280
SOTHEBY'S/PRIVATE COLLECTION

such a parody takes nothing away from the subject but, on the contrary, brings to it a note of pointedness. As for the colour of the costumes I have taken into account the impressions suggested to me by the nature of the character. Zeus, the master of thunder, is dressed in a costume the tones of which vary between red and yellow, the colours of fire; the dress of Artemis the chaste is white and silver; the dresses of the dryads are the colour of leaves; the amazons, gentle friends of the huntress, are dressed in a gentle nattier blue; Acteon, the hunter, brings a note of audacity and tragedy into this group, his costume is black, dark green and silver.

But his theories were not entirely successfully put into practice. The original idea of designing a 'Greek' ballet like a miniature *Sleeping Princess* was not seen to be controversial by the critics who either did not appreciate the theories or simply ignored them. They were dismissive of Bakst's staging along the lines of 'we know the art of Bakst well, he asserts himself again in *Artemis Troublée*, but there is nothing new.' They were right, but as *The Sleeping Princess* had not been produced in Paris they did not know the reason.

Ida Rubinstein had seen *Le Martyre de Saint Sébastien* as a vehicle she could use but when she decided to revive it for six performances she realized that the original play was too long and decided to cut the second act completely. This made the play even more incomprehensible and the vehicle, without one of its wheels, collapsed. Only Bakst survived. He tried to give the staging some cohesion by making a number of new costume designs, a new set design, a curtain for the beginning of the first act, and adapting other set designs. The play, however, remained a muddle and was still very long and very boring although everyone still loved looking at Rubinstein's legs, and Bakst's sets and costumes. Aware of his glittering contribution and publicity value, he was offended by being left out of the advertising. He wrote to Rouché and announced: 'I have decided not to produce any more ballets or plays at the Opéra with Madame Rubinstein. Let her choose another painter, but I do not want to go to such effort and then be stripped of my bouquets.' But this was Bakst being petulant again because on Saturday 24 June 1922, the day after *Le Martyre de Saint Sébastien* completed its run, Ida Rubinstein appeared in a costume he designed as the Adriatic sparkling in diamonds and gold at the Grand Prix Ball at the Opéra.

In November 1922 Mrs Garrett invited Bakst to America for the first time for the opening of his second exhibition at Knoedler's which she had arranged. He arrived at New York on the *Mauretania* on 24 November 1922. Bakst, as a celebrity, was asked for an opinion and declared with some imagination: 'The view of the New York skyline at the Battery is more interesting than Venice.'

Five days later, the *New York Times* gave an advance notice of the exhibition and carried the story 'the great work which the artist has just completed, the great work of his life, he says, is a set of mural decorations for the grand salon of the new Park Lane mansion of James Rothschild. These are in seven panels and are M. Bakst's conception of the fairy tale of the Sleeping Beauty, with a fourteenth century setting, North Italian, which is practically French, as well. He has followed in the footsteps of the early masters in using modern portraits . . . In the panels practically all of London society is to be found, the artist says. There are forty-two members of the Rothschild family alone. Included are the attendants, the valet of Mr Rothschild, his jockey, his horses and dogs, all in a gay color scheme.' The fairy story, apart from the canopy for 'The Awakening' (p. 203), is interpreted quite differently from the two productions; the panels are three centuries earlier in style. This work, although not theatrical, is unlike any of his other work and helped to sustain him during the difficult years of the war and the period after the revolution.

Mrs William K. Vanderbilt, Jr gave a lunch for Bakst on 5 December. The *New York Times* reported: 'Following this the hostess and guests walked down the avenue to the show. Practically everyone in the Social Register appeared at some time during the afternoon.' There were eighty-one exhibits divided into three sections: 'Portraits', 'Sujets Décoratifs', 'Contes

Perrault' (designs from *The Sleeping Princess*), and four designs from *Judith*. The 'Decorative Subjects' were large scale watercolours which Bakst made specially for this exhibition. Many of them were either based on, or were copies of earlier theatre designs and have often been confused with them. Their unusually large size and their date, almost always 1922, provide the clues as to their real purpose. They do not have the spontaneity of the original designs, they lack that free-flowing sense of movement which is so characteristic of Bakst's work for the theatre, and they are stiff, often literally so with thick, almost encrusted gold and silver paint. But the drawings appealed to New Yorkers even though they probably had not seen the production for which they had originally been invented; Bakst was fashionable and the exhibition was a financial success.

Bakst stayed in America after the exhibition with the Garretts at their house Evergreen in Baltimore. While he was there he was commissioned by Mrs Garrett to convert the gymnasium into a private theatre to which she could invite her friends for her own singing and dancing performances. Considering her tiny talent she was extremely fortunate to have such a theatre designed for her. It is unique in Bakst's decorative work. The walls of the gymnasium had been lined with bookcases for books overflowing from the adjoining library. (Later the bookcases were removed and replaced by mirrors. Bakst would not have approved.) Between the library was a passage with huge supporting columns. The gymnasium was converted into the auditorium and stage, and the passage into a foyer. Bakst left the original bookcases but decorated the ceilings, columns and proscenium arch, after first having them plastered and painted white, with cut stencils painted in solid blocks of pure colour, blue, yellow, green, crimson. The decorative motifs he used for the stencils were stylized birds and flowers, and abstract patterns based on Russian folk and American Indian art designs. The original theatre was opened in May 1923 and given to the John Hopkins University in 1942. Mrs Susan Tripp, Director of the University Collections, has recently supervised the complete restoration of the theatre and the colours which had faded somewhat have been brought marvellously back to life. The theatre reopened in September 1990.

While Bakst was in Baltimore he lectured to students at the Maryland Art Institute and became interested in the textile design classes. A report in the *Baltimore Sun* of 13 May 1923 stated: 'Mrs Garrett drove him to the Institute where he popped in for "a brief 15 minutes" but then he became so interested in the work and enthusiasm of the pupils that he left her sitting in the car for an hour and a half before he remembered her.' On another occasion he gave this advice to American artists: '... study what is associated with your daily life, create a school of art distinctly American ... You have the same sky and sea, plains and trees that the Indians know. Paint what inspired their art and it should inspire yours. Create an American school from an American environment. I am glad to see disposition on the part of American sculptors, painters and architects and workers in textiles to develop from Indian art, a national art.' Bakst always retained his curiosity and a fresh eye and was ahead of his time in urging American artists to look at their indigenous art for inspiration.

His interest in textile design led to a commission by the American silk manufacturer Arthur L. Selig. Bakst quickly produced twelve designs based not only on Russian but also on early American Pueblo Indian, Mexican and Peruvian motifs some of which were identical to those he used in the Evergreen Theatre. Judging from the metric width of the several fragments which remain in the collections of the Baltimore Museum of Art it is clear that the silks were manufactured in France. Some forty designs, found in New York after Bakst's death, were exhibited between 1927–30 at various centres in the United States. He also made at least one design specifically for wall-paper which was produced by Arthur Sanderson and Sons in 1924. As the *New York Times* said of the exhibition: '... the opulent talent for design which the great Russian designer displayed in his ballet designs is present in these colored designs for textiles.' (One of them has been used for the endpapers of this book.)

While he was in America Bakst did not neglect his theatre work in Europe. He had chosen to neglect, however, his threat about not working for Rubinstein any more and was busy on two productions for her, *Phaedre* by d'Annunzio and his own *Istar*. On 26 February he wrote about his work for *Phaedre*: 'Which is going to be audacious (and new) and which requires serious study for each setting. I am moved by the tragedy – one of the most beautiful by d'Annunzio, if not the most beautiful, the most "theatrical" (good). It's true that there are one or two boring passages (the scene between Hippolytus and the Phoenician) – but you will have to cut wisely and battle with Mr Doderet [the translator] . . . as for the costumes, don't worry about them, I do not have time now, but it will sort itself out in Paris where I can control their production (in a new style) for without me present to criticize the costumier will only make something old-hat and conventional, inspite of a good design. Mme Rubinstein should not worry – I will be in time for both *Phaedre* and *Istar*.'

In 1923 Bakst published his travel notes on his journey to Greece in 1907. This trip must have been very much on his mind when he was designing *Phaedre* because his palace settings (pp. 226–27) are his interpretations of the Palace of Minos at Knossos. D'Annunzio's *Phaedre* is the same legend as dramatized by Euripides and Racine but with typical d'Annunzian differences. Phaedre (Ida Rubinstein) kills herself neither by hanging as in Euripides, nor by taking poison as in Racine, but by having arrows shot at her by Artemis. The other big difference, as usual with Rubinstein productions, was that there was a very large cast of extras who all needed costumes. Bakst again used motifs and patterns which he had seen and drawn in Crete. He also reused many of his earlier 'Greek' designs for *Daphnis and Chloë* and for Racine's *Phèdre* (1917) which, in their new context, would not necessarily have been familiar to the audience. Most of the new drawings were hurried sketches on a template system; some were mirror images of tracings. Even the several costume designs for Rubinstein herself were repeats or reverse repeats of the same figure (p. 225). In spite of his earlier assurances to Rouché, Bakst seems to have been somewhat overwhelmed by this production and less inspired although the final effect convinced Robert de Beauplan who wrote in *Théâtre et Comoedia Illustré*: 'The sets and the costumes by Léon Bakst are the most sumptuous and audacious recreation of a myceno-phoenician style. In their contrasting polychromy the blues, oranges, greens, reds, blacks are accurately inspired by recent archeology. By their grandeur, the colossal temple with monstrous idols in the first act, and the piles of colonnades superimposed on heavy foundations in the palace of Phaedre in the second, symbolically crush the paltriness of the human being, and the chaos of rocks on the beach where the body of Hippolytus lies in the third act gives an unexpected savagery to the mediterranean mellowness.'

By July Bakst was on to gentler things and working hard on *La Nuit Ensorcelée*. This was originally titled *Nocturne* and sometimes referred to as 'the Chopin ballet' in deference to the music adapted by Emile Vuillermoz. Bakst again wrote a number of letters to Rouché which show how he was always obsessed with trying to get everything as perfect as possible. Having heard that there would be no special curtain between the two scenes of the ballet, Bakst protested: 'That will be a disaster, because we have the music – an intermezzo, for the change of scene and if the audience sees the house curtain of the Opéra it will just go to the buffet and foyer, and we won't have the impression of continuity between the first and second acts which the curtain provides so successfully!' In September there were problems over the costumes. He wrote on the 4th:

I have succeeded in knocking Muelle's price down by 50 francs for each costume; but you should not insist too much because for a ballet which will last you need materials that will last, and as I am also something of a dressmaker myself I choose (as I always have done) the quality of the materials. I know how to be intransigent, bearing in mind the necessary goal for the success and the lasting quality of the costumes, and if I was indulgent over a hurried order for *St Sébastien* – and I accepted the process of making the women's costumes at the last minute – I will never allow the same thing for a piece which in my estimation (and my experience is as few directors have) will have an enormous number of performances. All I ask, beg, insist is for the best and *your success at the Opéra . . .* and your appreciation of my efforts; I stayed here without a holiday *in order to paint better, to supervise, and teach the dancers the ballet* as I understand it, and if you think that I will be less exacting than Staats [the choreographer] – the reverse is true . . . to battle, above all, as author, I change my skin – you will see me at the rehearsals.

The first night was on 12 November 1923. The action of *La Nuit Ensorcelée* takes place in Paris during the Second Empire. 'Two Princesses, before going to bed, look at a cupboard where their dolls are sleeping. Then they decide to say goodnight to them. In Scene two, the little happy group finds a perfect place to hold a dance in the spacious hall at the bottom of the grand staircase'. The first act was a symmetrical set (p. 226) with two beds on one side, a fireplace with an ornate carving surround on the other, and a large chinoiserie cupboard for the

Set design (preliminary drawing) for Act
I of *Phaedre*, 1923
215 × 280
SOTHEBY'S/PRIVATE COLLECTION

Bakst based all his set designs for this
production on the Palace of Minos at
Knossos in Crete which he had seen in
1907 being excavated at the time by Sir
Arthur Evans. Although the designs are
archaeologically exact Bakst has also
used his imagination

Set design for Act I of *Phaedre*
320 × 550
MUSÉE NATIONAL D'ART MODERNE, CENTRE
GEORGES POMPIDOU, PARIS

Scene (Act 2) and characters in *Phaedre*
from *Le Théatre et Comoedia Illustré*
BIBLIOTHÈQUE NATIONALE, DÉPARTEMENT DES
ARTS DU SPECTACLE, PARIS

Opposite, above
Set design for Act 2 of *Phaedre*, 1923
335 × 523
THYSSEN-BORNEMISZA COLLECTION

Below
Compare scaled and squared up
drawing of the set (the squares equal
0.50 metre) made for the scene painters
RICHARD NATHANSON, LONDON/BIBLIOTHÈQUE
NATIONALE, MUSÉE DE L'OPÉRA, PARIS

227

Costume design for *Phaedre* 1923 and comparative illustration from *Theatre Arts Monthly*, January 1924

The design shows how Bakst adapted an archaeological relic to suit his costume design. On the left is a portion of a fresco from Tiryns in Crete. Bakst's costume design, however, is much more lascivious and grotesque than the original

dolls centre stage at the back. Bakst got his strange drop curtain between the acts, painted like a screen with an alternate pattern of larger than life-size Chinese figures. The grand staircase of the second act was like a greatly enlarged detail from *The Sleeping Princess* and, using the same trick as before, was painted to be in scale with the dolls and not with the human beings. Some of the costumes were remakes of those designed for *La Boutique Fantasque*, others harked back to the beginning of his career with *The Fairy Doll* and *Le Carnaval*. But the taste had changed. The ballet was much too puerile for a post-war audience. But Bakst could not see that. When he heard that 'this *Nuit*, which has filled and enthused the house' had been 'banished from the repertory for the month of December' he wrote to Rouché to ask 'why not slip this 35 minute ballet in after an opera? That would not harm anybody, and, on the contrary, would *reaffirm the impression of a dazzling success*. You know how pleased Diaghilev would be ... if he finds out that this little ballet which made him so angry and which deprives him of his supremacy is only given *rarely in the future*! I work for the complete success of your ballet, I love it and I admire it sincerely, but I must see some encouragement.' He then referred to his new ballet, *La Folle Jeunesse* which he was planning with Vuillermoz and Aubert as part of a double bill with *La Nuit Ensorcelée* and which he thought would be ready by the following June. He describes it in a letter of 14 December as a ballet in two acts, with 29 characters and no stars, but he also states:

> My idea is that this ballet, coupled with *La Nuit Ensorcelée* will strike a terrible blow at Diaghilev's ballet *in the spring*; and the victory, I am positive, with full houses, will be

at the Opéra. I have warned Diaghilev, as I usually do quite openly, that he is going to receive a decisive blow by the ballet at the Opéra – he does not forget, that the ballets (except *Petrushka*, on which I also collaborated) which had the most dazzling success were the ones for which I wrote the libretto as well as doing the design, such as *Schéhérazade*, *Thamar*, Schumann's *Carnaval*, *Après-midi d'un Faune* (Nijinksy did what I showed him), *Daphnis and Chloë*, *Narcisse*, and *Cléopâtre* completely transformed by me with Fokine.

I love the ballet and if I had been taught choreography more thoroughly I should have become a choreographer myself one day, but I am not so ambitious as to attack an art in which I do not feel completely at home.

Bakst now became increasingly agitated in a frenzy of self-justification and was determined to spite Diaghilev. He also probably realized that his creative inventiveness was fading. His two ballets were like going back over old ground and, although *La Nuit Ensorcelée* was revived by the Opéra in 1941, *Folle Jeunesse* was never produced.

At the same time Bakst was also preparing to go to America for the second time to give a lecture tour arranged by Mrs Garrett and in the same letter he asked Rouché to release him from designing *Istar*. He wrote:

There are 15 days left until the 31st. In these 15 days I have to abandon all my work for America and make a costume – with seven transformations – for Mme Rubinstein, eight costumes for the entrées, one for two partners and one for the fiancé – that is 12 extremely difficult costumes, as they have to be *original*, and *then*, what amounts to *seven terribly complicated costumes for Mme Rubinstein* on which I will spend my whole time supervising the smallest detail, because Mme Rubinstein always orders costumes from dressmakers and not theatrical costumiers, and I have to teach the dressmakers every stitch of the needle! During these same 15 days I have to be present at *every* rehearsal at Mme Rubinstein's because Staats told me he does not know what I want, and as you know, you can only explain by demonstrating the steps. Well, it is an *impossible* task because I have neither the time nor the head for it, and the result will never be seen by me as I am leaving on the 2nd; I will not be able to light the entrances, or the set, direct things or make the thousand corrections – without which the work will be a fiasco . . . .

Bakst sailed on 2 January 1924 in the *Majestic*. The production of *Istar* was postponed as Rubinstein had been preoccupied with mounting a production of *La Dame aux Camélias* by Alexandre Dumas, which Bakst had tried, unsuccessfully, to prevent her from undertaking because he thought the part was beyond her capabilities. He therefore stayed in America lecturing and doing more textile designs for Arthur L. Selig before returning to Paris at the beginning of May 1924.

Istar, twenty minutes long, was given one performance only at the Opéra on 10 July 1924 in aid of the Olympic games. It was Bakst's last production but he never saw the performance. It was just as well, the libretto is a farrago of absurdity. Ida Rubinstein, however, later remembered: ' . . . Léon Bakst, fired with enthusiasm for the very beautiful legend of Istar, worked on it with love, with passion. He was at the dress rehearsal but he was already in a great deal of pain. *Istar* was his last thought. He only left my dressing room to return home, and we never saw him again.' We do not know what his 'pain' was but he was still busy making plans for the future. There was to be a new production in New York for Morris Gest and a trip to Palestine in the spring of 1925. He was the master of his profession, he knew all the tricks of his trade. He was still appreciated, even venerated, by managements, critics and audiences. The theatre had been his life for more than twenty years. Was he now depressed because he was exhausted from over-work or because he realized that his work had reached the end? It is a mystery.

Léon Bakst fell into his final, fatal depression. Prince Peter Lieven wrote: 'There was talk of artero-sclerosis and kidney and heart trouble, but nothing was definite or clear. It seemed as though his organism had suddenly heard him and, obeying his sick soul, refused to work any longer.' At first he stayed in his flat, but then he was moved to a clinic in Rueil-Malmaison outside Paris where he died at 4.30 in the morning of 27 December 1924. His brother-in-law, having escaped from Russia, arrived in Paris via the Far East in time to arrange the Jewish funeral on 31 December 1924. Among those present were Jacques Rouché,

Costume design for Mireille in *La Nuit Ensorcelée*, 1923
450 × 292

Set design for scene 1 of *La Nuit Ensorcelée*, 1923
Pencil, 143×255
MR AND MRS N.D. LOBANOV-ROSTOVSKY
COLLECTION

Scene 1 of *La Nuit Ensorcelée*, 1941
BIBLIOTHÈQUE NATIONALE, MUSÉE DE L'OPÉRA,
PARIS

The original production in 1923 was
revived with the same sets in 1941 at the
Opéra, Paris

Drop curtain for *La Nuit Ensorcelée*, 1941
between scenes 1 and 2
BIBLIOTHÈQUE NATIONALE, MUSÉE DE L'OPÉRA,
PARIS

Scene 2 of *La Nuit Ensorcelée*, 1941
BIBLIOTHÈQUE NATIONALE, MUSÉE DE L'OPÉRA,
PARIS

Robert de Rothschild, Maurice de Brunoff, Pablo Picasso, Serge Prokofieff, Léo Staats, César Franck, André Levinson, Jean Cocteau, and Ida Rubinstein. His divorced wife, too, came from Russia.

Bakst is buried in the Batignolles cemetry in Paris with his sister, Sophie Kliatchko-Bakst, a brother-in-law, André Barsacq, director of the Atelier Theatre, Paul, son of Sophie and Eugene Constantinowitz, another brother-in-law. Nearby is the grave of Alexandre Benois. Incessant traffic drones overhead on the Périphérique.

Diaghilev sent a telegram from London to José-Maria Sert: 'Please convey my deepest condolences to Bakst's family on the loss of a friend. Masses of touching memories over the long period of our collaboration and 35 years of friendship.'

Newspapers all over the world recorded his death and carried panegyric obituaries. The *New York Times* in a leader on 4 January 1925 provided the perfect epitaph: 'Like so many of his distinguished contemporaries, Bakst long painted in the conventional manner – and, what is something quite different, painted conventionally. Then he discovered the strong joy of barbaric color, the intoxication of the tortured line, and set all the world aglow with a flame that was of the senses wholly.'

Set design (preliminary drawing) for
Istar, 1924
210 × 270
THEATRE MUSEUM, LONDON

234

Costume design for Ida Rubinstein in
the title role in *Istar*, 1924
482 × 314

Appendix 1

The 1909 season of the Ballets Russes was a great artistic success but lost money. Diaghilev was left in debt to Gabriel Astruc, the French impressario, who sequestered the scenery, costumes and props. Astruc then made a deal with Raoul Guinsbourg, director of the Société de Monaco, who agreed to buy most of them for 20,000 francs but would release them if Diaghilev repaid the debt by a certain date. A deed of sale was drawn up with an inventory and this extremely interesting document not previously published (in French in the Gabriel Astruc papers in the Dance Collection of the New York Public Library at Lincoln Center) is revealing because it lists various sets and costumes in detail. It included the following productions:

Cléopâtre	75 costumes	1 decor
Armide	105 costumes	2 decors
Sylphides	24 costumes	1 decor
Festin	50 costumes	1 decor
Rousslan [sic]	50 costumes	
Igor	130 costumes	

Cléopâtre and Le Festin are the only two known productions designed by Bakst to have inventories which list the different components of his sets and costumes. This is the inventory for Cléopâtre (except for Rubinstein's costume it is almost complete):

1 floor cloth
1 sky cloth
2 black drapes
1 black border
1 wing prompt side
1 wing o.p. side
1 tarpaulin
1 ground row parapet prompt
1 ground row parapet o.p.
2 sphinx prompt
2 sphinx o.p.
1 canopy in 5 pieces
3 gondolas
9 runners for gondolas
1 cyclorama

Costumes:

Slaves (women):
11 cashmere dresses of different colours (one in knotted satin silk trimmed with gold braid and paint, with ribbons of silk muslin)
11 orange cashmere collars trimmed with gold braid
11 yellowish silk tights
11 yellowish body stockings
10 pairs ballet shoes

Priestesses (Servants in the Temple):
8 taffeta dresses painted blue with pendant in white painted faille (coarse grained silk) embroidered in silver
8 collarettes in white painted faille
8 white faille hair ribbons
8 olive green silk body stockings
8 olive green silk tights
8 pairs ballet shoes

Jewesses:
1 blue coat with painted gold spots
6 deep red cashmere coats with painted gold spots
7 voile, muslin and foulard silk painted dresses with metal motifs and precious stones
7 head scarves of painted crêpe de chine
14 gold metal bracelets

Greeks:
2 painted and spangled water-green crêpe tunics
2 body stockings
2 silk head-dresses, painted and trimmed with gold and spangles
4 white voile tunics painted and trimmed with gold
4 cream crêpe de chine tunics painted green
4 voile scarves painted green
4 white silk net head-dresses, with metal motifs
10 painted cashmere shawls

Berenice (Pavlova):
1 crêpe de chine dress embroidered with pearls and precious stones
1 skirt sewn to under dress in white chiffon embroidered with gold
1 painted cashmere scarf with wool and gold fringes
1 nut-brown body stocking

Amoun (Fokine):
1 silk, multi-coloured loin cloth with gold embroidered pendant
1 orange silk collar with white cloth appliqué
1 nut-brown silk trunk-hose
1 green silk body stocking
1 green silk doublet
1 nut-brown silk body stocking
3 nut-brown silk tights
1 gold cloth belt
1 glass collar
1 pair bracelets and spangled fabric

Slave (Nijinsky):
1 tunic with wool and silk pendant embroidered with gold and trimmed with pearls
1 silk and wool loin cloth

1 grey silk trunk-hose
1 grey silk body stocking
1 grey silk tights
1 silk and wool belt embroidered with gold
1 pair white soft leather ballet shoes
2 Egyptian head-dresses

High Priest (Boulgakov):
1 skirt in painted voile
1 pendant with silk belt with metal embroidered motifs
1 silk collar with gold braid
1 tiger skin (plush, cardboard head)
1 cardboard head-dress trimmed with pearls
1 pair red leather sandals
1 ½ silk yellowish colour body stocking
1 ½ silk yellowish tights

Servants of the Temple:
2 loin cloths with draperies and pendants in white voile
2 voile capes painted gold
2 brown silk trunk-hose
2 white voile head-dresses
2 brown cotton body stockings
2 brown cotton tights

Egyptians:
8 white cashmere loin cloths with pendants
8 brown velveteen trunk-hose
8 brown cotton tights (with soles)
8 brown cotton body stockings
8 pairs brown cotton gloves
8 white cashmere head-dresses

Jews:
2 purplish-red silk tunics with gold painted fringes
2 painted velveteen capes embroidered with gold

2 blue and heliotrope-coloured silk scarves
2 cambric shirts
2 blue and heliotrope-coloured head-dresses
2 pairs red and blue leather shoes

Satyrs:
2 orange cashmere tunics
2 brown velveteen cloth belts
2 brown cotton body stockings
2 brown cotton tights
2 pony tails with sash
2 pairs white leather sandals

Greeks:
6 painted nut-coloured velveteen tunics
6 white painted velveteen loin-cloths
6 brown velveteen trunk-hose
6 velveteen tiger skins
6 nut-coloured cotton body stockings
6 nut-coloured cotton tights
6 pairs white and green leather sandals

Slaves:
8 velveteen and green cloth tunics
8 brown cotton body stockings
8 brown cotton tights with brown cotton soles
8 brown head-dresses with painted silver spots

Negroes:
4 painted velveteen doublets
4 velveteen cloth and painted silk loin-cloths
4 silk belts with silver tassels
4 grey velveteen trunk-hose
4 violet painted cloth head-dresses
4 dark grey cotton body stockings
4 dark grey cotton tights

Appendix 2

Raymond Cogniat conducted an enquiry on 'The Evolution of Decor' for the newspaper *Comoedia*. Léon Bakst's reply was published on 3 September 1923. It is his last testament about theatre art:

'The crisis in beautiful stage scenery stems from a much more serious reason than economic problems or a lack of true specialist designers. In the modern theatre there are three important and well defined tendencies which in one way or another directly affect the character of a stage set.

The first tendency, which I call "protestant", has taken as its point of departure the denial of beautiful, rich, and impressive scenery on the pretext that it interferes with the perfect hearing of the text. It is as if a believing Protestant, faced with the cathedral of Notre Dame, were to complain that the beauty and splendour of the magnificent but religious architecture made it impossible for him to concentrate on the word of God. Such a person requires a drab and dull framework without the magical effect of perspective to occupy the stage box: a mass of constructions, representing the real grandeur of the space in which the action takes place. It always has a shabby effect without that breath of poetry which is the only and principal reason for scenery. In other words it is a negative aesthetic dictated by fear. Furthermore, when a director no longer knows how to "dress" a play he decides to set it by using grey, black or white "drapes", or nothing at all . . . Testimonimus paupertatis!

All the success of the theories of Gordon Craig, a second-rate designer but a first-rate talker, consists of this negative aesthetic which, by the way, has the added attraction of being economical. When you talk to the English that is what they sarcastically never fail to throw at the paradoxical head of Craig. This "protestant" gentleman also has the drawback of making all his productions the same, for, by using such shabby components (neutral drapes, theoretical walls, conventional stepped rostra) dictated not by the particular nature and vitality of any particular play but by a *formula* which is adapted to any work of art, one finishes up by making something monotonous, which in the long run is irritating. As far as I am concerned I cannot see the difference between these various "protestant" stagings, whether they were for *Hamlet* in New York, or a Maeterlinck in Paris, or for Bernard Shaw in London.

A drape to the right, a wall to the left, a so-called "huge" column in the background, and "steps" (why?) in the centre . . . Change all this around and then you can perform the second act, or another play – the effect will be the same. Poverty, monotony, and above all, deceit. A man of taste will always be exasperated, maddened by seeing fake columns, steps, rocks made of papier mâché!

If you are looking for economy at any price why not sit the actors down facing the audience against a uniform background – and just make them read the play? The words, bereft of the actors' movements to and fro, will certainly benefit; and it will not shock the meditation of neurasthenics.

The other movement, let us call it "clown-like", comes to us a bit from medieval productions, from Switzerland, from Reinhardt and also from Russia and its crazy directors who are searching for the "extraordinary" at all costs. Circus clowning and the descriptions of medieval plays have the attraction of being naive and sincere performances, as well as amusing when the subject requires. The spice of an important text spoken by a grotesque character, a clown, or a fool is in the end the secret dream of this "sincere" interpretation of every theatrical masterpiece. While the old fashioned director did everything he could to stop overlong monologues from being boring by having "performing links", the new director of "clown-like" theatre makes the actor say them jumping from a staircase, doing a somersault, running across the auditorium in a costume which he puts on on stage and, even more ridiculous and irresponsible, a woman's bodice for a man, a wicker basket to represent a large stomach, or a bristle brush on his head for an aigrette . . . All this in the middle of a thousand useless, inexplicable, cumbersome objects on stage over which the actor is forced to jump; in

this jumble of traditional as well as unexpected and hazardous scenery, with its piles of triangles, cubes, circles, an ordinary lantern instead of a theatrical moon (that is hideous too!) it is a question of who will most play the fool, who will be the most absurd . . . Now, think what a painter can do here who would simply seek to render by means of paint the atmosphere, the spirit of the play?

There remains the third tendency, that of the "music-hall", which takes and spoils everything a painter does. It strives for the sumptuousness of tinsel and the richness of glitter no matter the cost. Here scenery is an imitation. Symbolic of this kind of show is the so-called real richness of an exterior or an interior set in false "bright" colours, in awful and nauseating taste. But things are evolving here too. Perspective, which prevents the whole set from being soulless and dreary, is giving way more and more to real wall papers, gold and silver materials, lace and embroidery, and costumes covered in spangles and precious stones. This tendency unites rival producers, especially in America, because over there critics are first and foremost interested in how many thousands of dollars have been spent on producing this miserable ostentation . . .

The hectic life, the thirst for instantaneous and immediate effect, the boredom which grips every ordinary spectator as soon as he is presented with a work of art which is beautiful, serious and thought provoking and the dislike of the effort he has to make in order to assimilate the thoughts of the author results, as we see only too often, in those who work for the theatre instinctively keeping up with the latest fashion. Instead of performances of theatrical art, we see vulgar dishes, served boiling hot, outrageously spiced, to be swallowed quickly but which burn the stomach and poison the brain. Anything, so long as the effect, the "sensation" is made, and quickly, quickly.

I see nothing wrong with the theatre calling upon the services of the painter – quite the opposite. A knowledge of theatre, its particularities, the special problems of this "world of the boards" can be acquired in two or three years" study. But it is a mistake to think that every good painter is automatically a good theatre designer. That is obviously wrong, because the artistic imagination and talent of a good theatre designer depends more on a feeling for architecture and sculpture. I contend that to become a good theatre designer one must be born a theatre designer, just as one is born a sculptor, an architect, or an engraver. The theatre designer is inspired in quite a different way from even an excellent portrait painter or a good still-life painter, and we have seen what a wretched theatre designer a famous painter may turn out to be.

The child who kneaded bread and later clay may develop into a marvellous sculptor; another child who doodled in his exercise books and on walls may become a great draughtsman or painter. But the small boy who cuts up sweet boxes and builds theatres out of them, who dresses and paints dolls that he has made himself, and gaily decorates his sister's hat with table napkins and his grandfather's Indian handkerchiefs – in him slumbers the future designer of scenery and costumes.'

Productions, projects and individual designs

The credit for sets and costumes has been omitted where Léon Bakst designed both. If the set only is credited, it can be assumed that the costume was unspecified or is unknown, and vice versa.

The dates of the first performances and the production credits have been established wherever possible by reference to the programme and contemporary newspaper announcements and reports.

The original titles and those by which the productions are commonly known have been given.

The individual productions were often part of a programme with other items not designed by Bakst: these others are only included in the following list when they form an integral part of the particular programme.

Russian dates are given in the old style followed by the new style in brackets. The difference increases by one day every century; in the twentieth century there is a difference of thirteen days. When only one Russian date is given it has not been possible to determine whether it is in the old style or the new.

Most designs by Bakst are probably still in private collections. The names of some of the galleries, museums and collections holding designs are given together with the following abbreviations:

[sd] = set design
[cd] = costume design
[pd] = props or furniture design
[c] = costume

1901

Project for Mariinsky Theatre, St Petersburg

Sylvia

Ballet in 3 acts by Barbier and Baron de Reinach

COMPOSER: Léo Delibes
CHOREOGRAPHERS: Nicholas and Serge Legat
SETS: Act 1: Alexandre Benois; act 2: Léon Bakst; act 3 scene 1: Constantin Korovine; act 3 scene 2: Evgeny Lanceray
COSTUMES: Valentin Serov and Léon Bakst
[Not staged].
Leningrad, Russian Museum [cd]

1902

22 February (7 March), Hermitage Theatre, St Petersburg

Sertsa Markisi (*Le Coeur de la Marquise* or *The Heart of the Marchioness*)

Pantomime-ballet in 1 act with prologue and epilogue in verse by Frédéric Fevre

COMPOSER: G. Giran
CHOREOGRAPHER: Marius Petipa
San Francisco, Fine Arts Museums [cd]

14 (27) October, Alexandrinsky Theatre, St Petersburg

Hippolytus

Tragedy by Euripides, translated by Dimitri Merezhkovsky

DIRECTOR: Yuri Ozarovsky
COMPOSER: E. Overbeck
PRINCIPAL CHARACTERS:
    APHRODITE: Ekaterina Aga-Ogi-Gamza
    PHAEDRA: Vera Michurina
    HIPPOLYTUS: Georgi Yureff
    THESEUS: Ivan Schouvaloff
    NURSE: Olga Uvarova
    MESSENGER: Nikolai Khodotov

Leningrad, Museum of Theatrical and Musical Arts [cd]
Leningrad, Russian Museum [sd]
Lugano, Thyssen-Bornemisza Collection [cd]
Moscow, Pushkin Museum [cd]

1903

7 (20) February, Hermitage Theatre, St Petersburg
[Transferred 16 February (1 March), Mariinsky Theatre]

Feya Kukol (*Puppenfee* or *The Fairy Doll*)

Ballet in 1 act, 2 scenes by Hassreiter and Gaul

COMPOSER: Josef Bayer
CONDUCTOR: Riccardo Drigo
CHOREOGRAPHERS: Nicholas and Serge Legat
PRINCIPAL DANCERS:
    FAIRY DOLL: Mathilde Kshessinska
    BABY: Olga Preobrajenskaya
    FRENCH DOLL: A. Tchoumakova
    JAPANESE DOLL: Vera Trefilova
    TYROLEAN DOLL: Makarova
    THE 2 NEGROES: Alfred Bekeffi and Alexander Schiraiev

Leningrad, Russian Museum [cd]
Moscow, Bakhrushin Musuem [cd]
London, Mr and Mrs N. D. Lobanov-Rostovsky Collection [cd]
London, Theatre Museum [cd]

19 March (1 April), Theatre of the Conservatoire, St Petersburg

Mignon

Comic opera in 3 acts by Michel Carré and Jules Barbier based on Goethe's *Wilhelm Meister's Lehrjahre*

COMPOSER: Ambroise Thomas
Costume for Leonid Sobinov as Wilhelm Meister: Léon Bakst

1904

9 (22) January, Alexandrinsky Theatre, St Petersburg

Oedipus at Colonus

Tragedy in 5 acts by Sophocles, translated by Dimitri Merezhkovsky

DIRECTOR: Yuri Ozarovsky
PRINCIPAL CHARACTERS:
    OEDIPUS: M. Gay
    CREON: M. Korvin-Krukovsky
    POLINICES: Georgi Yuref
    ANTIGONE: Mme Pushkareva

Moscow, Bakhrushin Museum [cd]
Paris, Bibliothèque Nationale, Département des Arts du Spectacle [cd]

13 (26) April, Novii Theatre (Moika 61), St Petersburg
Charity performance in aid of the sick and wounded in the Far East war

Antigone

1 act of the tragedy by Sophocles

DIRECTOR: Yuri Ozarovsky
PRINCIPAL:
    ANTIGONE: Ida Rubinstein (under pseudonym of I. L. Lvovsky)

1905

March–April, designs for Diaghilev's *Exhibition of Russian Portraits* at Tauride Palace, St Petersburg

1906

25 February (10 March), Mariinsky Theatre, St Petersburg
In aid of the society for the care of poor students of municipal and elementary colleges of St Petersburg
Tableaux vivants:
CONDUCTOR: Felix Blumenfeld
Gogol in a summer garden
PRINCIPAL CHARACTERS:
    GOGOL: M. Gay
    LADY-IN-WAITING: Maria Kavalieri
The Parting between Napoleon and Josephine
PRINCIPAL CHARACTERS:
    NAPOLEON I: Pavel Gerdt
    JOSEPHINE: Maria Kavalieri

9 (22) April
Flight of the Butterflies
Part of a revised *A Midsummer Night's Dream* to Mendelssohn's music with original choreography by Marius Petipa
Pas de deux to music by Chopin
CHOREOGRAPHER: Michel Fokine
COSTUMES: Léon Bakst
PRINCIPALS: Elena Smirnova; Vaslav Nijinsky

October, designs for Diaghilev's exhibition *Two Centuries of Russian Art*, Grand Palais, Paris

November, designs front cloth for Vera Kommisarezhevsky Theatre using his painting *Elysium*

1907

10 (23) February, Mariinsky Theatre, St Petersburg
Charity performance in aid of the Society for the Prevention of Cruelty to Children
Chopiniana (First version)
CONDUCTOR: Riccardo Drigo
COMPOSER: Chopin (Polonaise, Nocturne, Waltz, Mazurka, Tarantella) orchestrated by Alexander Glazounov
CHOREOGRAPHER: Michel Fokine
PRINCIPAL DANCERS:
    CHOPIN: Alexis Boulgakov

TAGLIONI: Anna Pavlova
PERROT: Mikhail Obukhov
Costume for Pavlova and Obukhov: Léon Bakst

Evnika (*Eunice*)
Ballet in 1 act, 2 scenes based on an episode in the novel *Quo Vadis* by Henryk Sienkiewicz
COMPOSER: A. Shcherbacheff
CHOREOGRAPHER: Michel Fokine
PRINCIPAL DANCERS:
    EUNICE: Mathilde Kshessinska
    PETRONIUS: Pavel Gerdt
    ACTÉ: Anna Pavlova
    CLAUDIUS: Alexis Boulgakov
Costumes for Kshessinska and Torch Dancers: Léon Bakst
[Programme began with *Stepik and Maniurochka*, comedy in 1 act by N. Evreinov and concluded with *Walpurgis Night* (From act 5 of Gounod's *Faust*)]

12 (25) March, Dramatichesky Peredvizhnii Teatr (Dramatic Touring Theatre), New Theatre, St Petersburg
Otvergnuti Don Juan (*Don Juan Rejected*)
Trilogy in verse by Serge Raffalovitch
COMPOSER: Mr Chernoff
PRINCIPAL CHARACTERS:
    DON JUNA: Mr Gaydeburov
    THERESA: Mme Skarskaya
    THERESITA: Mme Boguslavskaya
    LEPORELLO: Mr Goldfalden
London, Theatre Museum [cd]

22 December (4 January 1908), Mariinsky Theatre, St Petersburg
Charity performance in aid of New-Born Babies and Poor Mothers
Act 2 of Verdi's *La Traviata*
Costume for Dimitri Smirnov as Armand: Léon Bakst
Ballet divertissement
CHOREOGRAPHER: Michel Fokine
Costume for Anna Pavlova in **The Swan** with music by Saint-Saëns: Léon Bakst
London, Museum of London [c]
Costume for Tamara Karsavina in **Tanets s Fakelom** (Torch Dance) with music by A. C. Arensky: Léon Bakst
[Programme began with Elka (*The Christmas Tree*), comedy in 1 act by V. I. Nemirovitch Danchenko and *Zheleska* (*A piece of iron*), play in 1 act by Persiannovaya]

1908
La Traviata
Opera in 3 acts by Francesco Maria Pave based on *La Dame aux Camélias* by Alexandre Dumas
COMPOSER: Giuseppe Verdi
2 Costumes for Dimitri Smirnov as Armand: Léon Bakst
Moscow, Bakhrushin Museum [cd]

8 (21) March, Mariinsky Theatre, St Petersburg
Charity performance in aid of the Imperial Patriotic Society
Egipetskiya nochi (*Egyptian Nights*)
Ballet in 1 act
COMPOSER: A. C. Arensky
CHOREOGRAPHER: Michel Fokine
PRINCIPAL DANCERS:
    VERONICA: Anna Pavlova
    JEWISH DANCER: Tamara Karsavina
    AMOUN: Michel Fokine
    HIGH PRIEST: Alexis Boulgakov
    CLEOPATRA: Timé
    ANTONY: Pavel Gerdt
Costume for Karsavina: Léon Bakst
Leningrad, Russian Museum [cd]
Ballet to the music of Chopin (Second version of *Chopiniana*)
Costume for Anna Pavlova: Léon Bakst
[Programme began with *Na boikom meste* (*In a busy place*), play in 1 act]

11 (24) March, Pavlov Hall, St Petersburg
Bal Poudré
COMPOSER: Muzio Clementi orchestrated by Maurice Keller
LIBRETTO: Alexandre Benois
CHOREOGRAPHER: Michel Fokine
PRINCIPALS: Marie Petipa, Enrico Cecchetti
[The costumes, by Bakst, were later used in *Le Carnaval* in 1910]

3 (16) November, Mikhailovsky Theatre, St Petersburg
Charity performance in aid of the Russian Theatrical Society
Salomé
Play by Oscar Wilde (performed mimed not spoken)
DIRECTOR: Vsevolod Meyerhold
COMPOSER: Alexander Glazounov
CHOREOGRAPHER: Michel Fokine
PRINCIPAL:
    SALOMÉ: Ida Rubinstein

20 December (2 January 1909), Theatre of the
Conservatoire, St Petersburg
Concert of ballet and dance music
CONDUCTOR: A. Ziloti
Programme included:
Dance of the Seven Veils from *Salomé*
Play by Oscar Wilde
COMPOSER: Alexander Glazounov
CHOREOGRAPHER: Michel Fokine
COSTUME: Léon Bakst
SOLO DANCER:
    SALOME: Ida Rubinstein

1909
19 May, Théâtre du Châtelet, Paris
Le Festin
Suite of dances including:
L'Oiseau de Feu
COMPOSER: Peter Ilyitch Tchaikovsky (The Blue-Bird
pas de deux from *The Sleeping Beauty*)
CHOREOGRAPHER: Marius Petipa
CONDUCTOR: Emile Cooper
SET: Constantin Korovine
COSTUMES: Léon Bakst
PRINCIPAL DANCERS:
    THE FIREBIRD: Tamara Karsavina
    THE GOLDEN BIRD (HINDU PRINCE): Vaslav Nijinsky
COMPANY: Diaghilev's Ballets Russes
London, Theatre Museum [c]

[*L'Oiseau de Feu* was the third dance in the suite, the
others were: *Cortège* by Rimsky Korsakov, *Lesghinka*
by Glinka, *Czardas* by Glazounov, *Hopak* by
Moussorgsky, *Trépak* by Tchaikovsky, *Grand pas
classique hongrois* by Glazounov and *Finale* by
Tchaikovsky. Other costumes were designed by
Alexandre Benois, Ivan Bilibine, Constantin
Korovine]

2 June, Théâtre du Châtelet, Paris
Cléopâtre (*Egyptian Nights* revised)
Choreographic drama in one act
COMPOSER: Anton Arensky
with the following additional extracts: *Prelude* by
Serge Taneiew; *Arrival of Cléopâtre* by Rimsky
Korsakov; *Dance of the Veils* by Glinka; *Bacchanale* by
Glazounov; *Finale* by Moussorgsky
CONDUCTOR: Nicholas Tcherepnine
CHOREOGRAPHER: Michel Fokine
PRINCIPAL DANCERS:
    TA-HOR: Anna Pavlova
    CLÉOPÂTRE: Ida Rubinstein
    SLAVE: Tamara Karsavina

    SLAVE: Vaslav Nijinsky
    AMOÛN: Michel Fokine
    THE HIGH PRIEST: Alexis Boulgakov
COMPANY: Diaghilev's Ballets Russes
Jerusalem, Israel Museum [cd]
London, Mr and Mrs N. D. Lobanov-Rostovsky
Collection [cd]
Paris, Musée des Arts Décoratifs [sd]

7 June, Théâtre du Châtelet, Paris
Judith
Opera by Alexander Serov
[Orgy scene and Finale]
COMPOSER: Alexander Serov
CONDUCTOR: Emile Cooper
DIRECTOR: Alexander Sanine
SETS: Scene 1: Valentin Serov; scene 2: Léon Bakst
PRINCIPAL SINGERS:
    JUDITH: Félia Litvinne
    HOLOPHERNE: Feodor Chaliapin
COMPANY: Diaghilev's Ballets Russes

Costume for Anna Pavlova in first version of
Chopiniana (adapted for *Giselle* act I and *Les
Sylphides*): Léon Bakst

Costume for Anna Pavlova tour in *Swan Lake*
San Antonio, Robert L. B. Tobin Collection [cd]

1910
16 (29) January, Theatre of the Conservatoire,
St Petersburg
Charity concert: Recital by Maria Kousnezoff
Extracts from operas by Rimsky-Korsakov;
Ivanov; Serov; Rachmaninoff; Bernardi
and a staged scene from
Thaïs
Lyric comedy by Louis Gallet based on the novel
by Anatole France
COMPOSER: Jules Massenet
CONDUCTOR: Alexander Glazounov
Costume for Maria Kousnezoff: Léon Bakst
Oxford, Ashmolean Museum [cd]

22 January (4 February), Dvorianskoe Sobranie
Hall, St Petersburg
Ethnographic Concert and Ball
Bacchanalia
COMPOSER: Alexander Glazounov
CHOREOGRAPHER: Michel Fokine
PRINCIPAL DANCERS: Anna Pavlova, Laurent Novikoff

20 February (5 March), Pavlova Hall,
St Petersburg
[Revived 20 May, Theater des Westens, Berlin
and 4 June, Théâtre National de l'Opéra, Paris
by Diaghilev's Ballets Russes and with new set
6 February 1911, Mariinsky Theatre,
St Petersburg]
Le Carnaval
Ballet in 1 act by Michel Fokine and Léon Bakst
COMPOSER: Robert Schumann orchestrated by
Rimsky-Korsakov; Liadov; Tcherepnine; Glazounov
CONDUCTOR: Alexander Glazounov
PRINCIPAL DANCERS:
    HARLEQUIN: Leonid Leontiev (Vaslav Nijinsky)
    COLUMBINE: Tamara Karsavina
    FLORESTAN: Vasili Kiselev
    PANTALON: Alfred Bekeffi
    EUSEBIUS: J. Kshessinsky (Alexander Shiriaiev)
    PIERROT: Vsevolod Meyerhold
    CHIARINA: Vera Fokina
    ESTRELLA: Ludmilla Schollar
    PAPILLON: Bronislava Nijinska
London, Theatre Museum [cd]

20 February (5 March), Mariinsky Theatre,
St Petersburg
Vostochni Tanets (*Oriental Dance*) [Also
known as *Danse Siamoise*, developed into *Les
Orientales* see 25 June, Théâtre National de
l'Opéra, Paris]
COMPOSER: Christian Sinding, orchestrated by
Alexander Taneev
Costume for Nijinsky: Léon Bakst
Kobold
COMPOSER: Edvard Grieg, orchestrated by Igor
Stravinsky
CHOREOGRAPHER: Michel Fokine
PRINCIPAL: Vaslav Nijinsky

16 May, Palace Theatre, London
Les Amours de Diane
CHOREOGRAPHER: Marius Petipa
PRINCIPAL DANCERS: Anna Pavlova; Michael Mordkin
Costume for Pavlova: Léon Bakst

Danse Bacchanale
COMPOSER: Alexander Glazounov
COSTUMES: Léon Bakst
DANCERS: Anna Pavlova; Michael Mordkin

4 June, Théâtre National de l'Opéra, Paris
Schéhérazade
Choreographic drama in 1 act by Michel Fokine
and Léon Bakst (actually Alexandre Benois),

COMPOSER: Nicholas Rimsky-Korsakov
CONDUCTOR: Nicholas Tcherepnine
CHOREOGRAPHER: Michel Fokine
FRONT CLOTH (1911): Valentin Serov
PRINCIPAL DANCERS:
    SHAHRIAR: Alexis Boulgakov
    SHAH ZEMAN: Vasili Kissilev
    ZOBEIDA: Ida Rubinstein
    ZOBEIDA'S FAVOURITE SLAVE: Vaslav Nijinsky
    GRAND EUNUCH: Enrico Cecchetti
COMPANY: Diaghilev's Ballets Russes
Canberra, Art Gallery [cd]
Hartford, Wadsworth Atheneum [cd]
Jerusalem, Israel Museum [cd]
London, Mr and Mrs N. D. Lobanov-Rostovsky
Collection [cd] ,
Lugano, Thyssen-Bornemisza Collection [cd]
Paris, Musée des Arts Décoratifs [sd]
San Francisco, Fine Arts Museums [cd]
Strasbourg, Musée des Beaux Arts [cd]

25 June, Théâtre National de l'Opéra, Paris
L'Oiseau de Feu (*The Firebird*)
Russian fairy story in 2 scenes adapted by
Michel Fokine
COMPOSER: Igor Stravinsky
CONDUCTOR: Gabriel Pierné
CHOREOGRAPHER: Michel Fokine
SETS AND COSTUMES: Alexander Golovine
Costumes for Tamara Karsavina (Firebird): Michel
Fokine (Ivan Tzarevitch); Vera Fokina (beautiful
Tzarevna): Léon Bakst
COMPANY: Diaghilev's Ballets Russes

25 June, Théâtre National de l'Opéra, Paris
Les Orientales
Choreographic sketches by Serge Diaghilev
COMPOSERS: Alexander Glazounov, Christian Sinding,
Anton Arensky, Edvard Grieg, Alexander Borodin
CHOREOGRAPHER: Michel Fokine after Marius Petipa
SET AND COSTUMES: Constantin Korovine and Léon
Bakst
PRINCIPAL DANCERS: Tamara Karsavina; Vera Fokina;
    Catherine Geltzer; Michel Fokine; Vaslav
    Nijinsky; Alexander Volinine
Dances included:
Danse Siamoise
COMPOSER: Christian Sinding
CHOREOGRAPHER: Vaslav Nijinsky
COSTUME: Léon Bakst
DANCER: Vaslav Nijinsky
COMPANY: Diaghilev's Ballets Russes

Costume design for Maria Kousnezoff in
Puccini's **Madama Butterfly**

Project: Sets and costumes for *The Brothers
Karamazov* by Fyodor Dostoyevsky
[Not staged, no designs traced]

Project: *Faust* by Gounod
[see 26 June 1914, Royal Opera House, Covent
Garden, London, *Mefistofele*]

1911
19 April, Théâtre de l'Opéra, Monte Carlo
Le Spectre de la Rose
Ballet in 1 scene by Jean-Louis Vaudoyer from a
poem by Théophile Gautier
COMPOSER: Carl-Maria von Weber (*Invitation to the
Waltz*)
CONDUCTOR: Nicholas Tcherepnine
CHOREOGRAPHER: Michel Fokine
DANCERS:
    THE YOUNG GIRL: Tamara Karsavina
    THE ROSE: Vaslav Nijinsky
COMPANY: Diaghilev's Ballets Russes
Hartford, Wadsworth Atheneum [cd]
London, Theatre Museum [pd] [c]

26 April, Théâtre de l'Opéra, Monte Carlo
Narcisse
Mythological poem in 1 act by Léon Bakst
COMPOSER: Nicholas Tcherepnine
CONDUCTOR: Nicholas Tcherepnine
CHOREOGRAPHER: Michel Fokine
PRINCIPAL DANCERS:
    ECHO: Tamara Karsavina
    NARCISSE: Vaslav Nijinisky
    BACCHANTE: Bronislava Nijinska
    YOUNG BEOITIAN: Vera Fokina
COMPANY: Diaghilev's Ballets Russes
Leningrad, Museum of Theatrical and Musical Arts
[cd]
London, Mr and Mrs N. D. Lobanov-Rostovsky
Collection [cd]
London, Theatre Museum [cd] [c]
Moscow, Bakhrushin Museum [cd]
Oxford, Ashmolean Museum [cd]
Paris, Musée d'Art Moderne [sd]
Strasbourg, Musée des Beaux Arts [cd]

22 May, Théâtre du Châtelet, Paris
[Revised, See 17 June 1922, Théâtre National de
L'Opéra, Paris]
Le Martyre de Saint Sébastien
Mystery play in 5 acts by Gabriele d'Annunzio
COMPOSER: Claude Debussy
CONDUCTOR: André Caplet

DIRECTOR: Armand Bour
CHOREOGRAPHER: Michel Fokine
PRINCIPAL CHARACTERS:
    ST SEBASTIEN: Ida Rubinstein
    GIRL STRICKEN WITH FEVER: Véra Sergine
    MATER DOLOROSA: Adeline Dudlay
    THE EMPEROR: Desjardins
    THE PREFECT: Henry Krauss
    THE VOICE: Rose Féart
COMPANY: Ida Rubinstein
Boston, Isabella Stewart Gardner Museum [cd]
Jerusalem, Israel Museum [cd]
Oxford, Ashmolean Museum [cd] [sd]
Paris, Bibliothèque Nationale, Département des Arts
du Spectacle [cd]
Paris, Musée d'Art Moderne [sd]

6 June, Théâtre du Châtelet, Paris
Sadko
Ballet extract from the opera: *The Kingdom
under the Sea*
COMPOSER: Nicholas Rimsky-Korsakov
CONDUCTOR: Nicholas Tcherepnine
CHOREOGRAPHER: Michel Fokine
SET: Boris Anisfeld
COSTUMES: Boris Anisfeld and Léon Bakst
PRINCIPAL DANCERS: Liubov Tchernicheva; Vera
    Nemchinova; Léon Woizikovsky

Project: **La Péri**
Ballet in 2 acts by Théophile Gautier and Jean
Coralli (revised and adapted by Serge Diaghilev)
COMPOSER: Paul Dukas
CHOREOGRAPHER: Michel Fokine
DANCERS:
    LA PÉRI: Natasha Trouhanova
    ISKENDER: Vaslav Nijinsky
[Not staged by the Ballets Russes but performed by
Trouhanova with sets and costumes by René Piot,
22 April 1912, Théâtre du Châtelet, Paris]
London, Mr and Mrs N. D. Lobanov-Rostovsky
Collection [cd]
Lugano, Thyssen-Bornemisza Collection [cd]
Moscow, Bakhrushin Museum [cd]
New York, Metropolitan Museum [cd]

Théâtre du Gaieté-Lyrique, Paris
Sets for **Ivan le Terrible**

3 November, Royal Opera House, Covent
Garden, London
Costumes for Anna Pavlova and Vaslav
Nijinsky in **L'Oiseau d'Or**, *pas de deux* from
The Sleeping Beauty

1911–12

Costumes for Maria Kousnezoff for *Fortunio* and *Beatrice* by Messager; Mimi in *La Bohème* by Puccini; *Salomé* by Richard Strauss; *Madama Butterfly* by Puccini; Euridice in *Orpheus*; Volkhova in *Sadko* by Rimsky-Korsakov; Marguerite in *Faust* by Gounod; *Manon* by Massenet; Violetta in *La Traviata* by Verdi

Leningrad, Museum of Theatrical and Musical Arts [cd]

1912

8 January, Odéon, Paris
Bajazet
Tragedy in five acts by Jean Racine
Costume for Gilda Darthy as Roxane: Léon Bakst

10 (23) March, Mariinsky Theatre,
St Petersburg
Charity performance in aid of the Literary Fund
[Revived with new set by Mstislav Dobuzhinsky,
16 April 1914, Théâtre de l'Opéra, Monte Carlo]
Papillons
Pantomime ballet in 1 act by Michel Fokine
COMPOSER: Robert Schumann orchestrated by
Nicholas Tcherepnine
CHOREOGRAPHER: Michel Fokine
PRINCIPAL DANCERS: Tamara Karsavina, Michel
    Fokine
[The programme was as follows: *Sadko: The Kingdom under the Sea*, *Carnaval*, *Papillons*, *Islamey*]
Moscow, Pushkin Museum [cd]
Paris, Bibliothèque Nationale, Département des Arts du Spectacle [cd]

4 May, Théâtre du Châtelet, Paris
Hélène de Sparte
Tragedy in 4 acts by Emile Verhaeren
COMPOSER: Déodat de Sévérac
CONDUCTOR: Louis Hasselmans
DIRECTOR: Alexander Sanine
PRINCIPAL CHARACTERS:
    HELEN: Ida Rubinstein
    ELECTRA: Véra Sergine
    POLLUX: Edouard de Max
    MENELAUS: Desjardins
    CASTOR: Roger Karl
    ZEUS: Dorival
COMPANY: Ida Rubinstein
Boston, Museum of Fine Arts [cd]
Lugano, Thyssen-Bornemisza Collection [cd]

Oxford, Ashmolean Museum [cd]
Paris, Musée des Arts Décoratifs [sd]
San Francisco, Fine Arts Museums [sd]

13 May, Théâtre du Châtelet, Paris
Le Dieu Bleu
Hindu ballet in 1 act by Jean Cocteau and
Federigo de Madrazo
COMPOSER: Reynaldo Hahn
CONDUCTOR: Désiré-Emile Inghelbrecht
CHOREOGRAPHER: Michel Fokine
PRINCIPAL DANCERS:
    YOUNG MAN: Max Frohman
    YOUNG GIRL: Tamara Karsavina
    THE GODDESS: Lydia Nelidova
    THE BLUE GOD: Vaslav Nijinsky
    THE HIGH PRIEST: Michel Fedorov
    THE DRUNKEN BAYADÈRE: Bronislava Nijinska
COMPANY: Diaghilev's Ballets Russes
Boston, Museum of Fine Arts [sd]
Castle Howard, Castle Howard Costume Galleries [c]
Jerusalem, Israel Museum [cd]
London, Theatre Museum [cd] [c]
Lugano, Thyssen-Bornemisza Collection [cd]
Moscow, Bakhrushin Museum [cd]
Paris, Musée d'Art Moderne [sd]
San Antonio, Robert L. B. Tobin Collection [cd]

20 May, Théâtre du Châtelet, Paris
Thamar
Dance drama in 1 act by Léon Bakst after a
poem by Mikhail Lermontov
COMPOSER: Mily Balakirev
CONDUCTOR: Pierre Monteux
CHOREOGRAPHER: Michel Fokine
PRINCIPAL DANCERS:
    THAMARA: Tamara Karsavina
    THE PRINCE: Adolf Bolm
COMPANY: Diaghilev's Ballets Russes
Paris, Musée des Arts Décoratifs [sd]

29 May, Théâtre du Châtelet, Paris
L'Après-midi d'un faune
Ballet in 1 scene by Vaslav Nijinsky after the
poem by Stéphane Mallarmé
COMPOSER: Claude Debussy (*Prélude à l'Après-midi d'un Faune*)
CONDUCTOR: Pierre Monteux
CHOREOGRAPHER: Vaslav Nijinsky
PRINCIPAL DANCERS:
    THE FAUN: Vaslav Nijinsky
    THE NYMPH: Lydia Nelidova
COMPANY: Diaghilev's Ballets Russes
Hartford, Wadsworth Atheneum [cd]
Paris, Musée d'Art Moderne [sd]

8 June, Théâtre du Châtelet, Paris
Daphnis and Chloë
Choreographic symphony in 1 act and 3 scenes
by Michel Fokine
COMPOSER: Maurice Ravel
CONDUCTOR: Pierre Monteux
CHOREOGRAPHER: Michel Fokine
PRINCIPAL DANCERS:
    CHLOË: Tamara Karsavina
    DAPHNIS: Vaslav Nijinsky
    DARKON: Adolf Bolm
COMPANY: Diaghilev's Ballets Russes
Castle Howard, Castle Howard Costume Galleries [c]
Hartford, Wadsworth Atheneum [cd]
London, Theatre Museum [cd] [c]
New York, Cooper-Hewitt Museum [cd]
New York, Metropolitan Museum [cd]
Paris, Bibliothèque Nationale, Musée de l'Opéra [cd]
Paris, Musée des Arts Décoratifs [sd]
San Antonio, Robert L. B. Tobin Collection [cd]
San Francisco, Fine Arts Museums [cd]

13 June, Théâtre du Châtelet, Paris
Salomé
Play by Oscar Wilde
DIRECTOR: Alexandre Sanine
CHOREOGRAPHER: Michel Fokine
COMPOSER: Alexander Glazounov
CONDUCTOR: Louis Hasselmans
PRINCIPAL CHARACTERS:
    SALOMÉ: Ida Rubinstein
    HÉRODIAS: Odette de Fehl
    HEROD: Edouard de Max
    IOKANAAN: Roger Karl
COMPANY: Ida Rubinstein

[The performance was preceded by a concert with the following programme: *The Easter Festival* by Rimsky-Korsakov, *Pelléas et Mélisande* by Gabriel Fauré, *Coq d'Or* (*Introduction* and *Wedding March*) by Rimsky-Korsakov]

Oxford, Ashmolean Museum [sd]

Costume for Marchesa Casati in *Indo-Persian Dance*

1913

15 May, Théâtre des Champs-Elysées, Paris
Jeux
Choreographic scenes by Vaslav Nijinsky
COMPOSER: Claude Debussy
CONDUCTOR: Pierre Monteux
CHOREOGRAPHER: Vaslav Nijinsky
DANCERS:
    YOUNG MAN: Vaslav Nijinsky

YOUNG GIRLS: Tamara Karsavina, Ludmilla
Schollar
COMPANY: Diaghilev's Ballets Russes

San Antonio, Robert L. B. Tobin Collection [sd]

20 May, Royal Opera House, Covent Garden,
London
Il Segretto di Susanna
Interlude in 1 act by Enrico Golisciani
COMPOSER: Ermanno Wolf-Ferrari
CONDUCTOR: Ettore Panizza
SET: Léon Bakst
SINGERS:
    IL CONTE GIL: Mario Sammarco
    CONTESSA SUSANNA: Alice Nielsen
    SANTE: Ambrosiny

22 May, Théâtre des Champs Elysées, Paris
Boris Godunov
Opera in a prologue, 4 acts (7 scenes) by Modest
Mussorgsky after the play by Alexander
Pushkin
COMPOSER: Modest Mussorgsky revised and
orchestrated by Nicholas Rimsky-Korsakov
CONDUCTOR: Emile Cooper
DIRECTOR: Alexander Sanine
SETS: Konstantin Juon; scene 4: Léon Bakst
COSTUMES: Ivan Bilibine; Konstantin Juon; Léon Bakst
(Polish scene)
PRINCIPAL SINGERS:
    BORIS: Fedor Chaliapin
    MARINA: Nicolaeva
COMPANY: Diaghilev's Ballets Russes

San Antonio, Robert L. B. Tobin Collection [cd]

11 June, Théâtre du Châtelet, Paris
La Pisanelle ou La Mort Parfumée
Comedy in a prologue and 3 acts by Gabriele
d'Annunzio
DIRECTOR: Vsevolod Meyerhold
CHOREOGRAPHER: Michel Fokine
COMPOSER: Ildebrando da Parma
CONDUCTOR: Désiré-Emile Inghelbrecht
PRINCIPAL CHARACTERS:
    LA PISANELLE: Ida Rubinstein
    PRINCE OF TYRE: Edouard de Max
    THE BAILIFF OF VENICE: Mendaille
    THE QUEEN: Suzanne Munte
    SIRE HUGUET: Hervé
    MAÎTRE ANCEL: Desfontaines
    PSILLUDE THE CRETAN: Puylagarde
COMPANY: Ida Rubinstein

Boston, Museum of Fine Arts [sd]
London, Theatre Museum [cd]

Lugano, Thyssen-Bornemisza Collection [cd]
New York, Cooper-Hewitt Museum [cd]
San Francisco, Fine Arts Museums [cd]

6 October, London Opera House
Oriental Fantasy [retitled *Orientale* for
American tour]
Ballet in 1 act by M. Zajlich
Arrangement of music by Alexander Serov;
Rimsky-Korsakov; Moussorgsky
CHOREOGRAPHER: M. Zajlich
CONDUCTOR: Theodore Stier
PRINCIPAL DANCERS: Anna Pavlova; Laurent Novikoff

Boston, Museum of Fine Arts [cd]
Boston, Isabella Stewart Gardner Museum [cd]
London, Theatre Museum [cd]

23 December, London Hippodrome
Hullo, Tango!
Revue in 9 scenes by Max Pemberton and
Albert P. de Courville
COMPOSER: Louis A. Hirsch
LYRICIST: George Arthurs
COSTUMES: Léon Bakst
PRINCIPALS: Ethel Levy; Shirley Kellog; Harry Tate;
George W. Monroe

London, Theatre Museum [cd]

Bérénice
'Heroic tragi-comedy' by Albert du Bois
Costume for Mme Barthet as Bérénice: Léon
Bakst

Boston, Museum of Fine Arts [cd]

More costumes for the Firebird and Ivan
Tzarevitch

Poster for dance recital by Caryathis (Elise
Jouhandeau)

Project for 1914: Set and costumes for *Le Bal
Bakst*, Royal Albert Hall, London arranged by
C. B. Cochran

1914
Project: Sets and costumes for **Orphée**,
Mariinsky Theatre, St Petersburg
COMPOSER: Roger Ducasse
[Produced later, see 11 June 1926, Théâtre National de
l'Opéra, Paris]
Moscow, Pushkin Museum [sd] [cd]

16 April, Théâtre de Monte Carlo
[Revival of production 10 March 1912,
Mariinsky Theatre, St Petersburg]
Papillons
SET: Mstislav Dobuzhinsky
COMPANY: Diaghilev's Ballets Russes

14 May, Théâtre National de l'Opéra, Paris
La Légende de Joseph
Ballet in 1 act by Count Harry Kessler and Hugo
von Hofmannsthal
COMPOSER: Richard Strauss
CONDUCTOR: Richard Strauss
CHOREOGRAPHER: Michel Fokine
SET: José-Maria Sert
PRINCIPAL DANCERS:
    JOSEPH: Leonide Massine
    POTIPHAR'S WIFE: Maria Kousnezoff
    POTIPHAR: Alexis Boulgakov
COMPANY: Diaghilev's Ballets Russes

Leningrad, Russian Museum [cd]
San Francisco, Fine Arts Museums [cd]

2 June, Théâtre National de l'Opéra, Paris
Midas
Mythological comedy in 1 act by Léon Bakst
after Ovid's *Metamorphoses*
COMPOSER: Maximilien Steinberg
CONDUCTOR: René Baton
CHOREOGRAPHER: Michel Fokine
SET AND COSTUMES: Mstislav Dobuzhinksy replacing
Léon Bakst
PRINCIPAL DANCERS: Tamara Karsavina, Adolf Bolm
COMPANY: Diaghilev's Ballets Russes

26 June, Royal Opera House, Covent Garden,
London
Mefistofele
Opera in 4 acts with prologue and epilogue by
Arrigo Boïto after Goethe's *Faust*
COMPOSER: Arrigo Boïto
CONDUCTOR: Giorgio Polacco
DIRECTOR: Fernand Almanz
CHOREOGRAPHER: François Ambrosiny
SETS: Léon Bakst (except act 1 scene 2, act 3 scene 3
and epilogue: not credited)
PRINCIPAL SINGERS:
    MEFISTOFELE: Adamo Didur
    MARGUERITE: Claudia Muzio
    FAUST: John McCormack

San Antonio, Robert L. B. Tobin Collection [sd]

Costumes for Maria Kousnezoff in **Leila**

1915

29 December, Théâtre National de l'Opéra, Paris
'Représentation Russe' in aid of the British Red
Cross
Schéhérazade
[New production]
L'Oiseau de Feu
COMPOSER: Igor Stravinsky
New costumes for the Firebird, Tzarevitch and the
Beautiful Tzarevna: Léon Bakst
La Princesse Enchantée
COMPOSER: Tchaikovsky (*Pas de deux classique*)
DANCERS:
    PRINCESS: Xenia Maclezova
    PRINCE: Adolf Bolm

New costume for Flora Revalles as the 'Sultane
Favorie' in American tour of *Schéhérazade*

New set for American tour of *L'Après-midi d'un
Faune*

1915–22

Paints mural panels based on *The Sleeping
Beauty* for James de Rothschild's house in
London

1916

31 August, Hippodrome, New York
The Big Show
Revue in 3 acts presented by Charles
Dillingham
PRODUCER: Charles Dillingham
DIRECTOR: R. H. Burnside
CONDUCTOR: Raymond Hubbell
Act 2: **The Sleeping Beauty**
Ballet in 4 tableaux from the fairy tale by Charles
Perrault arranged by R. H. Burnside
COMPOSER: Piotr Ilyitch Tchaikovsky
CHOREOGRAPHER: Ivan Clustine
PRINCIPAL DANCERS:
    THE PRINCESS AURORA: Anna Pavlova
    THE PRINCE DESIRÉ: A. Volinine
    LILAS, THE GOOD FAIRY: Letty Yorke
    CARABOSSE, THE BAD FAIRY: Henry Taylor
Baltimore, Evergreen House Foundation [sd] [cd]
New York, Museum of the City of New York [c]
Paris, Musée des Arts Décoratifs [sd]

1917

12 April, Teatro Costanzi, Rome
Les Femmes de Bonne Humeur (*The Good-
Humoured Ladies*)
Ballet in 1 act after the play *Le Donne di Buon
Umore* by Carlo Goldoni adapted by Vincenzo
Tommasini
COMPOSER: Domenico Scarlatti
CHOREOGRAPHER: Leonide Massine
PRINCIPAL DANCERS:
    LUCA: Enrico Cecchetti
    SILVESTRA: Josephine Cecchetti
    COSTANZA: Lubov Tchernicheva
    MARIUCCIA: Tamara Karsavina
    LEONARDO: Leonide Massine
COMPANY: Diaghilev's Ballets Russes

Baltimore, Evergreen House Foundation [sd] [cd]
London, Theatre Museum [cd]
Paris, Bibliothèque Nationale, Département des Arts
du Spectacle [cd]

27 June, Théâtre National de l'Opéra, Paris
Charity performance in aid of Romanian
wounded and prisoners of war
Phèdre
Tragedy by Jean Racine, act 4 only
PRINCIPALS:
    PHÈDRE: Ida Rubinstein
    HIPPOLYTE: Edouard de Max
[Programme included an act from *Thaïs, La
Princesse qui ne sourit plus* by Louis Delluc and a
Romanian ballet, *Cobzar*]

Project: Sets and costumes for **Antony and
Cleopatra** by William Shakespeare translated
by André Gide with music by Igor Stravinsky
for Ida Rubinstein
[Eventually produced 14 June 1920, Théâtre
National de l'Opéra, Paris with music by
Florent Schmitt, designed by Jacques Drésa]

Project: Sets and costumes for **Sadko** opera by
Alexander Serov for Théâtre National de
l'Opéra, Paris
[Not produced]

Baltimore, Evergreen House Foundation [cd]
Baltimore, Museum of Art [cd]
Lugano, Thyssen-Bornemisza Collection [cd]

Project: Costumes for **The Firebird** by Igor
Stravinsky

New York, Museum of Modern Art [cd]

1917–18

Project: Sets and costumes for **La Chair
(Flesh)** with Madame Ricotti
[Set and costumes were designed, models were
made but the production has not been traced]

1917–19

Project: Set and costumes for **La Boutique
Fantasque**
Ballet in 1 act based on *The Fairy Doll*
COMPOSER: Gioacchino Rossini arranged by Ottorino
Respighi
[André Derain replaced Bakst in production by
Diaghilev's Ballets Russes, 5 June 1919,
Alhambra Theatre, London]
Chicago, Art Institute [sd] [cd]
Jerusalem, Israel Museum [cd]
Paris, Bibliothèque Nationale, Musée de l'Opéra [cd]

1918

Project for the Mariinsky Theatre, Petrograd
Narcissus and Echo
[Revival of Ballets Russes' *Narcisse* abandoned
because Fokine and Bakst could not or would
not travel to Russia]

1919

20 May, Théâtre Marigny, Paris
Aladin ou la Lampe Merveilleuse
Fairy story in 3 acts and 11 scenes by Rip
(pseudonym of Georges Thenon)
COMPOSER: Willy Redstone
CONDUCTOR: Léo Pouget
DIRECTOR: Mr Signoret
CHOREOGRAPHER: Robert Quinault
PRINCIPAL CHARACTERS:
    BARBIZON: Albert Brasseur
    ALADIN: Clermont
    FOUILLOCHE: Signoret
    SUZY: Yvonne Reynolds
    The Tiller Girls
Jerusalem, Israel Museum [cd]
New York, Museum of Modern Art [sd]

Set for **Nocturne**
[Subsequently retitled and produced, see
12 November 1923, Théâtre National de l'Opéra,
Paris, *La Nuit Ensorçelée*]

246

1920
4 October, Century Theatre, New York
Mecca
Melodrama by Oscar Asche
DIRECTOR: E. Lyall Swete
COMPOSER: Percy Fletcher
CHOREOGRAPHER: Michel Fokine
SETS: Joseph and Philip Harker
COSTUMES: Percy Anderson and Léon Bakst
PRINCIPALS:

> ALI SHAR: Lionel Braham
> SHARAZAD: Gladys Henson
> ZUMMURUD: Hannah Toback
> ZARKA: Kate Mayhew
> THE SULTAN: Orville R. Caldwell
> PRINCE NUR AL-DIN: Herbert Grimwood

1921
20 June, Théâtre National de l'Opéra, Paris
Daphnis and Chloë
[New production, see 8 June 1912, Théâtre du Châtelet, Paris]
PRINCIPAL DANCERS:

> DAPHNIS: Michel Fokine
> CHLOË: Vera Fokina

2 November, Alhambra Theatre, London
The Sleeping Princess
Ballet in 5 acts after the fairy story by Charles Perrault
COMPOSER: Piotr Ilyitch Tchaikovsky, with prelude to scene 3, the symphonic interlude *The Dream*, and *Aurora's Variation* in scene 3 orchestrated by Igor Stravinsky
CONDUCTOR: Gregor Fitelberg
CHOREOGRAPHER: Marius Petipa, reproduced by Nicholas Sergueieff, with choreography for the action scenes, *Hunting Dances*, *Aurora's Variation* in scene 3, and *Tales of Bluebeard*, *Schéhérazade* and *Innocent Ivan* by Bronislava Nijinska
PRINCIPAL DANCERS:

> KING FLORESTAN XXIV: Leonard Treer
> THE QUEEN: Vera Sudeikina
> CANTALABUTTE, MASTER OF CEREMONIES: Jean Jazvinsky
> THE PRINCESS AURORA: Olga Spessiva (Spessivtseva)
> THE LILAC FAIRY: Lydia Lopokova
> THE WICKED FAIRY: Carlotta Brianza
> PRINCE CHARMING: Pierre Vladimiroff

COMPANY: Diaghilev's Ballets Russes
Austin, University of Texas [pd]
Cambridge, Fitzwilliam Museum [cd]
Cambridge, Massachusetts, Harvard Theater Collection [cd]

Castle Howard, Castle Howard Costume Galleries [c]
Hartford, Wadsworth Atheneum [cd]
Jerusalem, Israel Museum [cd]
London, Mr and Mrs N. D. Lobanov-Rostovsky Collection [cd]
London, Theatre Museum [c]
London, Victoria and Albert Museum [cd]
Lugano, Thyssen-Bornemisza Collection [sd] [cd]
New York, Museum of Modern Art [cd]
Oxford, Ashmolean Museum [cd]
San Antonio, Robert L. B. Tobin Collection [sd] [cd]
San Francisco, Fine Arts Museums [cd]

1922
9 April, Théâtre Fémina, Paris
Spectacle d'Art Russe
DIRECTOR: M. Boleslawsky
CONDUCTOR: M. Aslanoff
PRINCIPAL: Maria Kousnezoff
Programme 1:
SETS AND COSTUMES: **L'Adoration** (libretto by Bakst and Tcherepnine); **La Lâcheté** (libretto by Bakst) [announced but not performed until Programme 2]: Léon Bakst
Les Comédiens; *Koutorok*; *Grounka*; *La Balançoire*: Sergei Soudeikine
Le Cauchemar; *Ohana'Sani*; *Le Bel Amour et l'Amour Terrible*; *La Foire Russe*: Not credited

16 May
Programme 2:
SETS AND COSTUMES: **Les Jeunes Filles; Danse Cocasse; La Lâcheté; La Rose et le Rossignol; Moscou d'Autrefois; Judith de Bethulis**: Léon Bakst
Les Comédiens; *Les joujoux russes*; *Koutorok*; *Scènes Arméniennes*; *Chanson Cruelle*; *Le Carrousel*; *La Balançoire*: Sergei Soudeikine
Passagère: Not credited

28 April/1 May, Théâtre National de l'Opéra, Paris
Artémis Troublée
Ballet by Léon Bakst
COMPOSER: Paul Paray
CONDUCTOR: Camille Chevillard
CHOREOGRAPHER: Nicolas Guerra
PRINCIPALS:

> ARTÉMIS: Ida Rubinstein
> ALKIPPÉ: Mlle Jasmine
> ZEUS: M. Severin
> ACTÉON: M. Swoboda

Jerusalem, Israel Museum [cd]
London, Mr and Mrs N. D. Lobanov-Rostovsky Collection [cd]

Project: Set for **Mavra**
Comic opera by Boris Kochno after Alexander Pushkin's poem *The Little House in Kolomna*
COMPOSER: Igor Stravinsky
[Léopold Survage replaced Bakst for production by Diaghilev's Ballets Russes, 3 June 1922, Théâtre National de l'Opéra, Paris]
London, Victoria and Albert Museum [sd]

17 June, Théâtre National de l'Opéra, Paris
[Revival in four acts instead of five]
Le Martyre de Saint Sébastien
Credits as original production, 22 May 1911, Théâtre du Châtelet, Paris, except:
MATER DOLOROSA: Suzanne Desprès
THE VOICE: Jane Laval
Lugano, Thyssen-Bornemisza Collection [sd]
San Antonio, Robert L. B. Tobin Collection [cd]

24 June, Théâtre National de l'Opéra, Paris
Costumes for the *Bal du Grand Prix* with George Barbier

13 October, Théâtre du Gymanse, Paris
Judith
Dramatic comedy in 3 acts by Henry Bernstein
DIRECTOR: André Antoine
SET: Sergei Soudeikine
COSTUMES: Léon Bakst
COMPOSER: E. C. Grassi
PRINCIPAL CHARACTERS:

> JUDITH: Mme Simone
> HOLOPHERNE: Grétillat

Jerusalem, Israel Museum [cd]
Lugano, Thyssen-Bornemisza Collection [cd]

Costume for Marchesa Casati as Queen of the Night

1923
Decorates Evergreen Theatre, Baltimore
Baltimore, Evergreen House Foundation [designs and stencils]

8 June, Théâtre National de l'Opéra, Paris
Phaedre
Tragedy in three acts by Gabriele d'Annunzio translated from the Italian by André Doderet
DIRECTOR: Armand Bour
COMPOSER: Ildebrando Pizzetti
CONDUCTOR: Philippe Gaubert

PRINCIPAL CHARACTERS:
    PHAEDRE: Ida Rubinstein
    ASTYNOMÉ: Suzanne Desprès
    AETHRA: Moreno
    HIPPONOÉ, THE THEBAN SLAVE: Sylvie
    THÉSÉE: Desjardins
    HIPPOLYTE: Yonnel
COMPANY: Ida Rubinstein
London, Victoria and Albert Museum [cd]
Lugano, Thyssen-Bornemisza Collection [cd]
Paris, Bibliothèque Nationale, Département des Arts
du Spectacle [cd]
Paris, Musée d'Art Moderne [sd]
Paris, Bibliothèque Nationale, Musée de l'Opéra [sd]

12 November, Théâtre National de l'Opéra,
Paris
La Nuit Ensorcelée
Ballet in 2 scenes by Léon Bakst
COMPOSER: Frederic Chopin adapted by Emile
Vuillermoz, orchestrated by Louis Aubert
CONDUCTOR: Philippe Gaubert
CHOREOGRAPHER: Léo Staats
PRINCIPAL DANCERS:
    THE FAIRY-QUEEN OF THE DOLLS: Carlotta Zambelli
    PAGANINI, THE ITALIAN PUPPET: Léo Staats
London, Mr and Mrs N. D. Lobanov-Rostovsky
Collection [sd]

Project: Set and costumes for **La Folle
Jeunesse** at the Théâtre National de l'Opéra,
Paris
Ballet in 2 acts by Léon Bakst

COMPOSER: Louis Aubert, popular airs adapted by
Emile Vuillermoz
[Not produced]

Project: *La Dame aux Camélias*
Play by Alexandre Dumas fils
[Produced by Ida Rubinstein at Théâtre
National de l'Opéra, Paris but without Léon
Bakst as designer]

1924
10 July, Théâtre National de l'Opéra, Paris
[Revived 23 February 1925, Théâtre National de
l'Opéra, Paris]
Istar
A 'danced poem' in one act by Léon Bakst,
performed in honour of the International
Olympic Committee, National Olympic
Committees and International Sport
Federations
COMPOSER: Vincent d'Indy
CONDUCTOR: Philippe Gaubert
CHOREOGRAPHER: Léo Staats
PRINCIPAL DANCERS:
    ISTAR: Ida Rubinstein
    THE RAMPANT VISION: Mlle Delsaux
    THE VISION OF PARADISE: Gelot, Sarazotti
    THE VISION OF CHILDHOOD: Lambert, Levinson,
    Dugué
    THE SON OF LIFE: Ryaux
    THE PRIESTLY VISION: Féronelle
    THE CELESTIAL VISION: Peretti

THE VISION OF FIRE: Baron
THE VISION OF WAR: Pacaud, Pavent
London, Theatre Museum [sd]

Project: Sets and costumes for Morris Gest in
New York
Play by d'Annunzio with Ida Rubinstein,
directed by Max Reinhardt

1926
11 June, Théâtre National de l'Opéra, Paris
Orphée
Ballet in 1 act
COMPOSER: Roger Ducasse
CONDUCTOR: Gustave Cloez
SET: Alexander Golovine
COSTUMES: Léon Bakst [from stock, see 1914]
PRINCIPAL DANCER: Ida Rubinstein

1928
16 July, His Majesty's Theatre, London
The Gods Go A-Begging
Pastoral ballet by Sobeka
COMPOSER: Handel arranged by Sir Thomas Beecham
CHOREOGRAPHER: George Balanchine
SET: from *Daphnis and Chloë*
COSTUMES (*Les Tentations de la Bergère*): Juan Gris
PRINCIPAL DANCERS: Alexandra Danilova, Lubov
    Tchernicheva, Felia Dubrovska, Léon
    Woizikovsky, Constantin Tcherkas

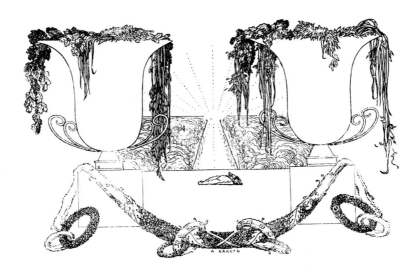

Exhibitions

These are listed in two parts and are confined to Bakst's theatrical work.

GROUP SHOWS: Major exhibitions of theatrical art in which Léon Bakst participated with other designers. When only the year is known the entries are in alphabetical order after the last date. This part also includes details of the specialist theatre and ballet auction sales arranged regularly by Sotheby's in London and New York from 1967 to 1987. Since then Bakst's work has been sold by Sotheby's and less often by Christie's and Phillips in 'Russian' sales in London. The viewing days of all these sales provided the most frequent opportunity for seeing Bakst's work. The date given is that of the sale. The titles of the sales have been omitted but the catalogues are useful if sometimes unreliable publications.

ONE-MAN SHOWS: Titles of exhibitions are included only when they were not *Bakst* or *Léon Bakst*.

GROUP SHOWS

1910
20 June–9 July, Paris, Galerie Bernheim
Les artistes Russes: Décors et costumes de théâtre et tableaux

1914
Zurich, Kunstgewerbemuseum
Theaterkunst

June, London, The Fine Art Society
Watercolours by Artists of the Gazette du Bon Ton

1917
Moscow
Exhibition of Paintings and Sculptures by Jewish Artists

1920
Kazan
First State Exhibition of Arts and Sciences

1921
Paris, Galerie Boëtie
Art russe ancien et moderne

1925
Paris, Hôtel Jean Charpentier
Exposition des arts du théâtre du XVe au XXe siècle

1927
London, Victoria and Albert Museum
Modern French and Russian Designs for Costume and Scenery

1928
3 February–3 March, London, Whitechapel Art Gallery
International Theatrical Art

May–June, Brussels, Palais des Beaux Arts
Art Russe Ancien et Moderne

1929
Paris, Musée des Arts Décoratifs, Pavillon de Marsan
Ballets Russes de Diaghilev

1930
March, London, Claridge Gallery
The Russian Ballet Memorial Exhibition

14–28 October, Paris, Galerie Billiet-Pierre Vorms
Exposition Rétrospective de Maquettes, Décors & Costumes exécutés pour la Compagnie des Ballets Russes de Serge de Diaghilew

1933
February–March, Vienna, Künstlerbund Hagen
Der Tanz

June, Paris, Musée Galliéra
L'Art décoratif au Théâtre et dans la Musique

2–18 November, New York, Julien Levy Gallery
Twenty-five years of the Russian Ballet from the Collection of Serge Lifar
[Also shown 22 April–20 May 1934, Cincinnati Art Museum; Smith College, Northampton, Massachusetts and Cleveland Art Museum]

1934
16 January–26 February, New York, Museum of Modern Art
International Exhibition of Theatre Art

Paris, Galerie Georges Petit
Nijinsky

1935
4 June–13 July, London, 1 Belgrave Square
Russian Art

1937
Paris, Musée de Arts Décoratifs, Pavillon de Marsan
Le Décor de la Vie de 1900–1925

1938
June–July, London, The Leicester Galleries
The Dance: An Exhibition of Paintings, Drawings and Sculpture by Artists, Past and Present

1939
March–1 July, Paris, Musée des Arts Décoratifs, Pavillon de Marsan
Ballets Russes de Diaghilew 1909–1929

1942
Cambridge, Massachusetts, Fogg Art Museum
Design for the Theatre in Modern Times

1943
5–31 October, London, National Gallery
Ballet Design
[Circulated in the UK by CEMA (Council for the Encouragement of Music and the Arts)]

1948–49
Paris, Galerie Charpentier
Danse et Divertissements

1950
Oxford, Ashmolean Museum
The Braikevitch Collection

16–29 November, London, Walker's Gallery
Russian Painting of the period known as Mir Iskusstvo

1951
Paris, Galerie Charpentier
Deux Siècles d'Elégance 1715–1915

1951–52
Moscow, Central House of Art Workers
Russian painting of the second half of the nineteenth and early twentieth century

1953
London, New Burlington Galleries
Ballet Designs from the John Carr-Doughty Collection

1954
22 August–11 September, Edinburgh, College of Art*
The Diaghilev Exhibition
[Enlarged and transferred 3 November 1954–16 January 1955 London, Forbes House]

Leningrad, Research Museum of the USSR, Academy of Arts
Paintings by Russian Artists (XVIII to the beginning of XX century) from Leningrad Private Collections

1956
London, London Museum
Anna Pavlova Commemorative Exhibition

Los Angeles, County Museum
Costume design for the Theater

1958
Kiev, Museum of Art
Works by Russian artists (second half of the XIX and early XX century) from Kiev Private Collections

1959
22 March–29 April, Indianapolis, Indiana, John Herron Art Museum
Fifty Years of Ballet Designs
[Also shown 3–31 May, Wadsworth Atheneum, Hartford, Connecticut and 11 July–16 August, Palace of the Legion of Honor, San Francisco, California. It was

subsequently split into two parts and circulated by the American Federation of Arts. Bakst's work had the following itinerary: 24 August–7 September, Corning Museum of Glass, Corning, New York; 2–22 October, Atlanta Public Library, Atlanta, Georgia; 4–24 November, Art Center, Pensacola, Florida; 2–28 December, J. B. Speed Museum, Louisville, Kentucky; 16 January–28 February 1960, Syracuse Museum, Syracuse, New York; 12 March–2 April, Denison University, Granville, Ohio; 14 April–5 May, Sophie Newcomb College, New Orleans; 1 July–20 August, White Museum, Cornell University, Ithaca, New York]

Moscow, Pushkin Museum
European, Oriental, Russian and Soviet Drawings and Watercolours

1960
Leningrad, The Hermitage, Department of the History of Russian Culture
Russian Engravings and Lithographs (XVIII to early XX century)

1961
17 June–16 July, Hove, Museum of Art
Russian Art and Life

1962
May, New York, Wildenstein Gallery
Stravinsky and the Dance

1963
Naples
Mostra internazionale de Scenografica Contemporanea

Moscow, Tretyakov Gallery
Drawings, Watercolours, Pastels and Gouaches of the late XIX and early XX centuries

1964
10 October–22 November, Eindhoven, Stedelijk van Abbe-Museum
Beeldend Experiment op de Planken

Leningrad, Research Museum of the USSR, Academy of Arts
Drawings and Watercolours by Russian Artists (late XVIII to early XX century) from Leningrad Private Collections

Milan, Galeria del Levante
Il contributo russo alle avant-guardie plastiche

Munich, Haus der Kunst, Pinakothek Bayerischen Staatsgemäldesammlungen
Secession - Europäische Kunst um die Jahrhundertwende

1965
25 September–14 November, Houston, Museum of Fine Arts, Junior Gallery
Theatre: The Magic Mirror

Hartford, Connecticut, Wadsworth Atheneum
The Lifar Collection of Ballet, Set and Costume Design

Odessa, Museum of Art
Drawings, Watercolours, Pastels, Gouaches of the late XIX and early XX centuries from the collection of the Odessa Museum of Art

1966
Leicester, Art Gallery
The John Carr-Doughty Collection

3 March–16 May, Paris, Musée des Arts Décoratifs
Les Années '25'

25 June–17 July, Spoleto, Palazzo Collicola
Tre secoli di Disegni Teatrali

Paris, Théâtre des Champs Elysées
Commémoration des Ballets Russes et du centenaire de la naissance d'Erik Satie

New York, Harkness House for Ballet Arts
Stage and Costume designs by Russian Painters from the collections of Mr & Mrs Nikita D. Lobanov-Rostovsky and Mr George Riabov

1966–67
Moscow, Tretyakov Gallery
Russian Watercolours (late XVIII to early XX century) from the collection of the Tretyakov Gallery

1967
Coventry, Belgrade Theatre
Diaghilev Ballet Designs

1 June–31 August, New York, Metropolitan Museum of Art
Russian Stage and Costume Designs for the Ballet, Opera and Theatre: A loan exhibition from the Lobanov-Rostovsky, Oenslager and Riabov Collections
[Circulated by the International Exhibitions Foundation, 1967–69]

13 June, London, Sotheby's

14 June–17 September, New York, Gallery of Modern Art
A Survey of Russian Painting: Fifteenth Century to the Present

13 July–24 September, Washington DC, Smithsonian Institution
Treasures of the Cooper Union Museum

24 October–18 November, London, Grosvenor Gallery
Aspects of Russian Experimental Art 1900–1925

Berlin, Akademie der Kunst
Avant-garde 1910–1930 Ost-Europa

1967–68
An exhibition of Ballet Designs, costumes and set drawings chiefly for Diaghilev Ballets drawn from the collection of John Carr-Doughty
[Toured by the Arts Council of Great Britain to Plymouth, Reading, Keighley and Birmingham]

1968
Stage Costume Design in the Twentieth Century
[Arranged and circulated by the Circulation Department, Victoria and Albert Museum]

17 July, London, Sotheby's, Scala Theatre

18 July, London, Sotheby's

19 November–31 December, London, Grosvenor Gallery
Ballet at the Grosvenor

Leningrad, Russian Museum
New Acquisitions

Moscow, Tretyakov Gallery
Pre-revolutionary Russian and Soviet Art, Paintings, Sculpture and Graphic Art. From New Acquisitions (1963–1968)

New York City, Shepherd Gallery
Russians in Paris: 1900–1930

1969
15 May–15 September, Strasbourg, Ancienne Douane
Les Ballets Russes de Serge de Diaghilev 1909–1929

9–10 July, London, Sotheby's

15–16 December, London, Sotheby's

19 December, London, Sotheby's, Theatre Royal, Drury Lane

San Antonio, Texas, Marion Koogler McNay Art Institute
Explosion: Color: Paris: 1909, Russian Theatre Designs, Drawn from the Collection of Robert L.B. Tobin

1970
May, New York, Hutton-Hutschnecker Gallery
Ballet and Theater Designs

6 May, New York, Parke-Bernet Galleries Inc.

1971
15 April–6 June, Norway, Henic Onstadt Museum
XX century Theatre Design

21 May–31 August, New York, Vincent Astor Gallery
Collection of Boris Kochno

3 June, London, Sotheby's

7 July, London, Sotheby's

17 November, London, Sotheby's Belgravia

1972
11–26 March, Milan, Museo Teatrale alla Scala
Ricordo di Serge de Diaghilev
[Also shown 5–20 April in Venice at the Teatro la Fenice]

23 June–3 September, Paris, Musée Galliéra
Hommage à Diaghilew, Collections Boris Kochno et Serge Lifar

25 October–15 January 1973, Paris, Galerie du Luxembourg
Illustrateurs des Modes et Manières en 1925

1972–74
Diaghilev and Russian Stage Designers. A loan exhibition of Stage and Costume Designs from the Collection of Mr and Mrs N. Lobanov-Rostovsky
[Circulated by the International Exhibitions Foundation]

1973
3 March, London, Sotheby's, Chenil Galleries

21 June, London, Sotheby's

New York, Cordier and Ekstrom Gallery
Stravinsky and Diaghilev

Petrodvorets, near Leningrad
Russian and Soviet Ballet. Material from the Collection of the Leningrad Theatre Museum

1974
16 April–26 May, Hempstead, Long Island, New York, Hofstra University, The Emily Lowe Gallery
Diaghilev/Cunningham

30 May, London, Sotheby's

20 June, Paris, Hôtel George V, Ader, Picard, Tajan (auctioneers)
Collection Serge Lifar, Les Ballets Russes

30 September–15 December, Danville, Center College of Kentucky
Selection of Painters for the Theatre

2 October–2 November, London, Annely Juda Fine Art
Theatre: An exhibition of 20th century theatrical designs and drawings
[Also toured November–December 1974, Galerie Bargera, Cologne; January–February 1975, Galerie Liatowitsch, Basel, and March–April 1975, Galleria Milano, Milan]

Leningrad, Russian Museum
Drawings by Russian Artists of the late XIX and early XX centuries

1975
5 June, London, Sotheby's

15 June–14 September, Venice, Palazzo Grassi
Omaggio ai disegnatori di Diaghilev

Chicago, University of Chicago
The Diaghilev Ballets Russes

Paris, Bibliothèque Nationale
Maurice Ravel

Leningrad, Russian Museum
The Portrait in Russian Painting of the late XIX and early XX centuries

1976
26 June, Monte Carlo, Sotheby's

7 July–31 October, Munich, Theatermuseum
Bühnenbilder des 20. Jahrhunderts

20 October, London, Sotheby's

Palm Beach, Florida, The Society of the Four Arts
The Golden Age of Ballet Design

Paris, Musée des Arts Décoratifs
Cinquentenaire 1925

1977
13 February–13 March, Austin, University of Texas, Art Museum
Russian Painters and the Stage 1884–1965. A loan exhibition of stage and costume designs from the collection of Mr and Mrs D. Lobanov-Rostovsky
[Circulated by the University of Texas Art Museum, 1978–79]

22 April–30 June, Le Mans, Musée du Mans
La Galaxie Diaghilev et les Ballets Russes

25 May, London, Sotheby's

29 November–16 March 1978, Paris, Centre Culturel du Marais
1909–1929 Les Ballets Russes de Diaghilev

15 December, New York, Sotheby's

Cambridge, Massachusetts, Harvard University
Diaghilev's Ballets Russes 1909–1929

Rome, Libreria e Galleria Pan
Diaghilev i balletti russi e il loro tempo

1978
17 May, London, Sotheby's

24 November, New York, Sotheby's

25 November–19 December, Newcastle-upon-Tyne, Hatton Gallery
Russian Graphic Art XVIII–XX centuries
[Toured the UK, 1979]

New York, Metropolitan Museum of Art
Diaghilev: Costumes and Designs for the Ballets Russes

1979
31 May–5 November, Paris, Centre National d'Art et de Culture, Georges Pompidou
Paris–Moscou

6 June, London, Sotheby's

20 August–14 September, Edinburgh, College of Art
Parade: Dance Costumes of Three Centuries

11 October–20 November, Norwich, England, Sainsbury Centre for Visual Arts
The Diaghilev Ballet in England
[A large part transferred 3 December 1979–11 January 1980, The Fine Art Society, London]

7–30 November, London, Institut Français
Hommage à Diaghilev

12 November, London, Sotheby's

6 December, New York, Sotheby's

Jackson, Mississippi, Mississippi Museum of Art
Dance Image: A tribute to Serge Diaghilev

Paris, Bibliothèque Nationale
Diaghilev: Les Ballets Russes

1980
19 January–9 March, San Francisco, Fine Arts Museums of San Francisco
Russian Theatre and Costume Designs
[Circulated by the Fine Arts Museums of San Francisco, 1980–82]

13 March, London, Sotheby's

22 May, New York, Sotheby's

14 October–January 1981, Paris, Musée d'Art Moderne de la Ville de Paris
Igor Stravinsky – la carrière européenne
[Part shown 1982, Teatro la Fenice, Venice and Teatro alla Scala, Milan]

23 October, London, Sotheby's

18 December, New York, Sotheby's

1981
8 April–26 July, London, Victoria and Albert Museum
Spotlight: Four centuries of Ballet Costume, a tribute to The Royal Ballet

22 May–16 August, Cleveland, Ohio, Cleveland Museum of Art
Art and the Stage

3 June–4 October, Moscow, Pushkin Museum
Moscow-Paris: 1900–1930

4 June, London, Sotheby's

12 June, New York, Sotheby's

29 October, London, Sotheby's

15 December, New York, Sotheby's

15 December–15 February 1982, Naples, Museo Diego Aragona Pignatelli Cortes
Mir Iskusstva–il mondo dell'arte

Fort Worth, Texas, Kimbell Museum
Costumes for the Ballet: Diaghilev to Balanchine

Houston, Texas, Museum of Fine Arts
The Diaghilev Heritage. Selections from the Collections of Robert L.B. Tobin

1982
4 March, London, Sotheby's

27 March, New York, Sotheby's

March–October, London, Theatre Museum, Victoria and Albert Museum
Show Business

18 June–29 August, Jackson, Mississippi, Mississippi Museum of Art
Russian Stage Design, Scenic Innovation, 1900–1930. From the collection of Mr and Mrs Nikita D. Lobanov-Rostovsky
[Also shown at the Elvehjem Museum of Art, Wisconsin; Phoenix Art Museum, Phoenix, Arizona; New York City and Archer M. Huntington Art Gallery, University of Texas, Austin, Texas, 1982–84]

28 October, London, Sotheby's

9 November–8 January 1983, Boston, Institute of Contemporary Art
Art and Dance
[Also shown 6 March–24 April 1983, Museum of Art, Toledo]

10 December, New York, Sotheby's

1983
9 June, London, Sotheby's

22 June, New York, Sotheby's

29 June, London, Christie's

26 October, London, Sotheby's

November–February 1984, Marseille, Musée Borely-Musée Provençal du Cinéma
Jean Cocteau: Magicien du Spectacle

15–16 December, New York, Sotheby's

Moscow, Tretyakov Gallery
Paintings and Graphic Works Donated to the Tretyakov Gallery by Evelyne Cournard

1984

6 March–3 June, Paris, Musée National d'Art et de Culture, Centre Georges Pompidou
Image et imagination d'architecture

17 April, London, Christie's

9 May, London, Sotheby's

6 June–9 September, Basel, Kunstmuseum
Strawinsky, Sein Nachlass, Sein Bild

16 October–6 January 1985, Detroit, The Detroit Institute of Arts
Designed for Theatre

17 November–12 January 1985, Bristol, Arnolfini Gallery
Artists Design for Dance 1909–1984

21 November, New York, Sotheby's

1985

25 January–17 May, Boulogne Billancourt, Centre Culturel
Mille et une nuits

29 April–31 May, London, The Fine Art Society
Spring '85
[Also toured, The Fine Art Society, Edinburgh and Glasgow]

April–May, Paris, Mairie du XXe arrondissement
4 Siècles de Ballet à Paris

28 May, London, Sotheby's

20 July–24 August, Buxton, Museum and Art Gallery
The Musical Stage

24 July–3 August, King's Lynn, Town Hall
Erté and the Folies Bergère

10 September–27 April 1986, London, Victoria and Albert Museum, Theatre Museum Galleries
130 set and costume designs from the Theatre Museum

16 October–6 January 1985, Detroit, Institute of Arts
Designed for Theater: Drawings and Prints from the Cooper-Hewitt Museum

San Antonio, Texas, Marion Koogler McNay Art Museum, The Tobin Wing
Bakst and Benois

1986

1 March–26 May, Frankfurt am Main, Schirn Kunsthalle
Die Maler und das Theater in 20. Jahrhundert
[Also shown in the summer, Palais des Papes and Maison Jean Vilar, Avignon]

2 March–25 May, Frankfurt am Main, Stadelschen Kunstinstitut
Raumkonzepte-Konstruktivistische Tendenzen in Bühnen- und Bildkunst, 1910–1930

18 March–6 July, New York, Cooper-Hewitt Museum
Bronislava Nijinska: A Dancer's Legacy
[Also shown 13 September–4 January 1987, The Fine Art Museums of San Francisco, San Francisco, California]

23 April, New York, Sotheby's

Jerusalem, The Israel Museum
One Hundred Works on Paper from the Collection of The Israel Museum, Jerusalem

1987

1 February, Monaco, Christie's, Hôtel Loews

22 October, London, Sotheby's

1988

18 May, London, Sotheby's

15 June–4 September, London, The Arts Club
The Art of the Theatre

9 September–6 December, Troyes, Musée d'Art Moderne

6 October, London, Christie's

3 December–26 February 1989, San Francisco, Fine Arts Museums, M. H. de Young Memorial Museum
The Art of Enchantment: Diaghilev's Ballets Russes, 1909–1929

6 December–4 February 1989, Milan, Museo Teatrale alla Scala
D'Annunzio: La Scena del Vate

Moscow, Pushkin Museum
Russkoe Teatralno-Dekoratzionnoe Iskusstvo 1880–1930 (Russian Theatre Design 1880–1930) from the Collection of Nikita and Nina Lobanov-Rostovsky

1989

14 February–21 May, Paris, Musée d'Orsay
L'Après-midi d'un Faiune: Mallarmé, Debussy, Nijinsky

6 April, London, Sotheby's

20 April–25 August, Baden Baden, Staatliche Kunsthalle

17 June–2 July, Granada, Auditorio Manuel de Falla
España y Los Ballets Russes

14 July–18 October, New York City, Museum of Modern Art
Painters for the Theater

19 September–21 October, New York City, Eduard Nakhamkin Fine Arts
100 Years of Russian Ballet 1830–1930: An exhibition from the Leningrad State Museum of Theater and Music

5 October, London, Christie's

15 December–17 February 1990, Paris, Musée-Galerie de la SEITA
Nijinsky

1990

27 March–20 April, London, Marina Henderson Gallery
Designs for the Stage 1900–1950

7 April–21 July, New York City, The Drawing Center
Theatre on paper (Set and costume designs from the collections of the Theatre Museum, London)

23 May, London, Sotheby's

12 June–5 August, Oxford, Ashmolean Museum
Russian Drawings in the Ashmolean Museum

19 June–13 July, London, The Arts Club
Great Russian Designers and Their Influence

3–31 October, London, David Harrington Gallery
Russian Theatrical Artists 1900's–1930's

26 November, London, Phillips

30 November, London, Sotheby's

ONE-MAN SHOWS

1911
6 July–15 October, Paris, Musée des Arts Décoratifs, Pavillon de Marsan

1912
June, London, The Fine Art Society

1913
June–July, London, The Fine Art Society

Berlin, B. P. Cassirer Gallery

1913–14
2–29 November, New York City, Berlin Photographic Company
[Toured December 1913, Art Club, Boston; 4 January–1 February 1914, Fine Arts Academy, Buffalo, New York; 8–28 February 1914, The City Art Museum, Saint Louis; 5 March–1 April 1914, Art Institute, Chicago; 6–28 April 1914, Cincinnati Art Museum, Cincinnati, Ohio; 4 May–1 June 1914, Museum of Art, Detroit]

1914
October, New York City, Berlin Photographic Company [A new exhibition]

1916
March, New York City, Scott and Fowles

1917
June, London, The Fine Art Society
Designs for the ballet 'La Belle au Bois Dormant' (for the production of *The Sleeping Beauty* by Anna Pavlova in New York, 1916)

1918
19 May–July, The Hague, Kunstzall Kleykamp
Tentoonstelling van aquarellen en teekeningen van den Russischen Kunstenaar Leo Bakst

1920
10–24 April, New York City, M. Knoedler & Co.
[Also shown at the Chicago Art Club, and in Denver, Dallas, Los Angeles, San Francisco, Santa Barbara]

1922
6–16 December, New York City, M. Knoedler & Co.
[Also shown 12 March–5 April 1923 at the Chicago Art Club]

1924
5–14 January, Cincinnati, Art Museum

December, New York City, Ferargil Gallery

1925
5–19 November, Paris, Musée des Arts Décoratifs,

1926
Brussels, Galerie du Centaure
[Also shown in Liège]

1927
April–1 May, New York City, Art Center
Textile Designs by Léon Bakst
[Also shown October 1927, Maryland Art Center, Baltimore; 1–15 March 1928, Saint Louis Art Museum; 10–23 February 1929, Museum of Fine Arts, Houston; 18 October–22 December 1930 at the Minneapolis Institute of Arts]

May, London, The Fine Art Society
Memorial Exhibition of the work of Léon Bakst

Paris, Hôtel Jean Charpentier

1929
The Hague, Kunstlerhaus

1938
14 July–6 August, London, Arthur Tooth & Sons

1957
Paris, Musée Galliéra

1965
London, Arthur Tooth & Sons

1966
Leningrad, Theatre Museum
L. S. Bakst centenary exhibition

1967
2–22 May, Milan, Galleria del Levante
Mostra commemorativa dell'opera di Léon Bakst
[Also shown May–September, Rome and October–November, Munich]

1968
17 January–3 March, The Hague, Geemeentemuseum
Ballet in beeld bij Bakst

1972
Paris, Peintres du Spectacle
Hommage à Léon Bakst

1973
3 December–4 January 1974, London, The Fine Art Society

December, London, Fischer Fine Art
[7 costume designs for the ballet *La Légende de Joseph*, 1914 which should have been identified for the well-known fakes they were]

1976
21 August–11 September, Edinburgh, The Fine Art Society
[Also shown 16 September–9 October, The Fine Art Society, London, and subsequently a major part of the exhibition toured in the USA including McNay Art Institute, San Antonio, Texas; and Davis & Long Gallery, New York City]

1984
7 August–7 October, Baltimore, Maryland, Museum of Art, Benesch Gallery

Select bibliography

This bibliography is in two parts. Part One, as comprehensive as possible, lists books and articles in periodicals exclusively on or by Bakst. Bakst's own writing is listed in chronological order. Anonymous references are listed alphabetically by title. Part Two lists major works which feature Bakst.

Both parts exclude references to contemporary notices and reviews of the productions designed by Bakst. For these refer to newspapers and periodicals of the relevant cities on or about the date of the first performances given in the list of productions.

PART ONE

Alexandre, Arsène
'Un Beau Livre à l'horizon: L'art décoratif de Léon Bakst', *Comoedia Illustré* (Paris, 20 December 1912)

Alexandre, Arsène and Cocteau, Jean
L'art décoratif de Léon Bakst: essai critique par A. Alexandre. Notes sur les ballets par J. Cocteau (Paris, 1913) [English edn *The Decorative Art of Léon Bakst* published London, 1913]

Aranovich, D.
'Lev Bakst' ('Leon Bakst'), *Iskusstvo Trudiashchemsiya* No. 18 (31 March–5 April 1925)

'Back to Bakst', *The Times* (London, 18 December 1973)

(Bakst, Léon) Lvov, B.
'Posmertnaya vistavka kartin Endogurova, Yaroshenko i Shishkina' ('The posthumous exhibition of paintings by Endogurov, Yaroshenko and Shishkin'), *Mir Iskusstvo* No. 5 (St Petersburg, 1899)

Bakst, Léon
'Zhenshchina v masterskoi khudozhnika' ('The woman in the artist's studio'), *Peterburgskaya Gazeta* (St Petersburg, 22 December 1902)

'Detskaya krasota' ('Childlike beauty') [interview], *Peterburgskaya Gazeta*, (St Petersburg, 22 November 1903)

'Kogda bilo luchshe?' ('When was it better?') [in answer to a questionnaire set by the newspaper], *Peterburgskaya Gazeta* (St Petersburg, 2 January 1907)

'Krasota ili pornografia?' ('Beauty or pornography?') [in answer to a questionnaire set by the newspaper], *Peterburgskaya Gazeta* (St Petersburg, 20 November 1908)

'Puti classitzizma v iskusstve' ('The paths of classicism in art'), *Apollon*, No. 2–3 (St Petersburg, 1909) [French version 'Les Formes Nouvelles du Classicisme dans l'Art', published in *La Grande Revue*, Paris, 25 June 1910]

(Bakst, Léon) R.
'Nagota na stzene' ('Nudity on the stage') [interview with Bakst on the appearances of Isadora Duncan and Ida Rubinstein], *Peterburgskaya Gazeta* (St Petersburg, 10 December 1909)

Answers to a questionnaire on the 50th anniversary of Chekhov's birth, *Odesskie Novosti* (Odessa, 17 January 1910)

Open letter to Repin, *Birzhevie Vedomosti* (St Petersburg, 6 March 1910)

Introduction to catalogue of exhibition of the work of students of Bakst and Mstislav Dobujinsky (St Petersburg, 1910)

'Nagota na stzene' ('Nudity on the stage'), *Peterburgskaya Gazeta* St Petersburg, 20 January 1911)

[*see also* Svetlov, Valarian]

'Kostium zhenshchini budushchego' ('The dress of the woman of the future') [interview], *Birzhevie Vedomosti* (St Petersburg, 20 March 1913)

'O sovremennom teatre. Nikto v teatre bolshe ne khochet slushats a khochet videts' ('On contemporary theatre. No-one in the theatre wants to listen any more; everyone wants to see') *Peterburgskaya Gazeta* (St Petersburg, 21 January 1914)

M. Ch.
'L. S. Bakst o sovremennikh modakh' ('L. S. Bakst on contemporary fashions'), *Utro Rossii* (St Petersburg, 9 February 1914)

'Moda' ('Fashion'), *Peterburgskaya Gazeta* (St Petersburg, 20 February 1914)

'Ob iskusstve segodnyashnego dnia' ('On art today'), *Stolitza i Usadsba* No. 8 (St Petersburg, 1914)

'Choréographie et Décors des nouveaux Ballets Russes', souvenir programme of Diaghilev's Ballets Russes (Paris, 1917 season)

'Tchaikovsky at the Russian Ballet', Alhambra Theatre souvenir programme for *The Sleeping Princess* (London, 1921)

'Tchaikowsky aux Ballets Russes', *Comoedia* (Paris, 9 October 1921)

'A propos de *Lâcheté*', *Le Journal* (Paris, 13 May 1922)

Serov i ya v Gretzii, Dorozhnie zapisi (*Serov and I in Greece, Travel notes*) (Berlin, 1923)

'L'Evolution du décor – opinion de M. Léon Bakst. Réponse à l'enquête de Raymond Cogniat', *Comoedia* (Paris, 3 September 1923)

La Nuit Ensorcelée. Ballet en deux tableaux. Musique de Chopin; adaptation musicale de Emile Vuillermoz (Paris, n.d. [?1923])

'Bakst', *Minneapolis Journal* (Minneapolis, 30 January 1916)

'Bakst and Benois clothe the Russian Dancers in Rich and Radiant Plumage', *Boston Evening Transcript* (Boston, 20 January 1916)

'Bakst and His Decorations', *Arts and Decoration* (New York, April 1920) p. 417

'Bakst and the Opera', *The New York Times* (New York, 5 October 1915)

'Bakst at his Best', *The Tatler* (London, 7 January 1914)

'Bakst Designs for the Ballet', *The Times* (London, 20 July 1938)

'Bakst Dolls', *Boston Evening Transcript* (Boston, 28 April 1920)

'Bakst Gives Lecture on Women's Dress', *The New York Times* (New York, 31 January 1923)

'Bakst, Magician of Dress', *Boston Sunday Globe* (Boston, 16 January 1916)

'Bakst Says Patti Inspired His Art', *The New York Times* (New York, 27 January 1923)

'Bakst Selects U.S. Beauties', *The Sun* (Baltimore, 13 May 1923)

'Bakst, the colorist of the Russian Ballet', *Literary Digest* (New York, 15 September 1923) pp. 30–33

'Bakst: the New Russian Designer of Modern Dress', *The New York Times* (New York, 2 November 1913)

'Bakst: the Weird Color King's Astonishing Next to Nature Fashion', *The Gazette Times Home Journal* (6 October 1912)

'Bakst to open studio', *New York Dramatic Mirror* (New York, 22 July 1916)

'Bakst to the land of "Ragtime and Revue"', *The Tatler* (London, 14 January 1914) pp. 56–57

'Bakst's Stage Decorations', *The New York Times* (New York, 11 April 1920)

Balance, John [pseudonym of Edward Gordon Craig]
'Kleptomania, or the Russian Theatre', *The Mask* Vol. 4 (Florence 1911–12) pp. 97–101

'Ballet according to Bakst', *New Republic* Vol. 6 (New York, February 1916) pp. 13–14

Barchan, Paul
'Léon Bakst', *Kunst und Kunstler* Vol. II No. 4 (Berlin, 1913) pp. 313–21

'Léon Bakst und das Theater', *Die Kunst für Alle* Vol. 41 (Munich, 1925) pp. 41–50

Baschet, Jacques
'L'Exposition Léon Bakst', *L'Illustration* (Paris, 21 November 1925) p. 549

'Beauty and the Primitives', *The New York Times* (New York, 4 January 1925)

Benois, Alexandre [*see also* Part Two]
'Salon i shkola Baksta' ('The "Salon" and the school of Bakst'), *Rech (Speech)* (St Petersburg, 1 April 1910)

'Novii baleti. *Nartzsiss*' ('New Ballets. *Narcisse*'), *Rech* (St Petersburg, 22 July 1911)

Birnbaum, Harry
'Bakst and the Russian Ballet', *Harper's Weekly* Vol. 55 No. 2971 (New York, 29 November 1913) pp. 13–15

Birnbaum, Martin
Léon Bakst, introduction to exhibition catalogue, Berlin Photographic Co. (New York, 1913)
[This introduction was reprinted in the catalogues of the same exhibition at the Buffalo Fine Arts Academy; Art Institute of Chicago; City Art Museum in St Louis; Cincinnati Museum; Detroit Museum of Art. The same introduction was reprinted, unattributed, in the *Catalogue of a Memorial Exhibition of the Works of Léon Bakst* at the Fine Art Society, London, 1927]

The Work of Léon Bakst, introduction to exhibition catalogue, Scott and Fowles (New York, 1916)

Léon Bakst, introduction (New York, 1919) pp. 29–39

Blanche, Jacques-Emile
'Léon Bakst dans le Ballet Russe', *L'Illustration* No. 4422 (Paris, 3 December 1927) pp. 599–606

Bloch, Jean-Richard
'L'Art de Bakst et les vitraux au Moyen Age', *Le Figaro* (Paris, 31 December 1924)

Boll, André
'Léon Bakst', *Revue Musicale* (Paris, June 1925) pp. 225–31

Léon Bakst, Galerie Billiet et Pierre Vorms (Paris, 1930)

Borisovskaya, N.
Lev Bakst (Leon Bakst) (Moscow, 1974)

Brock, H. I.
'Bakst "Orchestrated" His Stage Settings', *The New York Times Book Review* (New York, 10 April 1927)

Buckle, Richard [*see also* Part Two and Sokolova, Lydia]
'Bakst to the Wall', *The Sunday Times* (London, 16 December 1973)

Carrieri, Raffaele
  'I cartoni di Bakst i famosi balletti di Diaghilew', *Epoca* No. 869 (21 May 1969)

Carter, Huntly
  'The Art of Leon Bakst', *T.P.'s Magazine* Vol. II No. 10 (London, July 1911) pp. 515–26

  Léon Bakst, introduction to exhibition catalogue, Fine Art Society (London, 1912)

Casalonga
  'Le Ballet Russe: Réalisation', *Comoedia Illustré* (Paris, 20 May 1913)

  'Des Décors, de la Musique, de la Mise en Scène de la *Pisanelle*', *Comoedia Illustré* (Paris, 20 June 1913)

Celant, Germano
  'Léon Bakst', *La Biennale di Venezia* Vol. 17 No. 62 (Venice, June–September 1967) p. 46

'Le chapeau en 1913. Trois chapeaux de Léon Bakst. Les ornements', *Comoedia Illustré* (Paris, 20 April 1913)

Cheney, Sheldon [*see also* Part Two]
  'Bakst and the Dance Drama', *The New Movement in the Theatre* (New York, 1914) pp. 59–63

Chuzhoi, D.
  'L. Bakst', *Rabochii teatr* (*Workers' theatre*) (Moscow, 12 January 1925)

Cocteau, Jean [*see* Alexandre, Arsène]

Cogniat, Raymond [*see* 'Evolution du Décor, L'', etc. and Part Two]

'Colorful Art of Leon Bakst, The', *The Spur* (New York, 1 March 1916) p. 19

Craig, Edward Gordon [*see* Balance, John and Smith, C. G.]

Dalton, Elisabeth
  'In Search of Bakst', *The Dancing Times* (London, June 1967) pp. 458–59

'The Daring Russian who has shocked the world with his paintings depicting the Savage Instincts of European Women is Coming to the United States to Stage His Idea of our Primitive Female', *Chicago Sunday Herald* (Chicago, 30 July 1916)

de Colombier, Pierre
  'L'Exposition Léon Bakst', *L'Oeuvre* No. 98 (Liège, January 1926)

'De Diaghileff Gave Bask Her First Opportunity', *New York Preview* (New York, 30 September 1916)

'Disegni per modelli teatrali', *Emporium* (April 1911) p. 324

'Dioné, dessin de Bakst, réalisé par Paquin', *Journal des Dames et des Modes* (Paris, 1 May 1913) p. 73

Dobuzhinsky, Mstislav
  'O Bakste (iz moikh vospominanii)' ('About Bakst (from my reminiscences)'), *Segodnya* (*Today*) (Riga, 6 January 1925)

du Gard, Maurice Martin
  'Léon Bakst', *L'Art Vivant*, No. 2 (Paris, 15 January 1925)

Echea, E.
  'Leon Bakst y los ballets Russos' (n.p., n.d.)

Edelstein, Hermine
  'Influence of Modern Stage Setting on Music of Future', *Musical America* (New York, 9 September 1916)

Einstein, Carl
  Léon Bakst (Berlin, 1927)

'Evolution du décor – opinion de M. Léon Bakst. Réponse à l'énquête de Raymond Cogniat, L'', *Comoedia Illustré* (Paris, 3 September 1923)

Fern, Dale Edward
  'Ballet Design in Perspective – Léon Bakst', *Dance Magazine* (New York, December 1959)

Finck, Henry T.
  'Leon Bakst and Serge Diaghileff's Russian Ballet', *The Evening Post Saturday Magazine* (New York, 20 November 1915)

  'The Ballet Russe: Bakst and Nijinsky', *Nation* No. 103 (April 1916) pp. 464–65

Flagg, Harriet S.
  'Ballet Russe Succession of Most Amazing Scenes Ever Staged, Says Minneapolitan', unidentified newspaper (Minneapolis, 1916)

Flament, Albert
  'Bakst, artificier, décorateur et portraitiste', *Renaissance de l'Art Française* Vol. II (Paris, March 1919) pp. 88–95

'The Futurist-Bakst Ball', *Menton and Monte Carlo News* (Monte Carlo, 21 February 1914) p. 4

G., A. W. [Garrett, Alice Warder]
  'Leon Bakst as a Draughtsman', *Vanity Fair* (New York, May 1920)

  Bakst, foreword to exhibition catalogue, M. Knoedler & Co. (New York, 1920)

Gibson, Katharine
  'Textile Designs by Léon Bakst', *Design* Vol. 31 (Syracuse, 1929) pp. 109–13

Gleick, C. C. J. von
'Leon Bakst en de Russische Balletten van Diaghilef', *Spiegel Historiael*
Vol. III No. 2 (February 1968) pp. 114–20

Golynets, S. V.
L. S. Bakst 1866–1924 (Leningrad, 1981)

Gombault, Georges
'Une conversation avec Léon Bakst', unidentified newspaper (Paris,
28 May 1919)

Goodman, G. E. [*see also* Part Two]
'Notes on Decor: The Return of Leon Bakst', *The Dancing Times*
(London, July 1936) pp. 412–13

Gosling, Nigel
'Opulence and Decadence', *The Observer Review* (London, 9 December
1973)

Hall, Fernau
'Bakst', *The Daily Telegraph* (London, 1 September 1976)

Headlam, Cecil
'Great Christmas Stories as seen by Léon Bakst', *The Graphic* (London,
Christmas 1927) pp. 18–19

Howard, Deborah
'A sumptuous revival', *Apollo* (London, April 1970) pp. 301–308

'In a Treasure House Between Covers . . . the Manifold Riches of Leon
Bakst', *Boston Evening Transcript* (Boston, 2 June 1923)

Isakov, S.
'Lev Bakst', *Zhizn Iskusstvo* No. 1 (Moscow, January 1925)

Ivanov, V.
'Drevny uzhas: po povodu kartiny L. Baksta 'Terror Antiquus''
('Bakst's painting 'Terror Antiquus''), *Po svezdam: stat'i i aforizmi*
(*In the stars: articles and aphorisms*) (St Petersburg, 1909)

Janneau, Guillaume
'Bakst', *Bulletin de la Vie Artistique* (Paris, 15 January 1925) pp. 27–29

Kamensky, Alexander
'Lev Samoilovitch Bakst', *Ogoniek* No. 41 (Moscow, October 1989) p. 16
and colour supplement

'Kleine Nachrichten: Léon Bakst', *Kunst und Kunsthandwerk* Vol. 3 (1913)
pp. 206–13

Kozhevnikov, P.
'Elena Spartanskaya' ('Helen of Sparta'), *Stolichnaya molva*
(St Petersburg, 30 April 1912)

Kuzmin, M.
'L. Bakst', *Krasnaya gazeta* (*Red newspaper*) (Petrograd, 31 December
1924)

Lantz, Emily Emerson
'Russian Artist Follows Other Immortals', unidentified newspaper
(n.p., n.d.)

Lapidoth, Frits
'Leon Bakst', *Niewe Courant* (The Hague, 18 May 1918)

'L. Bakst', *Dni* (*Days*) No. 652 (Berlin, January 1925)

'Léon Bakst', *Comoedia Illustré* (Paris, 15 June 1910)

'Léon Bakst', *Comoedia Illustré* (Paris, 1 June 1911)

'Léon Bakst', *Harper's Bazar* (New York, October 1913)

'Léon Bakst', *Harper's Bazar* (New York, December 1915) p. 33

'Léon Bakst', *Harper's Bazar* (New York, February 1916)

'Léon Bakst', *Bulletin of the Minneapolis Institute of Arts* Vol. XIX No. 26
(Minneapolis, 18 October 1930) p. 129

'Léon Bakst as Artist of the Stage', *Chicago Post* (Chicago, 12 September
1916)

'Léon Bakst as a Draughtsman', *The Patrician* (June 1920) [*see also* G., A. W.]

'Léon Bakst: Designs for the Ballet Russe', *Harper's Bazar* (New York,
December 1915) pp. 46–47

'Léon Bakst is Here to Show Paintings', *The New York Times* (New York,
29 November 1922)

'Léon Bakst: Notice biographique et bibliographique', *Amour d'Art* No. 15
(Paris, December 1934)

'Léon Bakst on the Revolutionary Aims of the Serge de Diaghilev Ballet',
Current Opinion No. 59 (1915) pp. 246–47

'Léon Bakst, Stage Art Designer, Dies', *The New York Times* (New York,
28 December 1924)

'Leon Bakst, who Puts Poetry in Stage Settings – Career of the Man Who
Is Becoming World Famous', *The New York Times* (New York, 2 November
1913)

Levinson, André [*see also* Part Two]
Bakst: the story of the artist's life (London, 1923)

L'Oeuvre de Léon Bakst pour La Belle au Bois Dormant (Paris, 1922)
[English edn, London, 1923]

'Bakst – Vozvrashchenie Baksta' ('The return of Bakst'), *Jar Ptitza* No. 9 (Berlin, 1922) pp. 2–5

'Bakst: L'Oeuvre du Maître', *L'Art Russe* (Paris, 1924)

'Bakst, un grand artiste', *Comoedia* (Paris, 29 December 1924)

'Bakst', *L'Art Vivant* No. 23 (Paris, 1 December 1925) pp. 1–2

Li, 'Leon Bakst', *Krasnaya Panorama* (Moscow, 24 January 1925)

Lissim, Simon
    'L. S. Bakst', *Spolochi* (October 1922)

    'Léon Bakst, ses décors et costumes de théâtre', *L'Oeuvre* No. 2 (Paris, March 1924) pp. 38–39

    'Léon Bakst, 1866–1925', *L'Oeuvre* (Paris, Winter 1924–25)

    'Un rénovateur de la décoration théâtrale: Léon Bakst', *La Revue de l'Art ancien et moderne* (Paris, February 1925) pp. 101–12

    'Bakst as I remember him' [*see* Lister, Raymond *The Muscovite Peacock*]

Lister, Raymond
    'Bakst', *Apollo* Vol. 52 No. 307 (London, September 1950) pp. 90–92

    The Muscovite Peacock: a study of the art of Léon Bakst (Cambridge, 1954)

    'Léon Bakst (1866–1924): A Bibliography and some notes', *Theatre Research/Recherches Théâtrales* Vol. VIII No. 3 (Glasgow, 1967) pp. 145–55

Liubitel [P. D. Ettinger]
    'U Lva Baksta', *Birzhevie Vedomosti* (*The Stock Exchange Gazette*) (St Petersburg, 14 October 1909)

Lunacharsky, A.
    'Parizheskie pisma. Misteria o muchenichestva sv. Sebastiana' ('Letters from Paris. The mystery play 'The Martyrdom of St Sebastian''), *Teatr i Iskusstvo* (St Petersburg, 10 July 1911)

    'Parizheskie pisma. Elena Spartanskaya. Baletnaya burya' ('Letters from Paris. Helen of Sparta. A ballet storm'), *Teatr i Iskusstvo* (St Petersburg, 27 May 1912)

    'Pizanella', *Den* (*Day*) (St Petersburg, 15 June 1913)

M.
'U L. S. Baksta' ('At L. S. Bakst's'), *Den* (St Petersburg, 29 January 1914)

Makovski, Sergei
    'Zhenskie portreti sovremennikh russkikh khudozhnikov' ('Portraits of women by contemporary Russian painters'), *Apollon* No. 5 (St Petersburg, February 1910) pp. 5–22

'Vystavka v redaktsii Apollona. O shkole Baksta i Dobuzhinskogo' ('Exhibition at the ''Apollon'' offices. On the school of Bakst and Dobuzhinsky'), *Apollon* No. 8 (St Petersburg, May 1910)

Malherbe, Henry
    'Istar', *Le Temps* (Paris, 30 July 1924)

Mayer, Charles S.
    Bakst, introduction to exhibition catalogue, The Fine Art Society (London, 1976)

    'The influence of Léon Bakst on choreography', *Dance Chronicle* Vol. 1 No. 2 (New York, 1978) pp. 127–42

McBride, Henry
    'A Private Theater by Bakst', *The Arts* Vol. XI No. 5 (New York, May 1927) pp. 248–51

'The Masterpieces of This Color Master to be Seen when the Great Ballets Russes arrives ... Bakst Costumes at the Metropolitan Opera', *The New York Times* (New York, 17 January 1916)

Meyer, Annie Nathan
    'The Art of Léon Bakst', *Art and Progress* Vol. 5 (Washington DC, 1914) pp. 161–65

Michel, Georges-Michel [*see also* Part Two]
    'Léon Bakst, rénovateur du décor', *Paris-Midi* (Paris, 29 December 1924)

Milner, John
    'Designer-Dance', *TLS* (*Times Literary Supplement*) (London, 22–28 April 1988) p. 447

Misciatelli, Piero
    'Leone Bakst et l'Arte della Danza', *Vita d'Arte* No. 8 (1911) pp. 193–200

'Modern Fashion Owes to the Bakst Influence', *Greenboro Daily News* (Greenboro, 16 January 1916)

'Moderne Szenenentwürfe: Sven Gade und Léon Bakst', *Die Kunstwelt* (1 November 1913) pp. 90–96

'Modnaya znamenitost' Parizha. K priezdu v Petrburg khudozhnika Baksta' ('The fashionable Parisian celebrity. On the arrival of Bakst in St Petersburg'), *Berzhevie Vedemosti* (St Petersburg, 20 January 1914)

'Monografia o L. S. Bakste', *Jar Ptitza* No. 9 (Berlin, 1922) pp. 6–8

Mullaly, Terence
    'Two designers with a place in history', *The Daily Telegraph* (London, 10 December 1973)

N-n, E.
'O dekoratsiakh i kostiumakh khudozhnika Baksta' ('On Bakst's sets and costumes'), *Svobodnym Khudozhestvam* Vol. IV/V (St Petersburg, 1912)

Nolan, P. J.
'Léon Bakst: Wizard of Color', *Musical America* (23 December 1922) p. 3

Oliver, Cordelia
'Bakst', *The Guardian* (London, 1 September 1976)

Overy, Paul
'Bakst and the popular myth of Russian Art', *The Times* (London, 11 December 1973) p. 11

P. F.
'Kleine Nachriten: Berlin. Léon Bakst', *Kunst und Kunsthandwerk* No. 16 (1913) pp. 206–207

Pann, E. [*see also* Part Two]
'O Elene Spartanskoi' ('On Helen of Sparta'), *Studiya* No. 30–31 (St Petersburg, 1912)

Péladan, Joséphin
'Les Arts du Théâtre: Un Maître du Costume et du Décor: Léon Bakst', *L'Art Décoratif* Vol. 25 (Paris, 1911) pp. 285–300

Phillips, Sir Claude
'Russian Ballet; Léon Bakst', *The Daily Telegraph* (London, 20 June 1912)

'Portrait group by Léon Bakst, Noted Russian Artist, Exhibited', *The Sun* (Baltimore, 24 March 1924)

'Portrait of a Lady: A Notable New Canvas by Léon Bakst', *Vanity Fair* (New York, July 1920)

Powell, Anthony
'Ballet's Master Designer', *The Daily Telegraph* (London, 20 December 1973)

Pratt, George
'Emerald, Indigo, and Triumphant Orange', *Gallery Notes, Buffalo: Fine Arts Academy, Albright Knox Art Gallery* Vol. 27 No. 2 (Buffalo, 1964) pp. 25–31

Proujan [Pruzhan], Irina
Léon Bakst, Esquisses de décors et de costumes, arts graphiques, peintures (Leningrad, 1986) [English edn *Léon Bakst. Set and costume designs, book illustrations , paintings and graphic works* published London, 1987]

'Kartina L.S.Baksta "Drevnii Uzhas"' ('Bakst's painting "Terror Antiquus"'), *Soobshcheniya gosudarstvennogo Russkogo muzeya* (*The State Russian Museum reports*) Vol. 10 (Moscow, 1974)

Lev Samoilovitch Bakst (Leningrad, 1975)

Rainey, Ada
'Léon Bakst, Brilliant Russian Colourist', *Century Magazine* Vol. 87 (New York, 1914) pp. 682–92

Read, Helen Appleton
'Bakst Textile Design', *Art Center Bulletin* Vol. V No. 8 (New York, April 1927) pp. 142–43

Réau, Louis; Roche, Denis; Svietlov [*sic*], V. and Tessier, A., *Inedited Works of Bakst* (New York, 1927)

Repin, I.
'V adu u pifona' ('In hell with a python'), *Birzhevie Vedomosti* (St Petersburg, 15 May 1910)

'Restoration of Bakst's Theater in the Garrett House, Evergreen Foundation', *Baltimore Sun Magazine* (Baltimore, 29 January 1967)

'Review of R. Lister 'The Muscovite Peacock'', *Apollo* (London, March 1955) p. 55

Ritter, William
'Léon Bakst', *Emporium* Vol. 36 (Bergamo, December 1912) pp. 403–21

'Balletskizzen von Léon Bakst', *Deutsche Kunst und Dekoration* Vol. XXXI (Darmstadt, 1913) pp. 309–26

Roberts, Mary Fanton
'The New Russian Stage, a Blaze of Colour: What the genius of Léon Bakst has done to vivify productions which Combine Ballet, Music and Drama', *Craftsman* Vol. 29 (New York, 1915) pp. 257–69 and 322

'Les Robes de Bakst réalisées par Paquin', *Comoedia Illustré* (Paris, 20 March 1913)

'Robes modernes de Léon Bakst', *Comoedia Illustré* (Paris, 20 February 1913)

Roche, Denis [*see* Réau, Louis]

Ronkin, B.
'O balete L. Baksta' ('On the ballet of Bakst'), *Teatr* (Moscow, 4 December 1923)

Roosval, Johnny
'Couleurs et formes sur les décors des Ballets Russes à l'Opéra de Stockholm par Bakst', *Konst och Konstmarer* No. 2 (Stockholm, 1914) p. 18

Russell, John
'Léon Bakst's revolutionary stage designs', *The New York Times* (New York, 6 February 1977)

Savoy, John
'Leon Bakst's Expulsion from Russia Stirs London', *New York Review* (New York, 7 December 1912)

Schnitger, F. M.
'Oostersche schilderingen van Léon Bakst', *Elsevier's maanschrift* Vol. 86 (Leiden, 1933) pp. 145–53

Schouvaloff, Alexander [*see also* Part Two]
'Unmistakable Master: Léon Bakst and Diaghilev's Ballets Russes', *Country Life* (London, 16 April 1987) pp. 130–31

Shepherd, Michael
'Designing Dance', *Sunday Telegraph* (London, 9 December 1973)

Siordet, Gerard C.
'Léon Bakst's Designs for Scenery and Costume', *The Studio* (London, October 1913) pp. 3–6

Smith, C. G. [pseudonym of Edward Gordon Craig]
'This Little Theatre: Bakst', *The Mask* No. 11 (Florence, 1925) pp. 68–70

Spencer, Charles
Léon Bakst (London, 1973)

Léon Bakst at the Fine Art Society, introduction to exhibition catalogue (London, 1973)

'Léon Bakst at Covent Garden', *About the House* Vol. 4 No. 4 (London, Christmas 1973) pp. 26–30

'A great many lovely women with beautiful bodies', *The Sunday Times* (London, 2 December 1973)

'Spring Days in New York Galleries', *The New York Times* (New York, 3 April 1927)

Stebnitsky, G.
'L. Bakst', *Rabochii i teatr* (Moscow, 12 January 1925)

'Striking Designs by Léon Bakst', *The New York Times* (New York, 25 October 1914)

Strunsky, Rose
'Leon Bakst on the Modern Ballet', *New York Tribune* (New York, 5 September 1915)

Svetlov, Valerian [*see also* Part Two]
Sovremennii balet: izdano pri neposredsvennom uchastii L. S. Baksta (*The contemporary ballet: edited with the direct participation of L. S. Bakst*) (St Petersburg, 1911) [French edn *Le ballet contemporain; ouvrage édité avec la collaboration de L. Bakst* published St Petersburg, 1912]

'Favn' ('The Faun'), *Peterburgskaya Gazeta* (St Petersburg, 27 May 1912)

Svietlov, V. [*sic*] [*see* Réau, Louis]

Tessier, A. [*see* Réau, Louis]

Tevis, May
'The Scenic Art of Leon Bakst', *The Theatre Magazine* (January 1914)

Thomas, Louis
'Bakst, Student of the Archaic', *International Studio*, Vol. 76 No. 310 (New York, March 1923) pp. 479–84

'Le Réveillon avec Bakst', *Revue Critique des Idées et des Livres* No. 35 (Paris, 29 July 1923) pp. 395–401

'Le peintre Bakst parle de Mme Ida Rubinstein', *Revue Critique des Idées et des Livres* No. 36 (Paris, 25 February 1924) pp. 87–104

Tripp, Susan G.
'Bakst', John Hopkins magazine (Baltimore, June 1984) pp. 12–22

Tugendhold, Y. [*see also* J., Part Two]
'Teatral'ny sezon v Parizhe. Elena Spartanskays' ('The theatre season in Paris. Helen of Sparta'), *Studiya* No. 34–35 (St Petersburg, 1912)

Vanina
'Inauguration rue de la Paix des robes de "Léon Bakst", réalisés par "Paquin"', *Comoedia Illustré* (Paris, 5 April 1913)

Vaudoyer, Jean-Louis [*see also* Part Two)
Léon Bakst, introduction to exhibition catalogue (Paris, 1911)

'Léon Bakst', *Art et Décoration* Vol. 29 (Paris, 1911) pp. 33–46

'Léon Bakst et les Ballets Russes', *Nouvelles Littéraires* (Paris, 3 January 1923)

Veronesi, Giulia
'Leon Bakst', introduction to exhibition catalogue (Milan, 1967)

'Levensschets van Bakst', introduction to exhibition catalogue (The Hague, 1968)

Voloshin, Maximilian
'Arkhaism v Russkoi zhivopisi (The archaic in Russian Painting): Roerich, Bogaevsky, Bakst', *Apollon* No. 1 (St Petersburg, October 1909) pp. 43–53

Warnod, André [*see also* Part Two]
'Les aquarelles de Léon Bakst', *Comoedia* (Paris, 7 July 1911)

'L'exposition rétrospective de l'oeuvre de L.Bakst', *Comoedia Illustré* (Paris, 6 November 1925)

Wasmuth, Ernst
Léon Bakst, (n.p., n.d. but *c.* 1922)

Weidlé, Wladimir
'La Peinture en Russie' with 'Léon Bakst: Notice biographique', *L'Amour de l'Art* Vol. 15 (Paris, December 1934) p. 513

'Weird Art Ideas of Léon Bakst', *Ohio State Journal Sunday Magazine* (Ohio, 29 September 1912)

'We Nominate For the Hall of Fame', *Vanity Fair* (New York, March 1920)

Wykes-Joyce, Max
'Bakst and Batik 1910–1925', *Art* Vol. 1 No. 9 (London, 17 March 1955)

Zharovski, I.
'Posmertnaya vystavka Baksta' ('Posthumous exhibition of Bakst's work'), *Poslednie Novosti* (19 November 1925)

PART TWO

Annenkov, George P.
Russian Painters and the Rebirth of Theatre Arts, introduction to exhibition catalogue *Russian Stage & Costume Designs* (New York, 1967)

Bablet, Denis
Esthéthique générale du décor de théâtre de 1870 à 1914 (Paris, 1965)

Les Révolutions scéniques du XXe siècle (Paris, 1975)

'Les Peintres et le Théâtre', *Théâtre en Europe* No. 11 (Paris, July 1986) pp. 5–22

Bablet, Denis et al.
Die Maler und das Theater im 20. Jahrhundert (Frankfurt-am-Main, 1986)

Baer, Nancy van Norman (ed.)
The Art of Enchantment: Diaghilev's Ballets Russes, 1909–1929, exhibition catalogue (San Francisco, 1988)

100 years of Russian Ballet 1830–1930, introduction to exhibition catalogue (New York, 1989)

Bakshy, Alexander
The path of the Modern Russian Stage and other essays (London, 1913)

Barbey, Valdo
'Les Peintres Modernes et le Théâtre', *Art et Décoration* Vol. XXXVII (Paris, 1920) pp. 97–108 and 155–60

Barnes, Clive
'The Sleeping Beauty', *Dance and Dancers* (London, May 1961) pp. 5–14, and 23

Beaumont, Cyril W. [*see also* Polunin, Vladimir]
Impressions of the Russian Ballet 1918 (*No. 1, Cleopatra, No. 2, The Good Humoured Ladies*, No. 3, *Carnaval*) (London, 1918)

Impressions of the Russian Ballet 1919 (*Schéhérazade, L'Oiseau de Feu, Thamar*) (London, 1919)

Impressions of the Russian Ballet 1921. The Sleeping Princess (2 Vols) (London, 1921)

Anna Pavlova (London, 1932)

Michel Fokine and his Ballets (London, 1935)

The Diaghilev Ballet in London (London, 1946)

Ballet design past and present (London, 1946) [a combination and extension of the same author's *Five centuries of ballet design* and *Design for ballet*]

Complete book of ballets (London, 1951)

Bookseller at the ballet (London, 1978)

Benois, Alexandre [*see also* Part One]
'Uchastie khudozhnikov v teatre' ('Artists' participation in the theatre'), *Rech* (St Petersburg, 25 February 1909)

'Russkie spectakli v Parizhe' ('Russian performances in Paris'), *Rech* (St Petersburg, 19 June 1909)

'Russkie spectakli v Parizhe' ('Russian performances in Paris'), *Rech* (St Petersburg, 25 June 1909)

'Russkie spectakli v Parizhe' ('Russian performances in Paris'), *Rech* (St Petersburg, 12 July 1910)

'Russkie spectakli v Parizhe' ('Russian performances in Paris'), *Rech* (St Petersburg, 18 July 1910)

'Diaghilevskie spectakli' ('Diaghilev's performances'), *Rech* (St Petersburg, 25 June 1911)

Reminiscences of the Russian Ballet (translated by Mary Britnieva) (London, 1941)

Memoirs (2 Vols) (translated by Moura Budberg) (London, 1964)

Blumenthal, Arthur R.
  Theater Designs in the Collection of the Cooper-Hewitt Museum (New York, 1986)

Borovsky, Victor [*see* Schouvaloff, Alexander]

Bowlt, John E.
  Russian Painters and the Stage 1884–1965, introduction to exhibition catalogue (Austin, 1977)

  The Silver Age: Russian art of the early twentieth century and the 'World of Art' group (Newtonville, 1982)

  Russian stage design, scenic innovation 1900–1930, from the collection of Mr and Mrs Nikita D. Lobanov-Rostovsky (Mississippi, 1982)

Buckle, Richard [*see also* Sokolova, Lydia and Part One]
  The Diaghilev Exhibition, editor of exhibition catalogue, (Edinburgh, 1954)

  In search of Diaghilev (London, 1955)

  Nijinsky (London, 1971)

  Diaghilev (London, 1979)

Cheney, Sheldon [*see also* Part One]
  Stage Decoration (London, 1928)

Clarke, Mary and Crisp, Clement
  Design for ballet (London, 1978)

Cogniat, Raymond [*see also* 'Evolution du Décor, L'', etc., Part One]
  Décors de théâtre (Paris, 1930)

  Ballets russes: Bakst et Larionow – Décors du Théâtre (Paris, 1930)

  Les Décorateurs de Théâtre (Paris, 1955)

Collection des plus beaux numéros de 'Comoedia Illustré' et des programmes consacrés aux Ballets et Galas Russes depuis le début à Paris 1909–1921 (Paris, 1922)

Craft, Robert [*see* Stravinsky, Igor and Vera]

Davidova, M. V.
  Ocherki istorii russkogo teatralno-dekoratsionnogo iskusstva XVII-nachala XX veka (*Essays on the history of Russian theatre design from the eighteenth to the beginning of the twentieth centuries*) (Moscow, 1974)

de Cossart, Michael
  Ida Rubinstein (1885–1960), A theatrical life (Liverpool, 1987)

de Courville, Albert, *I Tell You* (London, 1928)

de Marly, Diana
  Costume on the stage 1600–1940 (London, 1982)

Diaghilev, Serge [*see* Zilberstein, I. S.]

Fizdale, Robert [*see* Gold, Arthur]

Fokine, Michel
  Memoirs of a ballet master (translated by Vitale Fokine; London, 1961) [Fuller Russian edn *Protiv techeniya. Vospominaniya baletmeistera. Stati, pisma* (*Against the tide. Memoirs of a ballet master. Articles, letters*) published Leningrad and Moscow, 1962]

Fuerst, Walter René and Hume, Samuel J.
  XX century stage decoration (London, 1928)

Fülöp-Miller, René and Gregor, Joseph
  The Russian Theatre (London, 1930, reissued New York, 1968)

Garafola, Lynn
  Diaghilev's Ballets Russes (New York, 1989)

Gavriulov, T. V.
  'Arkhitekturno-khudozhestvennii ansambl vistavki portreta v Tavricheskom dvortze' ('The architectural and artistic arrangement of the portrait exhibition in the Tauride Palace'), *Muzei* No. 8 (Moscow, 1987) pp. 229–36

Gold, Arthur and Fizdale, Robert
  Misia (New York, 1980)

Gontcharova, Nathalie; Larionov, Michel and Vorms, Pierre
  Les Ballets Russes de Serge de Diaghilev et la décoration théâtrale (Paris, 1955)

Goodman, G. E. [*see also* Part One]
  'Stage Designs at the Russian Exhibition: Notes on Decor', *The Dancing Times* (London, July 1935) pp. 402–403

  'Notes on Decor: Colonel de Basil's Ballets Russes', *The Dancing Times* (London, August 1935) pp. 527–28

  'Twenty-five years of Decor', *The Dancing Times* (London, October 1935) pp. 45–48

Grigoriev, S. L.
  The Diaghilev Ballet 1909–1929 (translated by Vera Bowen; London, 1953)

Harrison, Robert C.
  Scenic and costume design for the Ballets Russes (Ann Arbor, 1988)

Haskell, Arnold (in collaboration with Walter Nouvel)
  Diaghileff: His artistic and private life (London, 1935; reprinted 1955)

Holmes, M. R.
  Stage Costumes and Accessories in the London Museum (London, 1968)

Hume, Samuel J. [*see* Fuerst, Walter René]

Joseph, Gregor [*see* Fülöp-Miller, René]

Jullian, Philippe
Robert de Montesquiou, a fin-de-siècle prince (London, 1967)

d'Annunzio (London, 1972)

Karsavina, Tamara
Theatre Street (London, 1954)

Kochno, Boris
Diaghilev et les Ballets Russes (Paris, 1973)

Kostilev, N.
'Nash balet v Parizhe' ('Our ballet in Paris'), *Apollon* No. 9
(St Petersburg, 1913–14)

Krasovskaya, Vera
Russkii baletnii teatr nachalo XX veka (*Russian ballet at the beginning of
the 20th century*); Vol. 1 *Khoreografi* (*Choreographers*) (Leningrad,
1971); Vol. 2 *Tanzovchiki* (*Dancers*) (Leningrad, 1972)

Nijinsky (translated by John E. Bowlt; New York, 1979) [Russian
version, Leningrad, 1974]

Kuhlmann, A.E. [*see* Michaut, P.]

Larionov, Michel [*see* Gontcharova, Nathalie]

Lazzarini, John and Roberta
Pavlova: Repertoire of a Legend, (London, 1980)

Levinson, André [*see also* Part One]
'Russkie khudozhniki-dekoratori' ('Russian artists and theatre
designers'), *Stolitza i Usad'ba* No. 57 (St Petersburg, n.d.)

Lieven, Prince Peter
The Birth of the Ballets Russes (London, 1936)

Lifar, Serge
Serge Diaghilev: His life, his work, his legend (London, 1940)

*The Three Graces: Anna Pavlova, Tamara Karsavina, Olga Spessivtzeva,
the legends and the truth* (London, 1959)

Macdonald, Nesta
Diaghilev observed (New York/London, 1975)

Diaghilev observed encore (Mottisfont Abbey, Romsey, Hampshire,
forthcoming)

Mauclair, Camille
'Les Ballets Russes, Russie (Art Moderne)', *L'Art et les Artistes*, special
number (Paris, November 1917) pp. 43–47

Michaut, P. and Kuhlmann, A. E.
'Les Ballets Russes de M. Serge de Diaghilev', *L'Art Vivant* (Paris,
15 December 1929) pp. 718–21

Michel, Georges-Michel [*see also* Part One]
'Diaghilev et les peintres', *L'Art Vivant* (Paris, May 1930)

Moderwell, Hiram Kelly
'Music of the Russian Ballet', *The New Republic* (New York, 22 January
1916)

Money, Keith
Anna Pavlova, Her Life and Art, (London, 1982)

Nectoux, Jean-Michel
L'Après-midi d'un Faune, exhibition catalogue (Paris, 1989)

Nijinska, Bronislava
Early Memoirs (translated by Irina Nijinska and Jean Rawlinson;
London, 1982)

Nijinsky, Romola
Nijinsky and *The Last Years of Nijinsky* (London, 1980)

Pankratova, E. A.
Russkoe teatralno-dekoratzionnoe iskusstvo kontsa XIX nachala XX veka
(*Russian theatre design at the end of the nineteenth and beginning of the
twentieth centuries*) (Leningrad, 1983)

Pann, E [*see also* Part One]
'Russkii sezon v Parizhe' ('The Russian season in Paris'), *Maski* No.
7–8 (St Petersburg, 1912–13) pp. 58–75

Percival, John
The World of Diaghilev (New York, 1971; revised London, 1979)

'Dance to the music of time', *The Times Saturday Review* (London,
25 August 1990)

Polunin, Vladimir
The Continental Method of Scene Painting (edited by Cyril W. Beaumont;
London, 1927)

Pozharskaya, M. N.
Russkoe teatralno-dekoratsionnoe iskusstvo kontsa XIX-nachala XX veka
(*Russian theatre design at the end of the nineteenth and beginning of the
twentieth centuries*) (Moscow, 1970)

*The Russian Seasons in Paris: Sketches of the Scenery and Costumes,
1908–1929* (Moscow, 1988) [bilingual Russian and English
publication]

Propert, W. A.
The Russian Ballet in Western Europe 1909–1920 (London, 1921)

The Russian Ballet 1921–1929 (London, 1931)

Reade, Brian
Ballet Designs and Illustrations, 1581–1940 (London, 1967)

Ricketts, Charles
Self-Portrait (edited by Cecil Lewis; London, 1939)

Rischbieter, Henning (ed.)
Art and the stage in the 20th century (Greenwich, 1969)

Rood, Arnold
'''A rose by any name'' a. k. a. Edward Gordon Craig', *Victoria and Albert Museum Album* (London, 1987)

Salmina-Haskell, Larissa
Russian Drawings in the Ashmolean Museum (Oxford, 1970)

Russian drawings in the Victoria and Albert Museum (London, 1972)

Samkov, V. A. [*see* Zilberstein, I. S.]

Schouvaloff, Alexander [*see also* Part One]
The Thyssen-Bornemisza Collection: Set and costume designs for ballet and theatre (London, 1987)

Theatre on paper (London, 1990)

Schouvaloff, Alexander and Borovsky, Victor
Stravinsky on stage (London, 1982)

Serov, Valentin [*see* Zilberstein, I. S.]

Sert, Misia
Two or Three Muses (translated by Moura Budberg; London, 1953)

Shead, Richard
Ballets Russes (Seacaucus, New Jersey, 1989)

Simonson, Lee
'The designer in the theatre', introduction to catalogue *International Exhibition Theatre Art* (New York, 1934)

Sokolova, Lydia
Dancing for Diaghilev (ed. Richard Buckle; London, 1960)

Stravinsky, Igor
Chroniques de ma vie (2 Vols) (Paris, 1935) [English edn *An Autobiography* published London, 1936]

Stravinsky, Igor and Craft, Robert
Conversations with Stravinsky (London, 1959)

Memories and Commentaries (London, 1960)

Expositions and Developments (London, 1962)

Stravinsky, Vera and Craft, Robert
Stravinsky in Pictures and Documents (New York, 1978)

Svetlov, Valerian [*see also* Part One]
'Les peintres décorateurs Russes', *Comoedia Illustré* (Paris, 5 June 1913)

Tugendhold, J. [*see also* Y., Part One]
'Russkii sezon v Parizhe' ('The Russian season in Paris'), *Apollon* No. 10 (St Petersburg, September 1910) pp. 5–23

Vaillat, Léandre
'Les décors russes', *L'Art et les Artistes* (Paris, August 1910)

'Nouveaux propos sur les décors', *L'Art et les Artistes* No. 13 (Paris, September 1911) pp. 479–88

Vaudoyer, Jean-Louis [*see also* Part One]
'Impressions et souvenirs', *L'Art Vivant* (Paris, 15 December 1929) pp. 709–10

Vaughan, David
'Further Annals of The Sleeping Beauty: Anna Pavlova, 1916', *Ballet Review* Vol. 3 No. 2 (Brooklyn, N. Y., 1969)

Vlassova, R. I.
Russkoe teatralno-dekoratzionnoe iskusstvo nachala XX veka [*Russian theatre design at the beginning of the twentieth century*] (Leningrad, 1984)

Vorms, Pierre [*see* Gontcharova, Nathalie]

Warnod, André [*see also* Part One]
'Les peintres et les ballets russes', *La Revue Musicale* (Paris, 1 December 1930) pp. 78–89

Zilberstein, I. S. and Samkov, V. A. (eds)
Sergei Diaghilev i Russkoe Iskusstvo (*Serge Diaghilev and Russian Art*) 2 Vols (Moscow, 1982)

Valentin Serov v perepiske, interviu i dokumentakh (*Valentine Serov - correspondence, interviews and documents*) Vol. 1 (Leningrad, 1985), Vol. 2 (Leningrad, 1989)

Photographic acknowledgements

The following acknowledgements are listed according to location and the illustrations are referred to by page number.
Illustrations not listed from contemporary photography journals, newspapers and Souvenir Programmes are courtesy of the author.

AUSTIN
University of Texas, Harry Ransom Humanities Research Center, Theatre Arts Collections, pp. 67, 200

BALTIMORE
Evergreen House Foundation, Alice Garrett Collection, pp. 182, 183, 222

BOSTON
Isabella Stewart Gardner Museum, Art Resource, NY, pp. 124, 167
Museum of Fine Arts, Gift of L. Aaron Lebowich, 50.723, p. 165

CAMBRIDGE
Courtesy of the Syndics of the Fitzwilliam Museum, p. 208

HARTFORD
Wadsworth Atheneum, Ella Gallup Sumner and Mary Catlin Sumner Collection, W.A. 1933.394, p. 106; W.A. 1935.37, p. 151; W.A. 1933.392, p. 153

JERUSALEM
Israel Museum, p. 230

LENINGRAD
Museum of Theatrical and Musical Arts, pp. 41, 43, 45, 79, 111
State Russian Museum Publishing Company, pp. 19, 34, 38, 42, 49, 52, 55

LONDON
British Library, p. 170
Mr and Mrs N. D. Lobanov-Rostovsky Collection, pp. 74, 99, 119, 139, 232
Courtesy of Richard Nathanson, p. 227
Lady St Just Collection, endpapers
Courtesy of Sotheby's, pp. 11, 23, 26, 31, 38, 51, 64, 66, 70, 71, 72, 75, 85, 87, 98, 99, 103, 118, 121, 123, 125, 127, 129, 136, 141, 147, 152, 156, 159, 170, 174, 180, 181, 187, 188, 195, 196, 197, 198, 208, 210, 211, 214, 215, 217, 219, 220, 225, 226, 230, 231, 235
Theatre Museum, by courtesy of the Board of Trustees of the Victoria and Albert Museum, pp. 37, 56, 63, 85, 104, 116, 166, 234

LUGANO
Thyssen-Bornemisza Collection, pp. 91, 131, 143, 207, 227

MOSCOW
The Bakhrushin Museum, pp. 38, 46
Pushkin Museum of Fine Arts, p. 175
Tretyakov Gallery, pp. 59

NEW YORK
Metropolitan Museum of Art, Gift of Sir Joseph Duveen, 1922, p. 121
Museum of Modern Art, Joan and Lester Avnet Collection, p. 190; Gift of Joan and Lester Avnet, p. 199
New York Public Library at Lincoln Center, Dance Collection, pp. 6, 96
Parmenia Migel Ekstrom Collection, pp. 133, 162, 191
Sallie Blumenthal Collection, pp. 140, 186

OXFORD
Ashmolean Museum, pp. 26, 110, 158

PARIS
Bibliothèque Nationale, Département des Arts du Spectacle, pp. 126, 226
Bibliothèque Nationale, Musée de l'Opera, 62, 64, 68, 84, 85, 88, 90, 96, 107, 108, 129, 130, 137, 151, 161, 185, 196, 205, 207, 208, 225, 227, 232, 233
Musée des Arts Décoratifs, photo M.A.D./Sully Jaulmes, frontispiece, 94–95, 146–47, 154
Musée Nationale d'Art Moderne, Centre Georges Pompidou, pp. 31, 130, 137, 141, 150, 226

SAN ANTONIO
Marion Koogler McNay Art Museum, Robert L. B. Tobin Collection, pp. 58, 160, 187, 202, 212

SAN FRANCISCO
The Fine Arts Museums, Achenbach Foundation for Graphic Arts, Gift of Mrs Adolph B. Spreckels, 1962.39 TD, p. 36; 1959.38 TD, p. 171

STRASBOURG
Musée des Beaux Arts, pp. 86, 90, 115

WASHINGTON, DC
National Gallery of Art, Chester Dale Collection, 1963.10.173 (1837), p. 14

Index